ST.

Fac

Res

Academic
Admin

Managing
Human Resources Issues

William J. Heisler
W. David Jones
Philip O. Benham, Jr.

Managing
Human Resources Issues

Confronting Challenges
and Choosing Options

 Jossey-Bass Publishers

San Francisco • London • 1988

MANAGING HUMAN RESOURCES ISSUES
Confronting Challenges and Choosing Options
by William J. Heisler, W. David Jones, and Philip O. Benham, Jr.

Copyright © 1988 by: Jossey-Bass Inc., Publishers
350 Sansome Street
San Francisco, California 94104

&

Jossey-Bass Limited
28 Banner Street
London EC1Y 8QE

Library of Congress Cataloging-in-Publication Data

Heisler, William J., date.
  Managing human resources issues.

  (The Jossey-Bass management series)
  Bibliography: p.
  Includes index.
  1. Personnel management.   I. Jones, W. David, date.
II. Benham, Philip O., Jr., date.   III. Title.   IV. Series.
HF5549.H384   1988   658.3   88-42790
ISBN 1-55542-124-5

Manufactured in the United States of America

The paper in this book meets the guidelines for
permanence and durability of the Committee on
Production Guidelines for Book Longevity of the
Council on Library Resources.

JACKET DESIGN BY WILLI BAUM

FIRST EDITION

Code 8851

The Jossey-Bass Management Series

Contents

Tables, Figures, and Exhibits

Chapter Five

Chapter Eight

Chapter Nine

Chapter Ten

Chapter Eleven

Preface

Managing *Human Resources Issues* is an outgrowth of two separate but temporally related events. First, one of the authors of this volume has been a member of the Human Resources Group, University of Richmond, for the past two years. This group—whose original sponsor was Thomas Reuschling, formerly dean of the E. Claiborne Robins School of Business—is composed of training and human resources (HR) executives from the greater Richmond, Virginia, business community. The group was established to provide a forum for discussion of human resources issues and technologies. At one meeting, Reuschling polled the members to establish an agenda for future discussion. Second, at about the same time, Betty Hartzell, publisher of *Personnel Journal,* identified several current developments of importance to personnel management. The developments listed by Hartzell encompassed many of the topics posed by the Human Resources Group and, thereby, confirmed their strategic and operational importance to HR practitioners.

The list of issues and interest areas derived from these two sources included the following:

- Health care cost containment
- Employment-at-will
- Acquired immune deficiency syndrome (AIDS)

- Substance abuse
- Mergers and acquisitions
- Employee performance
- Retraining
- Terrorism
- Sexual harassment
- Employee Retirement Income Security Act (ERISA)
- Comparable worth
- Strategic human resources planning
- Recruiting strategies
- Downsizing

While many of these topics relate to traditional HR activities, others indicate new priorities and reflect greater cost, performance, and legal pressures.

Audience

Recognizing that few of these topics are addressed significantly by traditional HR texts, we set out to write a book that would fill this void and meet the growing list of challenges facing human resources managers. *Managing Human Resources Issues* should be a useful source of information for a variety of audiences. While the book may prove helpful to experienced human resources managers, it was written primarily with four distinct constituencies in mind: (1) human resources staff specialists who desire a more global view of the HR function, (2) executives who have been placed in the HR function with little previous formal training or experience, (3) human resources generalists in small organizations who are expected to personally administer a complete range of HR activities, and (4) undergraduate and graduate students at business schools with an applied professional orientation. For this last group, the book can serve as a companion volume to more traditional human resources or personnel texts or as a stand-alone text for a subsequent elective offering.

Before assuming our current human resources responsibilities in industry, we were employed as business school faculty members and administrators. Thus, we hope that the analysis and discussion in this volume will provide an applied perspective with sufficient conceptual rigor to be of value to all of these constituencies.

Organization of the Book

This book is organized around five major issues: health and safety, compensation and benefits, the changing employment environment, employee performance and productivity, and emerging challenges for the human resources manager. These issues constitute a conventional framework for the topics discussed in the book and facilitate cross-references between the contents of this volume and material from other, more traditional, personnel sources.

After a short introductory chapter, each chapter, with one exception, addresses a single challenge facing HR managers. Chapters typically begin with a discussion of an issue's origin and current importance. Then, alternative strategies are presented and specific practices are discussed.

In Part One we address two major health and safety issues that challenge virtually every organization today: substance abuse and AIDS. The very personal and private nature of these issues forces HR managers to make tough decisions that balance legal, moral, and cost concerns with organizational productivity. In Chapters Two and Three we provide insights into the problems accompanying these issues and offer broad-ranging strategies to manage them effectively.

Two distinct issues in the field of compensation and benefits are addressed in Part Two. With health care costs comprising an increasingly large share of corporate expenses, firms are faced with the dilemma of increasing their competitiveness through cost reductions while simultaneously attempting to satisfy employees' demands for comprehensive protection. In Chapter Four we suggest some alternatives for attaining effective health care benefits coverage at a cost consistent with the firm's objectives. The second issue, comparable worth, concerns how the value of a job is determined. In Chapter Five we consider apparent inequities in pay, especially between men and women. By examining the extent to which internal factors (such as accountability, skill, and physical demands) and external factors (such as market forces) influence compensation levels, we review the salient arguments on each side of the debate and provide practical guidelines for managing the organization's response.

In Part Three we address two important employment issues. Chapter Six looks at the pervasive problems of organizational downsizing as firms strive to improve their competitive position in an increasingly global economy. For organizations yet to face a work force reduction, we identify methods to avoid or delay downsizing. We also suggest ways to minimize the dysfunctional effects on those who must leave and on those who will remain when downsizing is required. Legal complications that arise in connection with downsizing are also given special attention. The other issue discussed in Part Three, employment-at-will, not only plays a role in downsizing decisions, but has much broader organizational implications as well. In Chapter Seven we review the history of employment-at-will rights and their recent erosion and take a critical look at approaches employers can use to protect these rights while providing for the fair and equitable treatment of employees.

A common concern throughout this book is how to make organizations more competitive. Part Four addresses this issue through discussions of performance management and retraining. In Chapter Eight we discuss the pressures forcing organizations to pay more attention to employee performance and to problems with current performance management and appraisal. We present an approach to overcome many of the limitations of these methods. In Chapter Nine we focus on factors behind the growing need to retrain workers whose skills are no longer appropriate to the technology employed by their companies. We provide alternative strategies for retraining and repositioning displaced workers so they may continue to be productive employees within the firm or within the broader economy.

Part Five serves two purposes. In Chapter Ten, we examine issues that some companies have come to grips with but that are just emerging in most firms and that may challenge many more organizations in the future. These include the human resources implications of mergers and acquisitions, of emerging employment trends arising from shifting demographic patterns, and of increasing terrorism in the workplace. In the last chapter, Chapter Eleven, we describe a means for organizations to systematically respond to challenges such as those presented in this book through strategic human resources planning and issues management. We trace the evolution of strategic human resources planning practices and their increasingly important role in organizational success. We present a framework for environmental scanning along with a model of strategic human resources planning, emphasizing the integration of operating and human resources concerns to create a firm that is flexible and proactive in the face of the shifting demands of an increasingly dynamic and competitive world.

Acknowledgments

We are indebted to our families for their patience during the development of the manuscript for this book. Their sacrifice of many hours of family time made it possible for us to complete the manuscript on an accelerated schedule, thus assuring its timely publication. We also wish to thank Thomas Reuschling and the members of the Human Resources Group for their seminal influence. Finally, we wish to publicly acknowledge and express appreciation for our secretaries—Barbara Connors, Evelyn Mathis, and Wendy Talley—who devoted many hours of their personal time to typing and retyping manuscript revisions. Without their continuous interest and support, this project would not have been completed.

The opinions and recommendations stated in this book represent the opinions and conclusions of the authors and do not necessarily represent the philosophy or practices of their employer, Newport News Shipbuilding.

Newport News, Virginia   William J. Heisler
September 1988   W. David Jones
                                Philip O. Benham, Jr.

The Authors

William J. Heisler is manager of management development and salaried employee training for Newport News Shipbuilding, a 28,000-employee subsidiary of Tenneco, Inc. In this capacity, he is responsible for management training, technical training for nonsupervisory salaried employees, succession planning, and human resources strategic planning. Heisler received his B.M.E. degree in mechanical engineering from Union College and his M.B.A. and Ph.D. degrees in business administration from Syracuse University. Prior to entering industry, he was an associate professor and director of the Executive M.B.A. Program at Wake Forest University and taught at the University of Notre Dame. He is the author or coauthor of more than fifty articles on organizational behavior and management education and has served as chairperson of the Management Education and Development Division of the Academy of Management.

W. David Jones is manager of employment for Newport News Shipbuilding. He received his B.S. degree in industrial management from the University of Tennessee, Knoxville, his M.B.A. degree from Augusta College, and his D.B.A. degree from Indiana University. Before joining Newport News Shipbuilding, Jones was an assistant professor of administration at Washington and Lee University, where he taught business policy and strategy, entrepreneurship, and organizational behavior. He has also worked for E.I. du Pont and Company as a manufacturing supervisor. Jones is the author or coauthor of several articles on strategic planning and management training.

Philip O. Benham, Jr., received his B.S. degree from the United States Military Academy and his M.B.A. and D.B.A. degrees from the University of Colorado, Boulder. Before taking his current position as program administrator for management training at Newport News Shipbuilding, he was assistant professor of management at Bucknell University. Benham has published and conducted research in management development and training methods. His most recent work, "Designing Effective Management Training: The Case Mapping Approach" (with W. J. Heisler), appeared in *Training Management Development Methods.*

Managing
Human Resources Issues

1

New Realities for
Human Resources Managers

The increasing importance and visibility of human resources management (HRM) in today's organizations are recognized by scholars and practitioners. HRM units are evolving from their more traditional and limited roles as processors and custodians of personnel information to expanded, more sophisticated, and more strategic roles. This evolution places both invigorating and sobering demands on human resources managers and their staffs. For the human resources manager it is perhaps—to invoke Dickens—"the best of times" and "the worst of times."

It is indeed the best of times because opportunities to make significant contributions to organizational effectiveness are emerging. The professionalization of HRM has created the capacity, as well as the expectation, to do more. Human resources managers now administer a wider array of activities using more sophisticated methods than ever before. Increasingly, human resources managers also have the opportunity to play a more crucial role in determining the strategic posture of organizations. As external environments become more complex, and the ensuing policy issues become more numerous and more consequential, human resources managers and their staffs become true partners with their cohorts in operations, marketing, and finance in guiding the economic affairs of the organization. Both in status and in substance, HRM activities are truly becoming codeterminants of organizational survival and prosperity.

1

It is perhaps the worst of times because of the plurality, pace, and complexity of change confronting human resources managers. Global competition, for example, is creating product and service market conditions that pressure organizations to reduce costs. Cost pressures are not new to organizational life, but they have intensified greatly during the last decade. Similarly, rapidly emerging technologies, which offer the hope of renewed competitiveness, pressure HRM to increase training. Demands for more training, however, are often accompanied by competing demands to reduce the training budget to achieve cost savings.

A more stringent and often hostile legal environment further aggravates these conditions. From labor law to health and safety legislation to compensation and benefits, federal and state agencies are extending and diversifying their opinions on acceptable practices within organizations. Additionally, a number of emerging societal issues (for example, substance abuse and AIDS) have become matters for legal scrutiny. The acceleration and proliferation of change in these areas make compliance an increasingly difficult and costly issue for organizations.

These challenges are not answered easily. Frequently the issues are not clear-cut. Neither are the solutions readily apparent. As a result, traditional practices and approaches may be insufficient. In general, human resources managers and their organizations may approach the emerging environment from one of four postures: denial, reaction, confrontation, and shaping.

Denial implies an "ignore it and it will go away" strategy. This approach is risky and potentially very costly. As a response option, denial selectively ignores emerging information and trends. It appears to say, What we don't know can't hurt us. Of course, just the opposite is true. Failure to acknowledge emerging demographic patterns, for example, may result in a poorly educated and inadequately trained work force. Insensitivity to changing demographics can also pose equal employment opportunity problems to uninformed employers who remain unprepared for the changes. The same can be said for health and retirement benefits as demographic trends suggest new conditions that must be prepared for. For almost any organization, denial is no longer an acceptable posture. Failure to remain informed on emerging issues, however, places an organization in a posture equivalent to denial. One cannot respond effectively to what one does not perceive and understand. Thus, human resources managers need to establish the means to identify and interpret the significance of the opportunities and threats they confront.

Reaction implies a "deal with it when we must" strategy. This approach is usually costly and disruptive. As a response option, reaction frantically searches for the quick fix. It seems to say, We'll fight this fire just like we fight all fires. Of course, reactionary policies often fail to distinguish between brush fires and holocausts—a failure that sooner or later can be devastating. Also, reaction usually results in inadequate responses. The inadequacies are evident in superficial and often inoperable policies that have been put together quickly to comply with a law or other adverse situation. Reactive strategies restrict their focus to "compliance-avoidance" behavior in countering environmental threats. They tend to be oblivious to opportunity, therefore, and thus do little to strengthen the organization's competitive position and enhance its image with both internal and external constituencies.

Confrontation implies an "if we have to deal with it, let's do it right" strategy. It employs a systematic approach to problem solving, emphasizing collaboration with affected stakeholders. It seems to say, We will have an effective and responsible policy on this (issue). Confrontation also implies an active search process to become aware of emerging situations that may require action. In confrontational organizations, human resources managers seek out those issues that are likely to require attention and seek out those opportunities that can add value to the organization. From a functional HRM perspective, confrontation seems both desirable and sufficient. In many instances, however, its "modular" characteristics may present an array of policies that lack coherence from the point of view of the larger organization.

Shaping implies a "let's look at this issue as part of the big picture" strategy. It emphasizes integration of the HRM functional considerations of an issue, trend, or situation into a comprehensive organizational framework. From this perspective, for example, human resources managers may attempt to influence organizational policies and practices to develop a labor force and organizational culture consistent with the business conditions of the future. Shaping also attempts to ensure that other organizational policies and practices regarding management style, performance appraisal, job design, and compensation are appropriately integrated and mutually reinforcing. Shaping considers the long-term planning implications of a policy response as well as the short-term directing and controlling implications. Shaping is the strategic posture that best serves the HRM, financial, and operational needs of today's organization. It is the posture advocated in this book through adoption of a strategic approach to human resources planning.

Development of effective HRM policies in response to the growing complexity of today's operating environments is a major challenge confronting employers. Responding to the challenge in an informed and enlightened manner is also rapidly becoming the only option for organizations. How they identify, interpret, and respond to key HRM issues of the present and the foreseeable future, therefore, will ultimately determine for each organization the extent to which this is the best or the worst of times.

PART ONE

Health and Safety

In an era of increasing economic uncertainty and changing social customs and practices, many corporate executives are preoccupied with major operational problems. Meeting production and delivery schedules, complying with budgets, and conforming to customer expectations command much of the attention and energy of top management. Health and safety issues may be regarded by many, therefore, as "rearguard actions" involving small numbers of personnel specialists and inconsequential shares of operating budgets. As the information provided in the next two chapters makes clear, however, the success of future corporate campaigns in the marketplace may well depend on how well these rearguard actions are fought. To obtain the quality and quantity of effort from a more diverse and demanding work force, employers must understand and respond successfully to these health and safety issues. Otherwise, morale and productivity will decline appreciably as health care costs escalate and charges of unresponsiveness and irresponsibility plague corporate America.

Increases in the incidence of substance abuse, the advent of a new public health crisis for which there is no known cure—AIDS, and escalating costs for the treatment of these conditions are now major issues confronting management. Complicating these issues are a series of legal pronouncements, to include Supreme Court decisions, that suggest an expanded scope of responsibility for managers as they attempt to develop policies and procedures to contend with these issues. What is clear at this point is that ignoring these issues is no longer an option for human resources managers.

Large organizations, in particular, are increasingly more vulnerable to damaging and expensive litigation resulting from improper responses to health and safety issues.

If managers cannot avoid these issues, what are their options? What information is necessary to make wise choices? What current practices are succeeding and why? These questions are explored fully in the next two chapters. The information contained in these chapters provides useful insights on what to do and what not to do. It provides these insights in the context of disciplined research and balanced analysis. Where the issues are sufficiently complex to preclude clear-cut recommendations, reasoned judgments are offered to clarify prudent courses of action to take as policy guidance.

Chapter Two is a comprehensive assessment of substance abuse in the workplace. Discussion focuses on the adverse consequences of substance abuse and the most prudent actions that management can take. Chapter Three examines the effect of AIDS in the workplace. It also focuses on the measures employers can take to respond effectively to this sensitive and increasingly important issue.

2

Substance Abuse:
Managing the
Conditions and Consequences
in the Workplace

The abuse of controlled substances (drugs and alcohol) in the workplace has become a problem of staggering proportions, pervading all occupations and levels of authority. Moreover, the problem is growing; the statistics on the conditions and consequences of substance abuse in the workplace are astounding.

One independent study conducted by a drug education and counseling firm in Phoenix reported that at least four million workers in the United States abuse drugs to the extent that they are referred for treatment (Mann, 1984). Conservative estimates place the total number of people in the work force who abuse drugs at approximately fifteen million, or 14 percent of the work force. Peter Bensinger of Bensinger, Du Pont, and Associates, a nationally prominent substance abuse consulting firm, contends that the problem is much greater. He estimates that there are 22 million marijuana users, 8 million cocaine users, and more than 10 million people who use prescription drugs without a valid prescription. Furthermore, more than one million workers traffic in drugs. An additional six to ten million people in the work force are estimated to be alcoholics, and the number of problem drinkers is much higher.

One of the most disturbing aspects of the drug abuse problem is its incidence among young workers. A National Institute of Drug Abuse Survey in 1981 reported that one in three workers age eighteen to twenty-five uses illegal drugs at least once a month. These practices are likely to persist as these younger workers mature and gain more responsibility for the decisions made in organizations. The consequences of substance abuse are therefore likely to intensify as we proceed into the next decade and the twenty-first century.

In succeeding sections of this chapter, the major issues regarding the consequences of substance abuse and the controversial practices companies employ to contend with substance abuse are examined. The first section assesses the financial impact of substance abuse on industry. The second section describes management's responsibilities in combating substance abuse in the workplace, and introduces the controversy over testing employees to identify substance abusers. Employer response to testing is then examined in terms of its conflicting consequences (that is, wrongful discharge versus reasonable accommodation). Employee Assistance Programs (EAPs) designed to help employees rehabilitate themselves from their dependency on drugs and/or alcohol are then described and evaluated. The chapter concludes with recommendations for developing and implementing an effective substance abuse program, emphasizing the active role that managers play in the success of the program.

Impact of Substance Abuse on the Workplace

The effects of substance abuse in the workplace have been documented in national surveys. Abusers have three to four times as many accidents on the job and four to six times as many accidents off the job as those who do not abuse drugs and alcohol. The abuser is absent from work two and a half times more often than the nonabuser, and medical costs and benefits run three times higher for the abuser. Wage garnishments imposed by employers on confirmed abusers are seven times higher than those imposed on nonabusers (Bensinger, n.d.). In terms of both human misery and financial loss, the deleterious effects of drug and alcohol abuse include illness, injury, and death; costs of replacing and training workers; increased workers' compensation and health insurance premiums and claims;

and costs of lower productivity stemming from lower-quality workmanship, employee theft, and absenteeism.

In 1981, a study conducted by the Research Triangle Institute estimated that drug use among the civilian work force of some 108 million cost private sector employers about $16.4 billion. A follow-up study in 1984 estimated the total cost of substance abuse at $60 billion, $33 billion of which was attributed to lost productivity (Castro, 1987). More recent estimates place the total loss figure at more than $100 billion annually. On a per employee basis, the attorney general recently estimated that each drug-abusing employee costs his or her employer $7,000 annually (Philips, 1986). Precise figures on costs are unavailable, but many contend that the figures frequently cited underestimate the true magnitude of the problem.

The costs of alcoholism are equally discouraging. The total dollar value approximates the costs reported for drug abuse. In New York State alone, conservative estimates on the costs of alcoholism to industry exceed $4 billion annually in lost work time, reduced productivity, increased health and welfare costs, property damage, accidents, and medical expenses (Handel, 1984).

Perhaps the most difficult aspect of measuring the costs of drug and alcohol abuse is understanding the financial implications of lost productivity. Employees under the influence of drugs and alcohol work at lower efficiency. They damage parts, misroute material and information, perform calculations inaccurately, and tend to work at a slower pace. Time spent away from the work station is greater for the user, as well as for those who traffic in drugs. The financial impact on a company can be significant.

One way to measure the profitability of a company is to calculate the product of its productivity and price recovery ratios. If price recovery, defined as the ratio of customer prices charged to costs incurred for labor, energy, material, and capital, is fairly stable, but productivity is declining, profitability declines dramatically. Exhibit 1 provides a simple illustration.

With productivity at 75 percent in timeframe 1 (t_1), profitability is indexed at 0.90. Conditions at t_1 include a drug-free work force adequately trained to meet performance expectations. In timeframe 2 (t_2), a 10 percent reduction in profitability is noted as the work force loses an average of 0.6 hour of productivity per work shift.

Exhibit 1. Impact of Productivity on Profitability.

	productivity		price recovery
Profitability =		×	
Profitability =	time performing job tasks correctly / time available to perform the job	×	prices charged to customers / costs incurred (labor, materials, and so on)
Profitability (t_1) =	$\dfrac{6.0 \text{ hours}}{8.0 \text{ hours}}$	×	$\dfrac{\$1.2 \text{ billion}}{\$1.0 \text{ billion}}$ = 0.90
Profitability (t_2) =	$\dfrac{5.4 \text{ hours}}{8.0 \text{ hours}}$	×	$\dfrac{\$1.2 \text{ billion}}{\$1.0 \text{ billion}}$ = 0.81

By decreasing the time spent performing job tasks correctly because of the adverse effects of substance abuse, the organization incurs a 10 percent reduction in profits at t_2.

The 0.6 hour represents 15 percent of the work force, a conservative figure, working at 25 percent efficiency because of drug and alcohol problems. The 25 percent figure is a "worst case" estimate. Studies of employee work efficiency in both factory and office work environments indicate a normal efficiency range of 50–75 percent, and substance abusers are generally half as efficient as other employees. Lost efficiency, therefore, consumes up to 75 percent of the time available to the substance abuser to perform assigned work. Part of the loss is attributable to time spent away from the work station in consuming, buying and selling, and suffering the ill effects of drugs and alcohol. Part of the time is lost to slower operating rates and error rates resulting in rework, schedule delays, and budget overruns. All of this time translates into lost profitability and, for most companies, a much weaker competitive position.

Referring to the situation in Exhibit 1, we note that had net income been $100 million in t_1, the 10 percent loss in productivity recorded in t_2 (5.4 hours worked versus 6.0) would cost the company $10 million in profits. The data generated from this example illustrate both the singular effect that substance abuse has on a billion-dollar company and the pervasive effect that substance abuse has on employers nationwide. Although the dollar amount lost to the company is large, it represents only 3.03 hundredths of a percent of the estimated $33 billion lost industrywide in 1984.

Recognizing the problem of substance abuse to be large and growing, employers are taking action to combat it. The next section describes current practices used to combat drug and alcohol abuse. It also reviews the responses of federal and state courts to these practices, and concludes with an endorsement for more training to prepare managers to deal with substance abuse competently.

Combating Substance Abuse at Work

Management must address three responsibilities in combating substance abuse. The first responsibility is to comply with laws pertaining to the possession, use, and disposition of controlled substances. Employers must demonstrate due diligence in this regard and report known and suspected violations of law to law enforcement authorities. The second responsibility is to provide a safe and healthy work environment for their employees. Employers must demonstrate this concern through written policies and effective practices designed to rid the workplace of the hazards posed by the abuse of drugs and alcohol. The final responsibility is to the stockholders. Management has to demonstrate the prudent use of assets to obtain an attractive return on invested capital. If earnings are adversely affected by poor management practices, the company's shareholders are likely to respond by withdrawing their investments or, in some cases, by attempting to remove the top management.

To meet these three responsibilities, managers must consider the means available for detecting substance abuse in the workplace, and then respond to those confirmed as substance abusers with some form of discipline and a rehabilitation program. Methods of detection include blood and urine testing, polygraph testing, random searches, undercover personnel, video surveillance, and, in some cases, trained dogs. Blood and urine testing, however, is the most commonly used method. Efforts to rehabilitate employees usually take the form of an employee assistance program sponsored by the company and conducted by an outside drug and alcohol treatment agency.

The detection and response issues are complex and pose many problems to corporate human resources policymakers. Liability and cost are the major criteria used to judge the feasibility of policy options. The judging process is complicated by the inability of managers to precisely determine future liability that may result from employees' drug and alcohol abuse. Therefore, indemnifying the organization through insurance is difficult because the level of risk in most cases is unknown. Consequently, many employers do little to combat substance abuse. The costs of doing something to detect, discipline, and rehabilitate drug and alcohol abusers are presumed to be greater than the costs of doing nothing. Although this rationale is fallacious in most cases, it contributes to the unwillingness of employers to support formal programs to detect and combat substance abuse.

A recent survey of companies by the American Management Association noted that only 25 percent of the Fortune 500 companies were testing for drugs. Although the number of companies testing is expected to increase, almost half of those now testing who responded to the American Management Association survey question its efficacy. As one corporate executive put it, "It costs us $25,000 to hire and train an average employee. It would be absurd to think about firing an employee on the basis of a test that isn't much better than flipping a coin" (American Management Association, 1987). Even when discipline is imposed, however, the risks are great. The courts, both federal and state, have offered no comprehensive and consistent guidelines on what constitutes just cause and appropriate response in disciplining employees who fail a test for drugs and alcohol. The practices defining the complexity of these and related issues are explored more fully in the sections to follow. As a preface to this discussion, Figure 1 provides a summary of employers' attitudes toward testing.

Preemployment Testing. The College Placement Council reports that of 497 national employers who responded to a recent survey, 140 (28.2 percent) currently use some form of drug testing as part of their preemployment screening process. An additional 20 percent of those surveyed indicated plans to begin screening applicants within the next two years. Table 1 lists the industries that reported the use of drug screening as part of preemployment testing.

The most important reason cited for drug and alcohol testing was safety. It was cited almost four times more than security, the second most important reason reported. Surprisingly, increased productivity and control of medical costs ranked a distant fifth and sixth, respectively.

A large majority of those responding (88.6 percent) stated they would not hire applicants who failed the preemployment tests. The penalty imposed for failing the test is not permanent, however, as 105 employers said applicants could reapply and receive favorable treatment in the future. Only 28 of the employers indicated that they would not consider a subsequent application from someone who failed a preemployment drug test (College Placement Council, 1986).

Among the major corporations that now require applicants to pass a urinalysis test as part of the preemployment screening process are Exxon, Federal Express, IBM, TWA, and Lockheed.

Employee Testing. Many employers also require the testing

Figure 1. Employer Attitudes Toward Testing.

48 percent
Yet to take
any action

21 percent
Currently testing
(preemployment
and/or for cause)

12 percent
Now developing a
testing program

9 percent
Rejecting the idea
of testing*

3 percent
No answer

8 percent
Now using techniques
other than testing to deal
with the problems

* Reasons for rejecting (percent):

68	Moral issues/invasion of privacy	28 Cost
63	Inaccuracy	17 Management opposition
53	Negative impact on morale	16 Employee opposition
43	Positive test shows use, not abuse or impairment	7 Union opposition

Note: N = 1,090. Because respondents could check more than one reason for rejecting testing, the total exceeds 100.

Source: Reprinted by permission of the publisher from *Drug Abuse: The Workplace Issues,* an AMA Research Study, p. 14. © 1987 American Management Association, New York. All rights reserved.

Table 1. Industries Reporting the Use of Preemployment Testing.

Industry	Respondents	
	Number	Percent[a]
Utilities—public (including transportation)	52	37.1
Chemicals, drugs, and allied products	13	9.3
Aerospace	12	8.6
Petroleum and allied products (including natural gas)	11	7.9
Glass, paper, packaging, and allied products	8	5.7
Research and/or consulting organizations	8	5.7
Metals and metal products	6	4.3
Building materials manufacturers and construction	5	3.6
Electrical and electronic machinery and equipment	5	3.6
Banking, finance, and insurance	4	2.9
Merchandising (retail and wholesale) and services	4	2.9
Automotive and mechanical equipment	3	2.1
Computers and business machines	2	1.4
Federal government	2	1.4
Local/state government	1	0.7
Accounting	—	—
Nonprofit organizations and educational institutions	—	—
Did not respond	4	2.9
Total	140	100.1

[a]Rounded to nearest tenth of a percent.

Source: Preemployment Drug Screening: A Survey of Practices Among National Employers of College Graduates. New York: College Placement Council, 1986, p. 6.

of current employees. In a recent survey by the Employment Management Association of human resources professionals' views on alcohol and drug testing in the workplace, 20.9 percent reported testing of current employees. In the American Management Association survey previously cited, 77 percent of the companies who reported using testing programs perform tests on current employees. "For cause" testing, or testing employees whose behavior confirms or suggests the use of drugs and alcohol, is by far the most prevalent reason for testing. Only 12 percent of the AMA survey respondents conduct periodic testing (for example, as part of an annual physical exam), and 8 percent perform random testing of employees.

Recently, Gomez-Mejia and Balkin (1987) analyzed the characteristics of forty-two industrial firms with drug testing policies and contrasted them against firms in the study that had no testing policies. The firms that test are larger, are involved in manufacturing, are located in the Northeast, and have a younger work force, the majority of whom are blue-collar production workers. Among the firms that do not test employees, the primary reasons cited are respect for individual privacy and the risks of adverse legal action against the firm.

Employees whose occupations and positions involve high risk to safety and health are more likely to be subjected to random testing as a condition of employment. Operators of public transportation vehicles and handlers of radioactive materials are two occupational groups that submit to drug tests. For these and other occupations, safety is a business necessity that permits what might otherwise be construed as an excessive invasion of privacy. In *New York City Transit Authority* v. *Beager,* the U.S. Supreme Court affirmed the appropriateness of business necessity as a cause for testing and taking subsequent disciplinary action based on the test results (Geidt, 1985). Again, the American Management Association survey suggests that if forklifts, oil rigs, eighteen-wheelers, and high-speed machinery are in operation, a company is most likely to show interest in testing.

A major oil company executive told the American Management Association researchers that "those refineries are high-temperature, high-pressure places, and we gotta watch out for the safety of our men. Our policy is simple: you got a [drug] problem, either you get it fixed or you get the hell out" (American Management Association, 1987). Other large companies seem to share these concerns. At Rockwell, for example, pilots and employees who handle explosives are tested annually. Kidder, Peabody, the New York–based investment banking firm, began testing its employees in August 1986 as part of a comprehensive drug prevention program. The major issue at Kidder, Peabody, according to Edwin Weihenmayer, vice-president of human resources, is the financial security of billions of dollars entrusted to the firm by its clients.

Acceptance of Test Results. The most controversial aspect of testing is the reliability of test results. The U.S. Centers for Disease Control submitted 100 urine samples to thirteen randomly chosen private laboratories for testing. Each sample was known either to be contaminated with an illicit drug or to be drug free. When the laboratory results were reported, the error rates were astonishing. False negative rates (laboratory results indicating the samples to be drug free when in fact drugs were present) were as high as 100 percent on amphetamines, cocaine, codeine, and morphine. False positive rates (laboratory results indicating drugs to be present when in fact the samples were drug free) were as high as 66 percent for methadone and as high as 73 percent for amphetamines (Waldholz, 1986; Extejt, 1987).

The problems start with the accuracy of the test itself (95–97 percent accuracy according to the manufacturers) and proceed to human error, equipment malfunctions, and mishandling of specimens. Confirmation tests using more reliable and expensive methods ($60 to $100 a sample), such as thin-layer chromatography, gas chromatography, or gas chromatography/mass spectrometry, can reduce—but not eliminate—the risk of obtaining false-positive results. The most prudent course a company can follow is to investigate the testing laboratory's experience, its analytical methods, and the means used to protect the identity and integrity of each sample.

A second and equally important matter pertaining to test reliability is safeguarding the reputation of an employee. False-positive results can produce unintended consequences with both legal and moral implications. A company can be liable for slander if it disciplines an employee on the basis of false-positive results. Morally, a company can damage an employee's personal reputation by creating the impression of distrust and disloyalty in an employee who must submit to confirmation procedures to negate the initial false-positive readings. As suspicions and doubts are raised during the confirmation process, so are the risks to the employee's personal reputation and the continuing relationship between employer and employee. General Motors, Ford, Mobil, IBM, General Electric, Tenneco, Standard Oil, and Philip Morris are among those companies having drug testing policies. ITT has discontinued drug testing because the company considers it cost-ineffective (Extejt, 1987).

The Impairment Argument. Although the reliability of testing is a major concern, many contend that it is irrelevant. The real issue, according to these people, is impairment—the inability to perform a job satisfactorily. If an employee's erratic or unusual behavior impairs his or her ability to perform the job satisfactorily, an employer can focus more comfortably and confidently on job relatedness in proposing disciplinary action. In this context, substance abuse is not viewed narrowly in moral and legal terms. Instead, it is viewed in more utilitarian terms as the cause of poor job performance, which is the only legitimate concern of an employer regarding the behavior of employees. Industrial unions and the American Civil Liberties Union are strong advocates of this position. Richard Hawks of the National Institute of Drug Abuse (NIDA) reinforces this position by noting that "you cannot equate urine drug levels and impairment of performance. You can have a 20-fold variation in urine samples taken a few hours apart from the same individuals" (American Management Association, 1987).

Invasion of Privacy. Invasion of privacy is another objection voiced by opponents of testing. Images of people lined up outside lavatories awaiting the next available stall with specimen container in hand are abhorrent to many. Having laboratory personnel monitor the process is even more demeaning. In the public sector, recent court decisions have found testing procedures to be unreasonable searches and seizures and, therefore, violations of the Fourth Amendment. In one opinion, the judge noted that "testing of civilians by urinalysis, absent some form of individualized suspicion, is in almost all cases offensive to the mandates of the Fourth Amendment" (American Management Association, 1987). As the federal government imposes more precise and restrictive procedures to screen for the abuse of drugs and alcohol, Fourth Amendment rights are likely to become a more prominent issue for public sector employees. Federal regulations requiring tightly controlled testing procedures will surely provoke several court challenges. Finding the right balance between an employer's right to control testing procedures to ensure the validity of test results and an employee's right to be free from unreasonable search and seizure is a matter yet to be resolved.

Although the provisions of the Fourth Amendment do not extend to the private sector, the notion of privacy as an individual right is also gaining support from the courts. Recently, for example, several state courts have granted exception to the *employment-at-will* doctrine, which has long guaranteed the autonomy of employers in discharging employees in matters involving testing. Now hundreds of privacy laws exist under the auspices of the seldom-invoked Ninth Amendment. These laws limit the indiscriminate use of the employment-at-will doctrine to mandate testing of employees in the private sector.

Rehabilitation Versus Discipline. A final complication in the use of tests as a basis for subsequent disciplinary action is the interpretation of the Rehabilitation Act of 1973 as it applies to employees with a drug and/or alcohol dependency problem. A 1977 ruling by the Department of Health, Education, and Welfare (now Health and Human Services) declared alcoholism and drug addiction as physical and mental impairments and, therefore, handicaps for the purpose of rehabilitation. The act does not protect the handicapped employee, however, when the handicap "prevents successful performance on the job." Thus, employers who have eschewed the moral and legal positions on substance abuse and focused more narrowly on job impairment are more likely to sustain their acts of discipline as reasonable responses to drug and alcohol abuse in the workplace.

Employers must be careful to distinguish between employees whose performance is declining and those who cannot perform job tasks. Declining performance requires a reasonable accommodation by the employer to rehabilitate the employee. Employees in the latter category, however, are more vulnerable to severe disciplinary action and discharge.

In California, for example, the state legislature now requires employers to allow employees time off to participate in an alcoholic rehabilitation program, provided this does not impose an undue hardship on the employer's operation. The statute states further, however, that employers are free to discharge or refuse to hire employees if they are unable to perform job duties or they would endanger other employees on the job (Geidt, 1985).

Because of generous interpretations of the law by federal judges, the limits of reasonable accommodation are not well defined. In *Whitlock* v. *Donovan* (598 F. Supp. 126, 1984), for example, a judge ruled that despite four years of efforts to accom-

modate an alcoholic's disability, the federal government had acted
unreasonably in discharging him. The plaintiff was not given a
firm choice between discharge and rehabilitation early enough.
Consequently, the Labor Department, the plaintiff's employer, had
to give the plaintiff one more opportunity to rehabilitate (Geidt,
1985). Reasonable accommodation, therefore, appears to include a
clear statement of potential consequences to the employee at the
outset. Rehabilitation programs must be accompanied by this
statement of potential consequences. Omission of this disciplinary
warning makes an employer vulnerable to judgments of wrongful
discharge.

Arbitrators appear to be more willing to recognize alcohol
dependency as a treatable illness than to recognize drug dependency
as one. This distinction may have historical precedents. Some
officials see significant differences between alcoholism and drug
addiction in our society. On the one hand, they view drug addiction
stereotypically as the consequence of young hedonists' attempts to
feel good and escape their responsibilities toward others. On the
other hand, these officials regard alcoholics more leniently,
generally as older and coping with disappointment and failure,
albeit inappropriately. Whatever the cause of the distinction,
employers and employees alike should make note of it. It may
influence the outcome of a wrongful discharge case in which
substance abuse is at issue in determining impairment.

Developing a Substance Abuse Policy: Key Points

A group of HRM executives experienced in administering
testing programs has made the following recommendations for
developing a substance abuse policy that includes detection as well
as treatment (Gomez-Mejia and Balkin, 1987):

- Target the program at specific groups of employees whose performance affects the public
  safety and/or the safety of fellow employees.
- Conduct tests only when reasonable cause is present; that is, erratic behavior of an employee suggests the possible abuse of drugs and/or alcohol.

- Conduct a confirmation test for any employee whose initial test is positive to preclude false charges and accusations.
- Require employees confirmed as substance abusers to enroll in a treatment program to rehabilitate themselves.

These recommendations are consistent with similar factors reported by the American Management Association in its 1987 survey of Fortune 500 companies:

- *Public safety*—safety of clients and customers served
- *Workplace safety*—safety of employees
- *Ability to perform work*—acceptable behavior and results
- *Public trust*—confidence placed in those occupying certain positions of professional responsibility

Employee Assistance Programs

To answer the call for efforts to rehabilitate employees suffering from drug and/or alcohol dependency, many companies turn to outside agencies that provide employee assistance programs (EAPs). EAPs provide counseling, education, and, in many cases, treatment referral and crisis intervention hotline programs to help employees overcome their problems with drugs or alcohol. Some company-sponsored programs extend coverage to dependents of employees as well. The following lists summarize the attributes of a strong employee assistance program.*

Source: Handel (1984, p. 224). Reprinted with permission from *New Directions in Welfare Plan Benefits: Instituting Health Care Cost Containment Programs* written by Bernard Handel and published by the International Foundation of Employee Benefit Plans, Brookfield, Wis. Statements or opinions expressed in this book are those of the author and do not necessarily represent the view or positions of the International Foundation, its officers, directors, or staff.

Major Characteristics of an Effective
Employee Assistance Program

Written EAP policy
Clearly specified procedures
Top management endorsement
Union endorsement (need for nonadversial relationship)
Local program committee (to include employee representa-
    tion, mandatory when there is a collective bargaining re-
    lationship)
Training of management and supervisory employees
Training of union stewards
Employee and family orientation
Communication and planning at all levels
Active plan coordinators
Coordination with in-house health services (if in existence)
Active involvement with community referral agencies
    (Alcoholics Anonymous, United Way organizations, other
    voluntary groups in community; linkage to existing
    facilities—EAPs should not create new network)
Periodic assessment and updating
Evaluation of program
Active follow-up
Determination of extent to which treatment costs are covered
    by health insurance plan
Confidentiality at all times

Essential Elements of an Effective
Employee Assistance Program

Early identification
Motivation to participate
Linkage with community treatment networks
Low cost to innovate and operate EAPs
Separation of essential major subject areas but not limited to
    (alcoholism leads to treatment, leads to family counseling,
    leads to treatment of other substance abuse, emotional,
    and financial problems)
Maintain confidentiality at all times

Cost-Effectiveness of Employee Assistance Programs

Reduction in workers' compensation claims
Reduction in on-site claims
Reduction in hospitalization and medical treatment
Improvement of work quality and productivity
Reduction in absenteeism
Reduction in turnover of employees
Demonstration of employer commitment to employee health
　　and welfare
Improvement in employee morale

A 1986 study by the national compensation/benefits consultant firm Hewitt Associates noted that almost half of the 293
companies responding to their survey sponsor EAPs for their
employees and dependents. Another 10 percent are considering
EAPs. The EAP is a fairly recent phenomenon, however, as more
than a third of those responding instituted their programs since
1984.

EAPs are not seen as panaceas by every company, however.
One retailing chain reported that the repeat offender, or chronic
alcoholic or drug abuser, could not be rehabilitated. Consequently,
the company sees little utility in sponsoring an EAP. Management
at this company views chronic alcohol and drug abuse as the cause
of impairment, a condition warranting discipline up to and
including discharge. In essence, the large retailer regards the EAP
as providing care that is largely custodial for those who suffer some
form of chemical dependency. They regard custodial care as
nonrehabilitative and, therefore, not a justifiable expense.

Although rehabilitative efforts seldom cure the dependency
of the drug and alcohol abuser, they often produce substantial
improvements. For example, a study of work performance at the
Utah Copper Division of Kennecott Copper Corporation noted that
employees who received counseling for alcohol abuse reduced their
absenteeism by 50 percent. Medical costs for those employees also
declined by approximately 50 percent (Handel, 1984). Cost savings
reported by some companies that use EAPs are presented in Table 2.

The EAP currently represents the best "good faith" effort a

Table 2. Cost Savings Reported for Some Employee Assistance Programs.

Company	Number of Employees	Number Using EAP	Rehabilitation Rate (%)	Annual Cost Savings[a]
University of Missouri	7,000	1,002	80	$ 67,996[b]
Scovill Manufacturing	6,500	180	78	186,550
Illinois Bell Telephone (family)	38,490	1,154 100	80	254,448[c]
U.S. Postal Service	83,000	?	75	2,221,362
Kennecott Copper (with dependents)	7,000 28,000	1,200/year	n.c.	448,400[d]
New York Transit	43,000	?	75	2,000,000
E.I. du Pont (with spouse)	16,000	176/year	70	419,200[c]
New York Telephone	80,000	300/year	85	1,565,000

[a]Number rehabilitated × average salary.

[b]Plus a 40 percent decrease in use of health benefits.

[c]31,806 disability days were saved; off-duty accidents decreased 42.4 percent and on-duty accidents decreased 61.4 percent. There were also savings in health insurance utilization and job inefficiency.

[d]The total included absenteeism, sickness, and accident disability and health insurance use. Absenteeism decreased 53 percent, weekly indemnity costs (sick/accident) 75 percent, and medical costs 55 percent. Rehabilitation rate not calculated as it varies with type of case and definition. Health care plan calls for comparison of the number discharged with the number seen. Conservative calculation found a $5.78 return on $1 invested in program.

[d]Only alcohol program.

Source: Handel, 1984, p. 236. Reprinted with permission from New Directions in Welfare Plan Benefits: Instituting Health Care Cost Containment Programs written by Bernard Handel and published by the International Foundation of Employee Benefit Plans, Brookfield, Wis.

company can make to demonstrate its willingness to rehabilitate employees with a drug and/or alcohol problem. The efficacy of EAPs, however, is open to judgment. At present, EAPs have been shown to reduce absenteeism and medical costs. They have not been shown to cure those with a drug and/or alcohol problem; however, in fairness, those agencies that provide EAPs made no promises to cure employees of their afflictions. The response to treatment and counseling varies from person to person. Some abusers overcome their dependency problems; some do not. If a company can demonstrate a "good faith" effort, it has a good chance of sustaining disciplinary actions against employees dependent on drugs and alcohol.

Need for Management Training

To support the comprehensive efforts required to detect, rehabilitate, and discipline an employee with a drug and/or alcohol dependency problem, employers need managers who are trained to carry out these responsibilities, and who feel a sense of obligation to discharge them well. Many managers, for example, do not know how to confront and counsel an employee suspected of substance abuse. To them, it is a formidable task. The 1981 National Survey of Supervisory Management Practices noted that more than 7,000 managers expressed little confidence in their ability to counsel an employee who abuses drugs or alcohol. In fact, this ability ranked seventeenth among eighteen job activities rated in terms of confidence to handle that activity well (Bittel and Ramsey, 1983). Much of this lack of confidence can be attributed to factors already described, such as absence of a formal program or bad experience with a program that has been poorly administered or successfully challenged in court. Recognizing the complexity and sensitivity of the matter, many managers have chosen to ignore it.

Preparing Managers to Implement Substance Abuse Programs. The first step in preparing management to implement a substance abuse program is development of a comprehensive company policy on drug and alcohol abuse. Such a policy should detail the reasons for the policy, disciplinary consequences for specific acts of drug and/or alcohol abuse, participation in the employee assistance program, circumstances and procedures for testing, and the applicable population to include vendors and contract labor or temporary employees. Exhibit 2 summarizes these key points as highlights from Duke Power Company's Drug and Alcohol Abuse Policy.

To gain confidence in their ability to confront employees suspected of substance abuse, managers must be taught what to do

**Exhibit 2. Highlights of Duke Power Company's Drug
and Alcohol Abuse Policy.**

Overview

Employees shall not be involved with the unlawful use, possession, sale, or transfer of drugs or narcotics in any manner that may impair their ability to perform assigned duties or otherwise adversely affect the company's business.

Employees shall not possess alcoholic beverages in the workplace or consume alcoholic beverages in association with the workplace or during work time.

Off-the-job illegal drug activity or alcohol abuse that could adversely affect an employee's job performance or that could jeopardize the safety of other employees, the public, company equipment, or the company's relations with the public will not be tolerated.

Since the company considers alcoholism and other drug addictions to be treatable illnesses, absences directly or indirectly caused by company-approved treatment of alcohol or drug abuse will be excused.

Use of the Employee Assistance Program

Employees experiencing problems with alcohol or other drugs are urged to voluntarily seek assistance through the company's employee assistance program to resolve such problems before they become serious enough to require management referral or disciplinary action.

Employees whose job performance deteriorates may be referred by management to the employee assistance program for diagnosis of the performance problem(s).

Participation in the employee assistance program will not jeopardize an employee's job. In fact, successful treatment will be viewed positively. However, participation will not prevent normal disciplinary action for a violation that may have already occurred or relieve an employee of responsibility to perform assigned duties in a safe and efficient manner.

Consequences of Alcohol and Drug Abuse

The use, sale, or personal possession of illegal drugs while on the job (including during rest periods and meal periods) or on company property is a dischargeable offense and may result in criminal prosecution. Any illegal drugs found will be turned over to the appropriate law enforcement agency.

The use or personal possession of alcohol during work time or on company property is a dischargeable offense. For all employees, alcohol consumption is prohibited during the workday (including during rest periods and meal periods). On some occasions, when removed from the usual work setting, employees may consume alcohol in moderation if approved by management. Employees who consume alcohol under such circumstances shall not report back to work during that workday.

Any employee who is perceived to be under the influence of alcohol will be immediately removed from service and evaluated by medical person-

Exhibit 2. Highlights of Duke Power Company's Drug and Alcohol Abuse Policy, Cont'd.

nel, if reasonably available. Management will take further appropriate action (that is, referral to the employee assistance program and/or disciplinary action) on the basis of the medical information, past history, and other relevant factors (performance, record of disciplinary actions, and so forth).

Special Action

The company will take whatever measures are necessary to determine whether alcohol or illegal drugs are located on or being used on company property. These measures will not be taken unreasonably but when the company believes that they are completely justified and necessary. Such measures must be approved by a senior vice-president or higher company officer except in situations in which time is critical to the success of the search.

Searches of company property, facilities, or equipment may be conducted by authorized personnel. Federal, state, and/or local authorities may be called upon to assist in an investigation. Trained dogs may be used to search company property, facilities, or equipment; they will not be used to search people.

Searches of people and of personal property located on company premises may be conducted by security officers, if available, or by management if security officers are not readily available. Refusal to submit to a search (after the purpose of the search and the potential implications of refusing to be searched have been explained) will result in immediate removal from service and may result in dismissal for insubordination.

Unannounced drug screens of groups of employees may be conducted if a reason to suspect drug use exists. Refusal to participate in a drug screen will result in immediate removal from service and may result in dismissal for insubordination.

Routine and Discretionary Drug Testing

Drug tests will be conducted as a routine part of the preemployment physical examination for all regular full-time and part-time job applicants and co-op students prior to employment. If a drug screen indicates the presence of drugs or controlled substances, the applicant will not be considered further for employment.

Drug tests will be conducted as a routine part of promotion or transfer into positions for which a company-mandated physical is required and/or which may directly affect public safety or employee safety. If the drug screen indicates the presence of drugs, the employee will not be considered further for the position. In addition, the employee will be referred to the employee assistance program and/or considered for disciplinary action.

Drug tests will be conducted as a routine part of company-mandated physicals for certain positions considered to be sensitive from a health and

**Exhibit 2. Highlights of Duke Power Company's Drug
and Alcohol Abuse Policy, Cont'd.**

safety standpoint. Positive results on a drug screen will be cause for referral to the employee assistance program and/or consideration for disciplinary action.

Drug and/or alcohol tests may be conducted at the option of management as part of the investigation of an accident or near-accident in which safety precautions were violated and/or unusually careless acts were performed—or when an employee's work record indicates a history of accidents and/or near-accidents.

Drug and/or alcohol tests will be conducted when an employee's supervisor has cause to believe that the employee is "unfit for duty" or when there is reason to suspect the use or possession of illegal drugs.

After approval of a senior vice-president or higher company officer, all employees in a work group may be tested for drugs when there is a change in group behavior, a high rate of accidents or injuries, reliable information about drug involvement, and/or reason to suspect the use of illegal drugs within the group.

Consequences of a Positive Drug Test

When a drug screen is positive for the first time but no evidence of drug use on the job exists, an employee will be suspended without pay. The employee must visit the employee assistance program at least once to learn what drug counseling resources are available. The employee will be required to seek treatment for drug abuse from a recognized professional and/or institution. Refusal to do so will be viewed as insubordination, and the employee will be subject to discharge. The employee must have a negative test result in a screen administered by the company within a period of six weeks from the date of suspension; otherwise, the employee will be discharged. If the employee has a negative result within the six-week period, but cannot return to work for good reason (such as participation in a treatment program), the suspension period will be extended. After the employee returns to work, random drug screening will be conducted for an indefinite period of time.

If a physical examination is not required for a job and/or public and employee safety is not a factor, an employee will be allowed to return to work upon receipt by the company of a negative test result.

If a physical examination is required for a job and/or public and employee safety is a factor, an employee will be allowed to return to work only upon providing to the employee assistance program certified documentation from a recognized professional indicating that the professional has a reasonable degree of confidence that the employee is capable of performing his or her assigned job duties without impairment.

Employees who have been suspended for a positive drug test and allowed to return to work will be discharged for a positive result on any subsequent drug screen.

**Exhibit 2. Highlights of Duke Power Company's Drug
and Alcohol Abuse Policy, Cont'd.**

Applicability to Vendors and Contractors

Vendors and contractors supplying workers to the company or performing
work for the company in areas considered by management to be sensitive shall implement and administer an alcohol and drug abuse policy
acceptable to the company and at least as stringent as the company's.

Source: Reprinted by permission of the publisher from "A Positive
Approach to Alcohol and Drug Abuse," William H. Wagel, *Personnel*, Dec.
1986, pp. 8-9. © 1986 American Management Association, New York. All
rights reserved.

and how to do it. They must also know whom to contact for referral
assistance. Testing procedures, for example, would most likely be
coordinated by the company's medical department. Rehabilitation
efforts, most likely sponsored by a company EAP, would probably
be coordinated by the firm's benefits or medical department staff.

The most prudent posture for the company to take in
training its supervisors is to adhere to the issue of job impairment.
Supervisors must be careful not to judge prematurely and wrongfully accuse an employee of drug or alcohol abuse. The company
could damage the accused person's reputation and incur a substantial judgment against itself for false accusations. Managers can be
trained to observe instances of unusual or erratic behavior, however,
and then relate that behavior to impaired job performance. By
focusing on the instrumental effect that the behavior has on
performance, a manager can view the suspected substance abuse
more objectively.

Managers can be trained to associate the instances of erratic
or unusual behavior with poor performance. For example, an
employee who appears listless and inattentive may make frequent
computational errors or may damage parts when attempting to
assemble them into larger units. The poor performance is the error
rate or damage. The behavior contributed to the performance. Note
how some erratic or unusual behaviors can contribute to poor
performance:

Unusual or Erratic Behavior	*Performance Consequence*
Irritable, quarrelsome behavior	Alienates co-workers; causes schedule delays
Frequent absences from work station to visit lavatories, lockers, or lounges	Work rate slows down; co-workers cannot coordinate common tasks
Incoherent actions	Instructions are misinterpreted or ignored; work standards are not met
Listless, inattentive behavior	Details are overlooked; accuracy and completeness of work suffer
Drastic changes in mood and disposition	Coordination and cooperation with co-workers decline; some tasks are not completed or are performed inaccurately
Unexplained absences from work	Schedules are delayed; others must compensate by doing more work

Confronting an Employee Suspected of Abusing Drugs or Alcohol. Knowing what to look for is a necessary first step in the process of rehabilitating and, where appropriate, disciplining poor performers with drug or alcohol problems. Knowing how to confront an employee whose behavior may indicate a drug or alcohol dependency is the key step. A successful confrontation may well result in a referral for treatment and rehabilitation. The meeting will also serve as a formal occasion to document poor performance. Should the erratic or unusual behavior persist, and performance fail to meet the reasonable expectations of management, disciplinary action can be taken on the basis of performance. Performance-based discipline, moreover, may avoid the issue of drug or alcohol dependency.

The generally accepted procedure for confronting an employee whose performance is a problem and whose behavior suggests the abuse of drugs or alcohol is outlined here.

- First, explain to the employee that his or her performance is unsatisfactory, or that she or he has violated a work rule. Cite specific instances too. For example, invoices were misplaced and purchasing had to call the vendor to have a second invoice mailed before payment for services could be made. Another example would be noting that tolerances were not met on a production run, and now the pieces have to be reworked at additional cost and with a delay in shipment.
- Note the association between the poor performance and an unusual or erratic behavior. For example, the misplaced invoices may have been associated with listless and inattentive behavior; missed tolerances may have been associated with heightened anxiety and irritability plus frequent absences from the work station.
- Encourage the employee to confer with the company's EAP coordinator. Mention that if the employee has a personal problem, the EAP coordinator can provide useful advice. Emphasize that the initial meeting with the EAP coordinator and the subsequent visits to the EAP provider or agency will be kept confidential; supervisors and co-workers will not be informed of an employee's referral to or participation in an EAP.
- Remind the employee that continued poor performance will result in disciplinary action. Unusual or erratic behavior that disrupts the workplace and/or poses a health or safety risk to other employees will also result in disciplinary action against the employee.
- Encourage the employee to turn matters around and meet the standards of performance expected by the company.
- Afterward, document the meeting by highlighting the preceding information.
- Continue to monitor behavior and performance. If improvement occurs, commend the employee and encourage him or her to continue the good work. If problems persist, take the next step in the disciplinary process, usually an oral warning. If the oral warning fails to effect a favorable change in behavior, issue a written warning, followed progressively by suspension and discharge, if necessary.

Implementation of substance abuse and employee assistance programs requires training of both managerial and nonmanagerial employees. The nonmanagerial employees are informed of the content of the policies, with an emphasis on the procedures to follow to participate in the EAP. The managers, of course, receive the training described in the preceding paragraphs. Exhibit 3 outlines how a company might proceed to introduce substance abuse policies and an employee assistance program. The model described in Exhibit 3 was designed for a manufacturing company in which unions are present.

Summary

Substance (drug and/or alcohol) abuse is a major problem in industry. The costs are staggering and there is no clear indication that the situation is about to improve.

Employers have begun to address the problems posed by employees who abuse alcohol and drugs. To detect the problem, many use some combination of preemployment and employee testing programs. Testing has proved troublesome, however, because of false-positive results and challenges to the constitutionality of testing procedures.

Even in those instances in which positive test results are confirmed and probable cause for testing is demonstrated, federal and state courts have restricted the use of the employment-at-will doctrine in imposing discipline. Companies are therefore under increasing pressure to demonstrate that employees with drug or alcohol problems are impaired and cannot perform adequately on the job. Demonstrating impairment is often difficult, however, and unless employers make some effort to rehabilitate these employees, the courts are apt to rule against discharges. Companies must reasonably accommodate the dependency problem by providing some form of rehabilitative assistance.

Reasonable accommodation is most frequently demonstrated by sponsorship of an employee assistance program (EAP). EAPs are becoming more prevalent in industry, though they cannot cure the employee with drug and alcohol problems. Most EAPs, however,

**Exhibit 3. Information Flow: Substance Abuse and Employee
Assistance Program Training.**

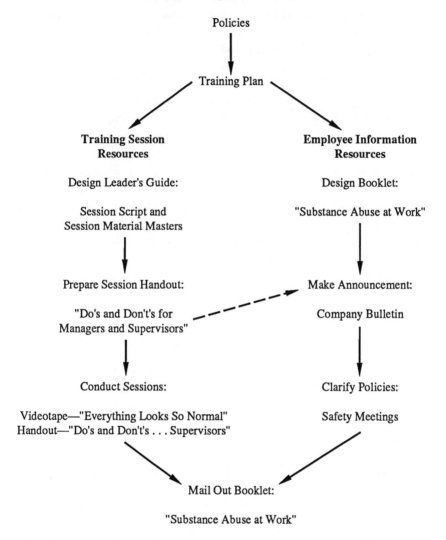

have alleviated absenteeism and have reduced medical program
costs for employees.

The most prudent course for employers seems to be institution of a program that emphasizes training and rehabilitative

assistance. Training supervisors to confront employees suspected of substance abuse is an important responsibility of employers. By associating poor performance with unusual or erratic behavior, supervisors focus on the impairment, not the legality or morality of substance abuse. They also avoid false accusations and wrongful actions should an investigation disclose that drugs and alcohol were not at issue.

The future of company detection and treatment or referral programs is uncertain. The private sector may join with the public sector to intensify educational efforts designed to inform people of the health and occupational consequences of drug and alcohol abuse. Employers are also likely to take a hard line in dealing with confirmed drug and alcohol abuse where the abuser is shown to be impaired and unable to perform adequately on the job. As the costs associated with substance abuse continue to escalate, employers are likely to become more involved in combating the effects of drug and alcohol abuse in the workplace.

3

AIDS:
The Critical Issues
for Management

With the advent of the 1980s, a public health issue—acquired immune deficiency syndrome (AIDS)—became a major and growing concern of corporate management. Laurance Baccini, a Philadelphia lawyer who advises companies on AIDS issues, claims that at some point "every corporation in America will have an AIDS problem" (Chapman, 1986). The dimensions and consequences of the problem are ominous:

- Between 1.0 and 1.5 million Americans carry the AIDS virus— HIV, LAV, and HTLV-III.
- Of those carrying the virus, between 20 and 30 percent will develop the disease within five years; another 40 percent will suffer a less severe form of infection called AIDS-related complex (ARC).
- Of those contracting AIDS, better than 50 percent will die within a year of the diagnosis and an additional 30 percent will die within two years; virtually all will die within five to seven years.
- Of those contracting the less severe ARC, some will die from infectious diseases; most will be too ill to work on a sustained basis.

Exacerbating the situation is the fact that at present there is no cure for AIDS, and the prospects for developing a cure are not very encouraging. As indicated by the mortality and disability figures summarized in the preceding paragraph, attempts to treat the disease have yet to succeed in forcing the disease into remission. And the disease is growing at an alarming rate.

Estimates by the U.S. Centers for Disease Control (CDC) indicate that by 1991 the number of confirmed AIDS cases in the United States will be 268,081 (McAuliffe and others, 1987), 175,000 more cases than reported for 1985. Other estimates, however, by the Rand Corporation place the number of cases at close to 400,000 by 1991. Using the smaller estimate of the CDC, the surgeon general predicts that 179,000 of those afflicted will have died by the end of 1991. For the 145,000 AIDS patients estimated to need health and supportive services, the surgeon general places the cost of treatment at $8 to $16 billion in 1991 (U.S. Public Health Service, 1987). As the disease is transmitted in a variety of ways, some of which are not completely understood by medical authorities, this exponential growth in AIDS cases could well continue into the twenty-first century. Consequently, AIDS has been declared the number-one health priority in the country by the U.S. Department of Health and Human Services.

Profile of AIDS Victims

AIDS is primarily a disease of homosexual and bisexual males, who, collectively, account for about 73 percent of all cases among Americans. Drug abusers, who contract the virus from contaminated hypodermic needles, account for another 17 percent of the cases. Most of the remaining 10 percent contract the disease from contaminated blood obtained in transfusions. Others contract the disease from normal heterosexual relationships and accidents involving contaminated human fluids, usually blood (Chapman, 1986).

Although AIDS has been reported in all fifty states, it is most prevalent in urban areas. To date, for example, almost half the AIDS victims live in New York City, San Francisco, and Los Angeles. Officials estimate that this imbalance will change as we move into the 1990s. They note that four out of five new victims over the next few years will reside and work in largely urban areas other than San Francisco and New York City (Comarow, 1987).

Because the AIDS virus is carried by males and females, heterosexuals are increasingly at risk. As those infected with the virus may show no visible symptom for several years, spouses, fiancés, and casual acquaintances, many of whom will be prostitutes, may contract the disease before it is confirmed or suspected in their partners. Studies indicate, for example, that a woman who has frequent sex with a carrier of the virus has a 33 to 50 percent chance of becoming infected. Epidemiologists in Tennessee, however, found that even after four years of steady sexual contact, infected spouses convey the virus to their partners only about 20 percent of the time (Siwolop and others, 1987). Because of the uncertainty and potentially lethal consequences, however, carriers of the virus pose a significant threat to the community if they are promiscuous and incautious.

The dimensions and consequences of the AIDS problem make several demands of corporate management. In succeeding sections of this chapter, these demands are discussed under the topics of health care costs, morale and productivity, employee rights and company liability, and testing: the right to privacy versus the right to know.

The purpose of the discussion is twofold: to identify the key policy issues pertaining to AIDS in the workplace and to explain how some companies are responding to these issues to protect themselves and their employees from both the legal and health risks associated with AIDS in the workplace.

Health Care Costs

Medical costs for a typical AIDS patient range from $50,000 to $150,000 (McAuliffe and others, 1987; Letchinger, 1986). At the national level, the U.S. Public Health Service predicts the cost of caring for AIDS patients could reach $16 billion by 1991, nearly 2.4 percent of the projected $650 billion for all personal health care expenditures (Chapman, 1986). The American Council for Life Insurance and the Health Insurance Association report that for 1986 some $292 million was paid in claims for AIDS cases (Collingwood, 1988). The cumulative cost is estimated to be more than $37 billion by 1991, and the costs for AIDS-related deaths are expected to reach $50 billion by the end of this century, according to the Society of Actuaries. Much of this burden will fall on corporations, as 70 percent of the population is covered by health insurance provided by employers (Chapman, 1986).

As discussed elsewhere (see Chapter Four), health care cost containment is a major economic policy issue at present and in the foreseeable future for corporations. The threat of an AIDS epidemic in the next decade, therefore, places new and intense pressures on corporations. Johnson and Higgins, a New York–based benefits consulting firm, estimates the cumulative cost to companies over the five-year period 1987–1992 to reach $14 billion in benefits (Lord and others, 1987). As a cure for the disease may require another five to ten years of research, no short-term relief from the expense of caring for AIDS patients is likely.

Current treatment with a drug (AZT) that stops the AIDS virus from reproducing is gaining widespread acceptance. The drug provides symptomatic relief and a brief reprieve to thousands who currently receive it. Many medical professionals believe that a second form of treatment is also required, however, to rehabilitate the patient's immune system. The combined costs of these treatments could well escalate the expense of care for a growing number of patients. Under these conditions, most companies would have to restructure their health insurance programs to remain viable.

To meet the care needs of patients and the financial needs of companies and their insurers, an innovative technique called case management is being adopted by some companies. The intent of the case management approach (Bompey, 1986) is to provide options for treatment that are preferred by the patient, agreed to by the patient's physician, and, in some cases, acknowledged by the health care provider as a less expensive alternative to conventional treatment plans. Often the options include home or hospice care, for example, which costs less and provides greater comfort to the patient as well.

Of course, employers should place considerable emphasis on educating the work force about AIDS. A well-informed work force will be less fearful and suspicious of the disease. Informing those employees who contract the disease of its limited means of transmission and various options for treatment could translate into more productive time at work and less time off the job. The key point that managers should remember is that an informed work force is more likely to support various initiatives to accommodate the disease and to control the costs of treatment.

Morale and Productivity

Because AIDS is a fatal disease, many people react with strong emotions to the current crisis. In some cases the reactions border on hysteria, posing a serious threat to productivity and morale. Employers have noted that diminished productivity among the "worried well" is noticeable and considerable. Even where no documented cases of AIDS exist, some employees make inferences about the presence of the disease based on known or suspected lifestyles. If not addressed by informed and responsible action from management, rumors of risks to health and safety can severely damage productivity and morale.

An emotionally distressed work force can develop "AIDS phobia." This condition is analogous to "cancer phobia," the fear of cancer, which is often associated with the presence in work settings of carcinogenic material used in the fabrication or processing of products. Despite precautionary and protective measures taken by management to safeguard employees in these situations, some employees suffer severe bouts of distress. As some courts have sustained claims for cancer phobia (for example, *Ayers v. Township of Jackson*, 189 N.J. Supp. 561, 1983, and 493 A.2d 1314, 1985; and *Ferrara v. Galluchio*, 5 N.Y. 2d 16, 1958), there is a legal precedent for such action based on the legitimate fear of future injury (Kandel, 1986). Employers can reduce the adverse consequences of AIDS phobia by educating their employees about the causes and means of transmitting the disease. If employers fail to take this initiative, they risk being found negligent in either miscommunicating or failing to communicate information and, thus, inflicting emotional distress on employees.

Employees suffering from emotional distress caused by AIDS

phobia are unlikely to be very productive. Distressed employees still on the job are likely to avoid certain tasks, to work at slower rates, and to spend excessive amounts of time complaining about conditions to management. They will also engage other employees in conversations about the situation. As these conversations progress, work will go undone and anxiety levels will likely rise. AIDS phobia, under these conditions, becomes a far greater nemesis to the employer than does the disease itself.

To combat the adverse effects of AIDS phobia on morale and productivity, managers should actively educate their employees on the risks of contracting the disease in the workplace. Current information from AIDS specialists indicates that the danger of contracting AIDS in the workplace is negligible. The CDC assert that the normal person-to-person contact occurring in the work-place does not pose the risk of transmission of the virus from an infected person to others.

Several companies have instituted formal programs to educate their employees on the risks of AIDS and, in so doing, to combat the fear and confusion that could jeopardize morale and productivity. As a recent study conducted by the Center for Work Performance at the Georgia Institute of Technology indicates, however, many people in the work force remain uninformed and apprehensive. The center reports, for instance, that 66 percent of those responding to the survey expressed concern about using the same restroom as someone with AIDS. Forty percent would be reluctant to eat in the same cafeteria, and 37 percent would not share tools or equipment with an AIDS victim. And 33 percent doubt assurances that AIDS can be transmitted only through sexual contact and contaminated blood.

Although AIDS will continue to remain an emotionally volatile issue for some time, employers can combat the confusion, fear, and, on occasion, hysteria associated with the risks of contracting the virus. Education programs, if well designed and effectively conducted, can add appreciably to the ongoing efforts of management to maintain morale and to facilitate improvements in productivity. Fortunately, much information about the disease and a variety of support groups and agencies is readily available to employers and employees. For example, *Personnel Journal* provides referral information as a public service in its monthly issues. A list of telephone hotlines and information sources available to employers, AIDS victims, and their families has been compiled by the Office of the Surgeon General and is reproduced as an appendix at the end of this chapter.

For companies that desire to make a more extensive effort, including strategies for policy development carefully explained in a manual for top executives and augmented by a guidebook for managers, the San Francisco AIDS Foundation offers a comprehensive program entitled "AIDS in the Work Force."

Although AIDS phobia among the worried well is a major concern, lost time among AIDS victims exacerbates this concern and its effect on productivity. As the disease progresses and its deleterious effects become more evident, prolonged absences increase. As the number of cases is increasing exponentially too, the total loss of time at work by AIDS patients will cause significant problems for employers in the decades ahead. With AIDS cases estimated to total between 270,000 and 400,000 by 1991, the long-term financial costs attributed to lost productivity and earnings among AIDS patients is expected to exceed $55.6 billion (Lord and others, 1987).

Employee Rights and Company Liabilities

Although some employers are making a conscientious and concerted effort to educate employees on the facts of the disease and to treat AIDS victims responsibly, many employers have either ignored AIDS as an issue in the workplace or they have acted improperly in responding to AIDS-related incidents on the job. Passivity and hostility, however, are likely to increase management's vulnerability to expensive legal action. Employers could face employment discrimination charges for the actions of employees at all levels if AIDS victims are singled out as a special class of people to receive disparate treatment. Succeeding paragraphs present a comprehensive analysis of the major liabilities confronting employers in responding to AIDS-related incidents at work. Topics for discussion include compliance with federal and state statutes, reasonable accommodation, and testing.

Federal and State Statutes. The Occupational Safety and

Health Administration (OSHA) requires the workplace to be free from recognized hazards to safety and health. The National Labor Relations Act (Wagner Act) states that employees cannot be penalized for refusing to work out of a legitimate fear for their safety. The Justice Department issued an opinion in 1986 contending that the provisions of the Rehabilitation Act of 1973 barring discrimination against the handicapped do not apply to AIDS patients. On March 3, 1987, however, the U.S. Supreme Court ruled that contagious diseases are indeed covered by the Rehabilitation Act. The Court declined to rule on the Justice Department's contention that the act did not apply to carriers of the disease who are not suffering from the effects of the disease. The justices did instruct the lower courts to defer to public health officials' professional judgments in determining whether or not a victim of a contagious disease poses a threat to the health of other workers.

It should be noted that the Rehabilitation Act has broad coverage too: sections 501 and 503 apply to all federal employees and employees of all federal contractors whose contracts are for $2,500 or more; section 504 applies to all recipients of federal funds.

Forty-seven states and the District of Columbia have laws prohibiting discrimination against the disabled in both public and private employment. Although the definition of disability, the inclusion of short- and long-term disabilities, and the extension of impairment to the ability to fight off infection may vary from state to state, state jurisdictions are likely to interpret the laws quite liberally in support of AIDS patients. The New York State Division of Human Rights, for example, has made it emphatically clear that discrimination based on AIDS as a disability is prohibited by state law (Kandel, 1986).

Although the weight of the legislation suggests that employers have little discretion in developing policies for employees afflicted with AIDS, the issue for many remains unresolved. Much of the uncertainty is attributed to the growing confusion over how the disease is contracted. At present, the CDC attribute 3 percent of all diagnosed AIDS cases to "undetermined causes" (Seib, 1987). Should this figure increase over time as more cases are diagnosed, pressures to take more stringent precautions to protect employees will increase as well.

To date, the OSHA rule requiring the removal of hazards to health and safety has been tested. Nurses in a San Francisco hospital were denied permission by the state OSHA board to wear special gloves and masks in treating AIDS patients. In another incident, two pregnant women at Bank of America lost their jobs because they refused to work near an employee with AIDS. At a large department store, however, a homosexual employee whose deteriorating physical condition caused a decline in employee morale was asked to leave. In this instance, because the employee did not contest the directive, no legal action was taken to countermand the company's dismissal.

The provisions of the National Labor Relations Act have not been tested. Conceivably, a member of the bargaining unit—an hourly employee—could refuse to perform some task or work procedure with a co-worker infected with the AIDS virus. Fearing a legitimate risk to his or her health, the employee could refuse to work with the AIDS victim. If management then disciplined the employee for failing to follow the instructions of management, the union could file a grievance alleging an unfair labor practice. The matter would probably proceed to arbitration for final disposition. In the unlikely event the union contract did not contain an arbitration clause, the charge would most likely be referred to OSHA for disposition.

Although there are no precedents in matters covered by the National Labor Relations Act, arbitrators are likely to show great deference to past rulings, invoking the provisions of the Rehabilitation Act of 1973 or, where appropriate, applicable state and local statutes. Until incontrovertible evidence can be presented to indicate that AIDS can be acquired through more casual and indirect contact, managers can be fairly confident that the provisions of current federal, state, and local laws will apply to all AIDS cases in the workplace.

Reasonable Accommodation: The Appeal to Fairness. An employer reviewing the legislation and court rulings defining illnesses and diseases as handicaps may conclude that no adverse action can be taken against an employee afflicted with a disease. This is not the case. An employer is expected to make reasonable accommodations only. Furthermore, these accommodations need only incur minimal costs and disruptions.

Reasonable accommodations could well take the form of allowing more frequent breaks, providing a flex-time work schedule, giving sick leave for medical treatment, and restructuring the job (Feuer, 1987). At Bank of America, for example, an employee with AIDS who was suffering visibly from Kaposi's sarcoma, a form of cancer in which purple lesions on the skin are quite noticeable, was allowed to work at home on his personal computer (Chase, 1988). If the requirements of the position are not met despite good faith efforts to make reasonable accommodations, an employer could proceed with considerable confidence to discharge the employee. To substantiate the discharge, an employer would have to demonstrate that reasonable accommodations have been made and that performance standards are not being met.

Reasonable accommodation seeks to define a balance in the relationship between employer and employee. The employer is obliged to make accommodations to preclude the possibility of a handicap becoming a convenient excuse to eliminate a class of people from the workplace. On the other hand, the law and the courts, in varying degree, recognize the need for limits to these accommodations. Limits acknowledge the property rights of an employer to obtain productive work from an employee in exchange for compensation in the form of wages or salaries and benefits. Limits also acknowledge an employer's social obligations to other employees, moreover, to provide a work environment that is safe and healthy. If a physician certifies it safe for an employee to return to work, an employer would have to demonstrate that a person with AIDS threatens the health and safety of others. In the unlikely event that an employee contracted AIDS and claimed the disease was communicated by another employee with AIDS in the workplace, the exclusive remedy in most states would be workers' compensation (Kandel, 1986).

Testing: The Right to Privacy Versus the Right to Know

Testing employees and applicants for employment to determine whether or not they have the AIDS antibody or ARC is a controversial issue. Except in Wisconsin, California, and Florida, it is not unlawful per se for employers to require a medical exam for a current or prospective employee. Employers must limit the use of the results from these exams, however, to the person's current ability to do the job. If current ability to do the job is the issue, the practices of the federal government can justifiably be questioned.

The federal government has succeeded in requiring members of the armed forces, the foreign service, and other agencies to submit to mandatory testing. Should this practice continue to spread, it could become a matter of public policy. As public policy, requirements for testing could supersede state and local laws that currently proscribe or limit testing. Detection practices that are now either limited or prohibited, therefore, could become permissible in the future as more is learned about the causes and effects of AIDS.

The Case for Testing. Advocates for testing cite historical precedents in support of their position. Earlier widespread concern over tuberculosis and syphilis resulted in rational testing policies. In both instances, as Robert Redfield, a physician at Walter Reed Army Medical Center, notes, testing began before cures were found (Seib, 1987). Another argument forcefully advanced by proponents of testing for AIDS is that many people who test positive will take precautions to prevent further spread of the disease. Finally, mandatory testing of diverse groups of people within a community or organization will avoid the stigma that currently discourages many people in high-risk categories, homosexuals and drug users, for example, from voluntary testing.

The Case Against Testing. Opponents of testing cite what they regard as an unreasonable breach of privacy as their major argument. Safeguarding information on promiscuous persons would be difficult; for example, test results could embarrass or discredit someone who tested positive for the AIDS antibody. Cost is another factor cited by opponents. New Hampshire's governor has proposed a fee of $8 to $10 for each applicant for a marriage license. For an expected 22,000 applicants annually, the fees would total $88,000 to $110,000. This is the cost, cite the critics, to confirm the two cases of AIDS that are likely to occur in New Hampshire annually. The CDC estimate that the cost of confirming AIDS carriers by testing low-risk people is $18,197 per confirmed carrier (Seib, 1987).

Taking a Stance on Testing. For employers the controversy over testing is best approached with caution. As long as current medical opinion regarding the means of transmission of the disease remains valid, employers should avoid testing for the mere presence of the disease or its antibody. As in all cases, employers should focus their evaluative efforts on an employee's ability to do the job with no more than the reasonable accommodation used by the employer to help someone classified as handicapped to meet normal job performance expectations. Additionally, of course, employers must take reasonable and prudent measures to provide a safe and healthy work environment for all employees. Again, with respect to AIDS, no special measures seem necessary except for health care institutions, where health care workers are judged to be at risk.

Developing an AIDS Policy

There are many parallels between AIDS and substance abuse as policy issues for management. Both AIDS and substance abuse pose threats to productivity and to efforts to contain health care costs. They also present a formidable challenge to the traditional notion of employer rights expressed in the employment-at-will doctrine. Employers can no longer terminate employees at will for behavior the employer regards as unacceptable when the courts regard such action as discriminatory and illegal. Companies find it necessary to follow a lengthy and often elaborate set of procedures to provide counseling and rehabilitative services to employees as part of an increasingly extensive commitment to safeguard employee rights.

In many cases, employees afflicted with chemical dependencies (drugs and/or alcohol) and AIDS are classified as handicapped and entitled to the same treatment as any handicapped employee. The treatment consists of efforts to accommodate the handicap reasonably. It may also include medical insurance, an employee assistance program (EAP), and a concerted effort by the employer to educate the work force on the causes and effects of the disease. To date, however, the corporate response to these matters nationwide has been weak. A March 1987 poll conducted by Louis Harris and Associates noted that 89 percent of the respondents had no specific policy for dealing with AIDS. In addition, 85 percent reported having no information program on AIDS for their employees, and 72 percent of those had no intention of implementing such a program (Masi, 1987). In light of what is known about the disease, it is somewhat astonishing to note too that one major automobile manufacturer stated that there was "no reason to believe that any of their 382,000 employees worldwide had AIDS" (Masi, 1987, p. 57).

A conference on AIDS in the fall of 1987 sponsored by Allstate Insurance Company reported that only 5 percent of U.S. employers have developed an AIDS policy. Reasons cited for avoiding the issue included fear of image problems—condoning homosexuality and intravenous drug use—and client backlash (Chase, 1988). These results are more discouraging than those obtained earlier in 1987 by Louis Harris and Associates and portend future problems for employers as the disease proliferates among the work force.

In developing a policy on AIDS, employers should be careful not to create a new class of contractual rights for workers with AIDS. As the report "Corporations Urge Peers to Adopt Humane Policies for AIDS Victims" points out, "Should a company wish to assure consistent treatment of employees with AIDS, but not wish to create contract rights, it may want to issue guidelines to its managers instead of distributing a specific policy to all employees" (Chase, 1988). The potential problem raised is the creation of inconsistent policies as artifacts of the law. The practical consequences to the employer can be devastating. Morale and productivity can decline as disgruntled employees rebel against the different standards for different classes of people. In some states, though, the issue can be circumvented by limiting the distribution of expectations on matters of policy to managers only. In these instances, issuing work rules that are fairly applied across the organization is a wise practice. A prudent regard for fair and consistent treatment of disabilities by an employer can contribute significantly to a corporate image of fairness and impartiality in policies regarding the health and welfare of employees.

Employers cannot avoid what could well become the major health issue of the 1990s and, in all likelihood, the early part of the twenty-first century. Because of the mystery still associated with the disease and its fatal nature, employers need to remember that employees with AIDS will become distraught before they become disabled. Mechanisms to deal with the disability issue are in place. Insurance, employee assistance programs, and reasonable accommodation policies provide the psychological and financial support to cope with AIDS-related disabilities. Some employers provide this support or are working toward that goal under the broad rubric of policies toward handicapped employees. Those employers who choose to remain ignorant of the disability issue are taking imprudent risks. The issue of distraught employees approaching disability is a more troublesome policy issue.

A few organizations have chosen to address the issue of distraught employees by implementing companywide comprehensive education programs on AIDS. Typically, these programs start with a widely disseminated statement of company policy such as the following from Bank of America (Feuer, 1987, p. 71): "Bank of America recognizes that employees with life-threatening illnesses including but not limited to cancer, heart disease, and AIDS may wish to continue to engage in as many of their normal pursuits as their condition allows, including work. As long as these employees are able to meet acceptable performance standards, and medical evidence indicates that their conditions are not a threat to themselves or others, managers should be sensitive to their condition and ensure that they are treated consistently with other employees."

Policies may continue with more explicit discussions of such issues as testing, health insurance coverage, EAPs, and precautions necessary for overseas travel, especially to countries where AIDS is a serious and widespread health problem.

A member of the human resources staff, perhaps the company's EAP coordinator, is identified as the person whom managers should contact for information on AIDS and other life-threatening illnesses. To initiate the education effort, the EAP coordinator should arrange a series of information briefings and discussions on the company's policies and procedures pertaining to AIDS and on the causes and effects of the disease. To reduce the risk of undue concern by employees, these discussions can be incorporated into regularly scheduled safety meetings and management updates. These efforts can also be augmented with printed material. Articles in company publications can reinforce key points addressed in the meetings and emphasized in the policy statements. The results of this approach can be dramatic. Since Bank of America initiated its education program, it has had no requests for transfers by employees based on fear of a co-worker's illness (Merritt, 1987).

Summary

AIDS in the workplace is a growing menace that demands attention. A rational, dispassionate response that is well grounded in medical fact and civil law can help substantially in providing needed assistance to AIDS victims and preventing undue labor turbulence and lost productivity. Management must obtain the facts, make them available to employees, and incorporate them into a comprehensive policy to assist handicapped employees. After reasonable efforts have been made to accommodate handicapped employees, employers can base subsequent personnel actions on an employee's demonstrated ability to meet the performance standards of the job.

As a policy issue, AIDS presents a unique situation in which concern for the dignity of individual employees coincides with concern for maintaining productivity and morale. The dilemma confronting employers, it seems, is avoiding the parochial appeals of the self-righteous, on the one hand, and the self-indulgent, on the other hand. AIDS is a volatile issue invoking judgments on limits to behavior. Some managers will be tempted to join the fray, to choose sides. Succumbing to the temptation, however, can only be self-defeating. As with substance abuse, the issue with AIDS is the ability to perform assigned work once reasonable accommodations have been made for an acknowledged handicap. Performance to standards, not conformance to rules, should be the philosophy on which an AIDS policy is based.

Appendix: AIDS Information Sources

AIDS Action Council
729 Eighth Street, SE
Suite 200
Washington, DC 20003
(202) 547-3101

American Association of Physicians for Human Rights
P.O. Box 14366
San Francisco, CA 94114
(415) 558-9353

Gay Men's Health Crisis
P.O. Box 274
132 West 24th Street
New York, NY 10011
(212) 807-6655

Hispanic AIDS Forum
c/o APRED
853 Broadway, Suite 2007
New York, NY 10003
(212) 870-1902 or 870-1864

Local Red Cross or American Red Cross AIDS Education Office
1730 D Street, NW
Washington, DC 20006
(202) 737-8300

Los Angeles AIDS Project
7362 Santa Monica Boulevard
Los Angeles, CA 90046
(213) 876-AIDS

Minority Task Force on AIDS
c/o New York City Council of Churches
475 Riverside Drive
Room 456
New York, NY 10115
(212) 749-1214

Mothers of AIDS Patients (MAP)
c/o Barbara Peabody
3403 E Street
San Diego, CA 92102
(619) 234-3432

National AIDS Network
729 Eighth Street, SE
Suite 300
Washington, DC 20003
(202) 546-2424

National Association of People with AIDS
P.O. Box 65472
Washington, DC 20035
(202) 483-7979

National Coalition of Gay Sexually Transmitted Disease Services
c/o Mark Behar
P.O. Box 239
Milwaukee, WI 53201
(414) 277-7671

National Council of Churches/ AIDS Task Force
475 Riverside Drive
Room 572
New York, NY 10115
(212) 870-2421

National Gay Task Force AIDS Information Hotline
(800) 221-7044
In New York: (212) 807-6016

National Sexually Transmitted Diseases Hotline
American Social Health Association
(800) 227-8922

PHS AIDS Hotline
(800) 342-AIDS or (800) 342-2437

U.S. Public Health Service
Public Affairs Office
Hubert H. Humphrey Building
Room 725-H
200 Independence Avenue, SW
Washington, DC 20202
(202) 245-6867

Source: U.S. Public Health Service, 1987.

PART TWO

Compensation and Benefits

Historically, compensation and benefit management in most organizations has been concerned with ensuring that people were properly paid, that wage rates were competitively set, and that benefit plans were appropriately administered. These functions are still important; however, the field of compensation and benefits has grown more dynamic and complex.

Today compensation professionals face increased cost pressures and legal challenges. As American business attempts to become more competitive, many firms seek ways to reduce costs, especially overhead (that is, those costs associated with programs or activities that do not directly support revenue-producing operations). One area that offers significant potential for cost avoidance or cost saving is employee benefits. And, of all employee benefits, health care costs have risen most significantly since the beginning of the decade. Although it is unlikely that these costs can actually be reduced, it is essential that every effort be made to control future increases.

Yet the issue is not simply one of cost reduction. If cost were the only criterion, the task of the human resources manager would be easy—eliminate or reduce employee benefits until the desired cost savings are realized. But seasoned practitioners know that benefit reductions can pose other challenges. Employee benefits constitute one of several systems rewards with which employers attract and retain people. If benefits are reduced excessively, the organization runs the risk of becoming less attractive as an employer than other organizations. Hence, recruitment can be adversely affected. And, because benefits may also be considered a hygiene factor, reductions may generate employee dissatisfaction and problems with retention. Therefore, decisions on the type and level of benefits offered by organizations must be made carefully, with full knowledge of the potential systemic effects of attempts to reduce costs. Chapter Four explores why health care costs have grown and discusses the options available to the employer for containing future escalation.

Although competitive pressures suggest a variety of new cost reduction efforts, the evolving legal environment presents other social and financial challenges. Notable among these, to many observers, is the issue of comparable worth. Although this issue is not new, steady growth in female employment and the continuing disparity in average pay rates between men and women have intensified the efforts of comparable worth advocates.

Since the passage of the Equal Pay Act of 1963 and the Civil Rights Act of 1964, the government has attempted to ensure economic justice in the administration of compensation programs. Historically, discrimination in pay has been assessed by an equal pay for equal work standard. But today, many suggest that the standard should be equal pay for comparable work. Because some firms allegedly employ artificial distinctions in job classifications to perpetuate lower pay for women, and occasionally for minorities, advocates of comparable worth propose that employees who perform work requiring similar skills under similar conditions should receive the same pay. Although few would challenge the concept of pay equity, employers recognize the administrative challenges posed by enactment of a comparable worth standard and its potential cost and labor market implications. Chapter Five explores arguments for and against the concept, traces its historical development, presents recent court interpretations, and discusses actions employers can take to minimize the potential for comparable worth litigation.

4

Health Care
Cost Containment:
Tough Decisions in
a Changing Environment

Skyrocketing medical costs have been front-page news for the past fifteen years. Although much of the growth in health care costs has been underwritten by the government, the impact on American business has been profound. What was once considered an employee benefit to be administered in a relatively perfunctory manner by the personnel department is now a major corporate cost component worthy of top-level, professional management. This chapter discusses the magnitude of the health cost issue, factors impacting health care cost growth, cost containment strategies, and employer preferences and actions.

Health Care Costs

Health benefits are now the third largest cost for most manufacturing organizations. Raw material costs and straight-time pay rank first and second. For most service organizations, health benefits are the second largest cost. The following data indicate the magnitude of these expenditures. In 1950, health care expenditures in the United States constituted 4.4 percent of the GNP. In 1985, it formed 10.7 percent of GNP. Table 3 presents the pattern of growth in health care expenditures from 1965 to 1985. Without strong cost controls, it is estimated that by the year 2000 health care spending may reach $790 billion annually, or 13.0 percent of the GNP. According to a different yardstick, health care costs amount to 24 percent of after-tax corporate profits.

Why are health benefit costs so prominent? For one thing, health-related benefits are among the most common fringe benefits offered by employers. In 1981, health insurance became the second most common employee benefit after holidays and vacations. Ninety-seven percent of full-time employees in industry receive some form of health insurance. Such insurance cost business more than $35 billion in 1977, a period preceding double-digit inflation. Overall, in 1987, health benefit costs constituted 9.7 percent of the payroll pie. The major components of these health care expenditures are broken down in Table 4.

Not only is the magnitude of health care expenditures great, but the rate of growth has been far out of proportion to other segments of the economy. From 1981 to 1983, the average annual rate of increase in health insurance premiums was 20 percent. The average rate of change in personal health care expenditures exceeded 10 percent. Although these increases have moderated recently, they still exceed increases in the Consumer Price Index. In 1986 the cost of medical care increased by 7.7 percent and the average cost of a hospital stay surged 19 percent; however, the rate of growth in the Consumer Price Index for the same period was only 1.1 percent. In 1987, according to a study by A. Foster Higgins & Company, a New York–based benefits consultant, the cost of health care benefits increased 7.9 percent while the energy-adjusted inflation rate was only 3.8 percent.

Many observers of the health care scene feel that the toughest test is yet to come (Nielsen, 1987). Retiree medical benefits constitute a potentially staggering liability. By the year 2000, it is estimated that the number of Americans age 65 and older will grow by 25 percent. And, by 2030, the percentage of the population older than age 65 will exceed 21 percent. In 1974, the average Fortune 500 company had twelve active employees for every retiree. Now it has three. In 1982, Bethlehem Steel had 70,000 active and 54,000 retired employees; in 1987, it had 37,500 active and 70,000 retired em-

Table 3. National Health Care Expenditures, 1965–1985.

Year	Total Spending (billions)	Spending Per Person	Spending as Percent of GNP
1965	$ 41.7	$ 211	6.0
1970	74.7	358	7.5
1975	132.7	604	8.6
1980	249.0	1,075	9.5
1985	425.0	1,780	10.7

Source: U.S. Department of Health and Human Services.

Table 4. Comparative Distribution of
Health Care Expenditures.

	1970	1980
Hospital care	37%	40%
Physicians' services	19	19
Dentists' services	6	6
Drugs	11	8
Nursing home care	6	8
Other personal health	8	7
Other national health	13	12

Source: U.S. Department of Health and
Human Services.

ployees. General Motors spent $837 million in 1985 on the medical bills of its 285,000 retirees or their survivors.

If left unchecked, one analyst projects that by the year 2000 health care expenditures could eliminate all profits for the average Fortune 500 company and the largest 250 nonindustrials. It is little wonder that 28 percent of the chief executive officers in a recent survey of 200 large industrial corporations said they were the most influential persons in their company's health care policymaking process (Herzlinger and Schwartz, 1985).

Factors Contributing to Rising Health Care Costs

A number of factors appear to be involved with rising health care costs. Some are structural; others are behavioral. Several key factors affecting cost growth are discussed here.

Changing Demographics. The advancing average age of the American population is increasing the demand for health services. Older persons require a greater quantity of more intensive and, thus, more expensive medical care. As a result, chronic diseases now outpace acute outbreaks of sickness or accidents as the major cause of illness.

Heightened Competition. Proliferation of the number and types of health care providers has produced increased competition. Unlike other industries, competition does not appear to lower service costs, perhaps because of the form that competition takes in the health care industry, that is, the use of advanced technology. As providers acquire the latest technological innovations to gain a new toehold in the market, costs rise for two reasons. First, the technology itself is expensive. Second, as providers strive to match the range of services provided by others, duplication occurs, the cost of which cannot be retrieved by an increase in usage rates alone. Heightened competition also results in increased promotional costs.

Cost Shifting. Several governmental strategies to reduce public sector outlays for health services have led to an increasing burden on private sector employers and individual consumers. Actions to restrict Medicaid rolls, increase deductibles and copayments, and narrow the range of services that Medicare will reimburse inevitably result in efforts by the provider to shift these unreimbursed costs to other consumer groups. In 1982, the Health Insurance Association of America estimated that $5.8 billion in charges was shifted from government sources to private patients (Wohl, 1984). Cost shifting also occurs to some extent within the private sector as some corporations, using more aggressive and sophisticated cost containment strategies, shift a portion of their costs to less aggressive organizations. Although this internal shift does not raise the total cost of health care, it allocates a disproportionate share of costs to smaller, less sophisticated organizations. The impact on these firms is the same as that of a general cost increase.

Provider Inefficiency. Most traditional health care providers have had little incentive to control per unit costs of services. Under private insurance, hospitals are reimbursed primarily on the basis of their costs. Additionally, most physicians are reimbursed on the basis of "usual and customary" fees, which reflect area and specialty pricing patterns. Hospitals can respond to decreased utilization by increasing rates or they can respond to lower reimbursement rates by increasing the length of patient stay. Part of the appeal of prepaid health plans (for example, health maintenance organizations) is that they provide the incentive to alter practice styles. This will be discussed more fully later.

Increased Malpractice Litigation. An increase in consumer willingness to litigate has substantially increased the cost of malpractice insurance premiums, and the failure of attempts to cap court awards in such cases has reinforced the rise. To protect themselves, medical practitioners prescribe additional, and often peripheral, tests to eliminate all potential sources of malpractice claims. A spokesman for Blue Cross and Blue Shield commented (1987) that about 20 percent of all diagnostic tests were unwarranted. In a 1983 survey of doctors by the American Medical Association, 41 percent said they ordered laboratory and diagnostic tests because they feared being sued. The American Medical Association further noted that one of the more frequent causes for litigation is a doctor's failure to properly diagnose a problem.

Lack of Employer Attention. Until recently, many companies failed to recognize the significance of changing health care patterns and costs. A Coopers and Lybrand survey of 225 employers found that only 29 percent of respondents had solid information about their health plans, including such data as the number of hospital admissions, average length of stay, and payments per employee (Coopers and Lybrand, 1983). Even fewer had detailed data on providers.

Cost Containment Strategies

Several strategies for cost containment are evident among the nation's businesses. In general, they range from promoting employee awareness of health care costs to effecting structural change in the health delivery system. A number of specific approaches are briefly discussed.

Promoting Employee Cost Consciousness. One of the first attempts at cost containment generally involves efforts by the employer to increase employee awareness of the company's health care cost situation and its potential impact on future health coverage, other fringe benefits, and, possibly, wages. Posters, newsletters, management orientation sessions, and similar devices are used to communicate the information (for example, provider price and cost differentials) aimed at influencing consumer (employee) choice for health services.

Typical of this approach are the actions of the Quaker Oats Company in Chicago and Maryland's attorney general office. Quaker Oats has produced a hospital pricing guide listing a range of selected diagnoses within 100 competing hospitals in the Chicago SMSA (Penzkover, 1984). The attorney general office in the state of Maryland is preparing a statewide directory of individual physician's fees for commonly performed procedures based on their Medicare claims ("Maryland to Publish First Statewide . . . ," 1986).

The goal of these informational efforts is a change in consumer choice. In the area of personal or family health, however, awareness alone is unlikely to impact employee behavior significantly. Even when used in conjunction with incentives (for example, sharing of savings with employees), cost reductions are likely to be modest. Nevertheless, this approach should complement other cost containment strategies implemented by employers.

Reducing System Utilization. A second set of options is available to employers attempting to reduce the overall level of use of health care services. These options include utilization reviews, mandatory second opinions, and wellness promotion programs. Utilization reviews are frequently employed by companies for certifying hospital admissions for nonemergency cases, for monitoring ongoing treatments, and for retrospectively assessing the value and appropriateness of care provided. Utilization reviews can be applied to specialty care situations, for example, disability and psychiatric care, and can also be instrumental for special case management when the levels of expenditure are likely to greatly exceed typical case outlays. More than one-half of the Fortune 500 companies have incorporated some form of utilization review into their cost management plans (Lee, 1986). In addition to the direct cost savings they produce, such reviews warn providers that their practices are being closely monitored. This factor alone can be significant in curtailing the escalation of health care costs.

One example of the benefits to be gained in this area is found in the Medical Case Management program of the Equitable Life Assurance Society of the United States. The program, last reported as having seventy clients nationally, targets twelve illnesses and injuries of a catastrophic nature (for example, precardiac bypass surgery, severe burns, major head trauma) for individual case management. Typical cost avoidance per case is cited at $8,000 to $200,000. One company that has referred seventeen cases to Equitable since July 1983 experienced a total cost avoidance of $600,000 (Employer's Health Costs Savings Letter, 1986).

In addition to the benefits gained from utilization reviews, good cost/benefit ratios have been reported for programs that make second opinions for surgery programs mandatory (Finkel, Ruchlin, and Parsons, 1981). These programs usually require a second confirming opinion from a physician for specific elective surgical procedures for which there is a high percentage of unnecessary surgery or for which a second opinion usually does not confirm the original diagnosis. Unnecessary surgery may be defined as a recommended elective (not life-threatening or emergency) procedure for which an alternative treatment may be preferable because (1) the surgery itself may be premature, (2) the risk to the patient may not justify the benefits of the proposed surgery, (3) an alternative medical treatment might be superior for both medical and cost-effective reasons, and (4) a less severe procedure might be preferable in the circumstances.

Some plans require second opinions on all elective surgery; however, this practice may not be cost-effective. It appears more beneficial for those common surgical procedures that are most likely not to be confirmed as necessary. Massachusetts, for example, has mandated a second opinion program for Medicaid participants for eight specific procedures. After the first year, significant declines were noted in seven of the eight procedures, with the greatest reduction in the number of hysterectomies. A cost/benefit ratio of nearly 1:4 was reported (Handel, 1984).

Finally, a more proactive approach to reducing the demand for health services is found in health promotion strategies. Through health insurance policies that promote a healthier way of life and the establishment of corporate "wellness" programs, six risk factors associated with diseases that cause 80 percent of all deaths can be eliminated or controlled. These six factors are smoking, high blood cholesterol, high blood pressure, obesity, alcoholism, and physical inactivity. All six factors involve behavior that can be changed. Because of its significance and growth in use, this cost containment strategy is addressed separately later.

Imposing Service Restrictions and Employee Cost Sharing. Several more direct and immediate avenues for employer cost savings can be identified within this category. For example, in the area of service restrictions, employers may impose limits on hospital stays, either case limits for specific procedures or global limits for a year. In the case of dental care, preventive examinations and cleanings may be limited to a specified number per year. Similarly, outpatient limits and physician service limits can be imposed.

Sharing a greater proportion of the burden of health costs with employees is another way of achieving reductions in outlays for health care. Common approaches include premium contributions, deductibles, and coinsurance. Requiring employees to make contributions to health care insurance premiums or increasing the level of employee contribution does not affect the use of health services, as employee payments, usually in the form of wage deductions, are independent of usage. Savings to the corporation, however, are direct and immediate. One study conducted in 1983 reported that only 11.8 percent of companies required no employee contributions to premiums, and 29.8 percent required a contribution of 20 percent or more of the cost of insurance premiums. A 1987 survey by A. Foster Higgins & Company indicated that 88 percent of employers required employees to pay a deductible.

Both the deductible (that is, requirement that employees pay for services to a set level before receiving any form of reimbursement) and coinsurance (that is, requirement that employees share in the cost of health services received according to some preestablished proportion) increase the employee's awareness of costs and reduce the employer's share of those costs. If the deductible and coinsurance amounts remain unchanged for several years, however, employees are less likely to be aware of cost increases.

By themselves, deductibles are more likely than coinsurance to discourage individuals from seeking unnecessary or convenience medical care if they are set at meaningful thresholds. In 1983, the annual deductible was only $100 per employee for about 60 percent of employer health plans, and only 15.6 percent reported annual deductibles exceeding $300 per family. However, on the basis of typical family incomes for covered employees, these deductibles provide little incentive to refrain from seeking unnecessary health care.

More than 80 percent of companies report employee copayments of 20 percent. Another 10 percent of companies have copayments of 10 percent. Less than 2 percent of companies have copayment schedules of 25 percent or higher. Even copayments of 10 to 20 percent can be significant for employees faced with a major or extended illness. Therefore, many companies have introduced annual out-of-pocket maximums above which the employee is no longer required to contribute. In the study cited previously, 51 percent of companies reported out-of-pocket maximums of $1,000 or less after the payment of a deductible. Forty-one percent had maximums ranging between $1,000 and $4,000, and only 2 percent of company maximums exceeded $5,000.

Finally, some companies have plans that pay all covered charges up to a dollar limit before employees pay anything. Of these companies, 83 percent set initial employee payment at $5,000 or more. This is an extremely expensive form of coverage for employers because few employees incur expenses greater than $5,000 per year. A less costly option for setting employer limits is to establish a benefit schedule under which certain benefits are paid up to a scheduled amount or up to a dollar limit over a lifetime. Most companies have a maximum of $5 million or less. As few consumers are likely to exceed this amount of medical services, a service maximum rather than a dollar limit is more likely to achieve desired cost containment objectives.

Undertaking Self-Insurance. Many larger companies can gain additional financial benefits by eliminating insurance premium payments and taxes through self-insurance. This option also provides for the ongoing use of reserve monies or their deposit into a tax-exempt trust. Self-insurance is most desirable for larger work forces because the greater the number of employees, the smaller the probability that actual claims will exceed expected claims. And, the volatility of medical claims is inversely related to the dollar amount of expected claims. In 1987, a study by consultant Johnson & Higgins indicated that 46 percent of corporations surveyed shunned conventional medical insurance for some or all of the health claims submitted by employees.

Although self-insurance offers potential cost advantages to employers, it should not be pursued without consideration of the additional administrative requirements it imposes. For example, a qualified health claims processing staff may be required to effectively assess claims for coordination of benefits, reasonableness of charges, appropriateness of treatment, and similar factors. Often, these functions are performed or supervised by individuals with nursing degrees. Alternatively, a third-party administrator can be used for claims processing, but the cost of producing these services can range from 3 to 10 percent of paid claims. The median is 5 percent.

Self-funding can also engender large financial risks. Catastrophic illnesses, such as those posed by AIDS, could be disastrous to a self-funded firm. To protect themselves, therefore, most self-insurers buy stop-loss coverage from insurance carriers, which takes over when an individual's claim exceeds a predetermined limit, for example, $50,000, or when all claims exceed a company's forecast by a specified amount.

Coordination of Benefits. Coordination-of-benefits reviews ensure that a company pays only allowable charges not covered by other insurance for which the employee or the employee's family is eligible, such as Medicare or dependent coverage with another employer. When both husband and wife are employed and are covered by separate employer health plans, determination of coverage applicability is relatively straightforward. The plan provided by the company in which the person incurring the expense works is considered the primary plan. Medical coverage for children is less clear, however.

Traditionally, when children incurred medical expenses and were covered as dependents by both parents' plans, the father's plan was considered primary; however, as a result of changing patterns of employment, the National Association of Insurance Commissioners (NAIC) has suggested use of the "birthday rule" to coordinate benefits for children covered by more than one group health plan. This guideline states that the plan of the parent whose birthday falls earlier in the year should be considered primary. More than half of the states have already adopted this guideline. Firms with a larger number of men with children should benefit from this rule, whereas companies with a high concentration of women with children could experience higher health care costs.

Shifting Service Demand Patterns. As some forms of health care service are less expensive than others, employers can implement strategies that attempt to shift employee demand from more expensive to less expensive forms of service. Some simple approaches involve financial incentives to shift demand patterns. For example, eliminating copayments on outpatient or ambulatory surgery can encourage employees to use outpatient treatment facilities. At Uniroyal, employees receive a $50 award for undergoing certain elective procedures on an outpatient basis. During the first four months of the program, 280 employees and retirees took advantage of the program. In total, they helped reduce medical costs by at least $70,000 (Employers' Health Costs Savings Letter, 1986).

The American Medical Association has endorsed the concept of ambulatory surgery for selected procedures. Some medical experts claim that as much as 20 to 40 percent of all surgical procedures can be performed on an outpatient basis, thereby eliminating overnight hospitalization and the resulting room-and-board and ancillary charges. However, the most recent data indicate that the demand for outpatient services is rising significantly. Outpatient visits grew by 8.1 percent in January–October 1986, compared with 4.1 percent for the same period in 1985. And, as demand grows, it can be anticipated that costs will rise and savings, compared with hospitalization, will be reduced. In particular, outpatient surgery may become as expensive as inpatient surgery if companies and insurers do not closely monitor the situation. Although outpatient surgery costs have traditionally ranged from 60 to 80 percent of inpatient surgery costs, in 1986 costs for four common outpatient surgical procedures ranged from 85 to 94 percent.

Additionally, as the number of hospital admissions decline as a result of outpatient initiatives, some experts contend that hospitals will attempt to maximize their revenue on a smaller pool of patients by adding extra charges for tests and supplies. A recent survey by Equicor–Equitable HCA Corporation suggests this concern may be valid. Equicor data indicate that the greatest increases in hospital charges during 1986 were for such ancillary services.

Another way of shifting patterns of service is by early detection through screening. Although primary prevention programs (for example, smoking cessation) attempt to reduce the risk of contracting specific diseases, secondary prevention programs (for example, colon cancer screening) attempt to reduce the impact of specific diseases by identifying and treating the illness early. As early treatment also reduces treatment costs, many companies have implemented workplace screening programs. The most common of these programs involve detection of cancer of the breast, cervix, colon, and rectum. Despite the potential utility of screening programs in improving employee health, these forms of cancer account for only a relatively small fraction of total cancer deaths in the United States for which screening is currently used. Thus, they are unlikely to result in significant cost savings. Also, the general effectiveness of workplace screening is still unknown. There is simply not enough evidence at this time to recommend that corporations sponsor widespread cancer screening programs (Herzlinger and Schwartz, 1985).

A third approach to shifting service demand patterns is flexible benefit programs. Basically, these programs allow employees to choose among different benefit plans. From the employer's point of view, choice increases employee cost consciousness and provides the potential to control benefit costs. Under the "medical bank account" model, for example, employees can elect to waive insurance protection for some basic health insurance, but continue to be covered under a liberal major medical plan. The employee pays for all routine medical and prescription drug expenses typically covered under the health insurance program. At the end of the year, the employee is paid a predetermined amount or a proportion of savings accrued from funds credited to the employee's medical bank account. Thus, flexible benefit programs may furnish incentives for employees to select health plans with lesser medical benefits in exchange for other benefits (for example, additional vacation days or additional life insurance). As a result, the employee may become a better purchaser of health care services.

The growing popularity of flexible benefit plans may also eliminate benefit coordination. Given the opportunities and structure of flexible benefit plans, husbands and wives can coordinate insurance coverage to avoid unnecessary and costly duplication of benefits.

Despite their potential for reducing the demand for certain types and levels of health service, companies considering the adoption of flexible benefit programs should consider some of the negative factors associated with their use. Among these are the administrative expenses to start and administer the program, the difficulty in communicating the concept and options to employees for informed choice, changing tax laws, and possible adverse selection of benefit plans by employees. Poor employee choices can lead to employee dissatisfaction and to public relations problems if employees voice disparaging comments about the company to the community.

Promoting Structural Change in the Health Delivery System. The strategies discussed so far are attempts to contain health benefit costs indirectly through employee choice and behavior. Structural change as a health care cost containment strategy refers to approaches that have as their outcome more direct employer impact on provider unit costs and practice styles.

Many health care observers believe that structural changes are best implemented through purchaser and purchaser–provider coalitions. Coalitions are local and regional organizations whose principal mission is cost containment. Since 1980, more than 100 health care coalitions have been established, and more than 1,000 employers now participate in one or more coalitions (Goldbeck, 1984; Alcaire and McGowan, 1986).

Early coalitions were informal groupings of benefit plan sponsors to discuss health care cost problems. As their number grew, however, more formal programs evolved. Many now involve the formation of a separate coalition organization with its own professional staff. Some of the more common approaches taken by coalitions to achieve their objectives include the following:

- Educating coalition members and others on health cost issues and strategies
- Developing a common data base for all employee benefit plans

in the area through the collection and analysis of utilization statistics

- Designing model benefit packages, health promotion activities, preferred provider plans, and self-funding programs
- Establishing a forum for interaction on behalf of employee benefit plan interests before state and local legislators and administrative organizations
- Encouraging peer utilization reviews
- Developing joint initiatives to explore cost-effective alternative methods of providing health care, for example, preferred provider organizations (PPOs) and health maintenance organizations (HMOs)

HMOs are the most prevalent alternative health delivery systems now in existence. They operate in specific geographic areas and provide services to voluntary subscribers on a prepaid capitation basis. Under the group practice prepayment type, the most common form of HMO, physicians are employed on a salaried basis and practice medicine as a team. The employee benefit plan pays a fixed premium to the HMO. As the HMO is at risk for the cost of covered health services, medical providers affiliated with HMOs have an incentive to avoid overutilization of medical services and to emphasize comprehensive, preventive, and ambulatory care.

Recent experience, however, indicates that offering HMO services to employees on a voluntary basis does not necessarily lead to meaningful cuts in health care costs. Cost savings are dependent upon which employees opt to join the HMO. If those with the least need for medical care (for example, younger, healthier employees) join the HMO and those with more frequent or chronic problems remain with the company's plan, an employer will still face a high health insurance bill. To achieve the savings desired, other variations in deductibles and coinsurance might need to be offered to create strong incentives for using the HMO.

A PPO is a panel of individual health providers who have obligated themselves to provide services at discounted fees. Unlike HMOs, providers are reimbursed on a fee-for-service basis rather than a monthly capitation premium. Reduced fees are offered in exchange for a potentially higher volume of patients. PPO members are committed to conservative styles of medical care with emphasis on outpatient care.

Coalitions have pursued a variety of approaches to reduce health care costs. For example, the Massachusetts Business Round-table, a statewide organization of business executives, participated in a coalition that helped enact a Massachusetts law that fixed the rate of increase of hospital costs and eliminated cost shifting of hospital charges. The Birmingham, Alabama Coalition designed a prototype benefit plan for member employers and arranged to pool employee health data.

In another effort, the Greater Portland Business Group on Health conducted surveys on member benefit plans and wellness programs. It is publishing a guide on employee health education and wellness programs. The work of the business group is currently conducted by five task forces: (1) health data systems, (2) employee health education and wellness, (3) legislative affairs, (4) alternative delivery/insurance systems, and (5) employee information and education. Staffing for the group is provided by Northwest Oregon Health Systems, and office space is provided by the chamber of commerce (Handel, 1984).

The experience of the city of Richmond, Virginia, in establishing a business/medical coalition ultimately led to the development of an HMO. Richmond's experience provides several useful lessons for business leaders who are ready and willing to take action (Reisler, 1985). First, business must provide the leadership. Second, the coalition approach is a politically effective strategy for dealing with local health cost problems. Third, although coalitions are useful for initiating action and coopting the opposition, they tend to be more useful for general education, needs assessment, and alternative identification. Because of their pluralistic nature, they tend to be less effective once substantive decisions have to be made. Thus, at this juncture, business leadership must take the initiative in pressing for effective action.

Reconceptualizing the Health Insurance Function. The final cost containment strategy to be discussed involves reconsideration of the basic function of health insurance. Unlike other forms of insurance (for example, life, disability, workers' compensation), health insurance does not protect solely against severe financial dislocations in people's lives. In 1980, for example, 25 percent of health insurance benefits were paid for annual expenses of under $1,000. Therefore, some industry observers and analysts have advocated the provision of a real insurance function that would protect against only financially catastrophic medical events.

The plan would protect only after health care expenses exceeded an established annual limit (for example, $1,000 or $5,000), and would provide coverage up to a high maximum (for example, $5 million or $10 million). For greater equity, annual limits could be scaled to income.

The potential savings from this option appear substantial. A study in one large company in 1981 showed that if medical payments had been limited to those claims that exceeded $5,000, the cost of health insurance would have been reduced by 56 percent. For a $1,500 limit, savings would have been 47 percent, and for a $1,000 limit, savings would still have been as much as 32 percent (Herzlinger and Schwartz, 1985). Additionally, the number of claims and claims processing costs would decrease dramatically, making in-company administration of the plan more attractive.

Employer Preferences and Actions. Given the variety of strategies available to employers, which options appear preferable? One study of 200 large corporations asked respondents how they would change health care practices within their organizations to achieve a 10 percent reduction in costs. As Table 5 reveals, the most favored approaches are changes in copayments or deductibles, self-funding, and reductions in benefit levels.

Another survey, conducted by the National Association of Employers for Health Care Alternatives, profiles the extent to which various cost containment approaches have been adopted by some of the nation's largest employers. It is apparent from the results of this survey that employers use a wide range of approaches. As Table 6 indicates, coordination of benefits, coalition participation, second surgical opinions, and health promotions are employed by 50 percent or more of the respondents. Preferred provider organizations are the least frequently reported cost containment strategy.

Health Promotion Strategies

Three primary prevention programs have well-documented success rates. These include control of smoking, control of alcohol use, and control of high blood pressure. Recent data also support

Table 5. Employer Preferences to Achieve a 10 Percent Reduction in Health Care Costs.

Option	High Priority	Medium Priority	Low Priority
Change copayment or deductible	79%	20%	1%
Convert to self-funding	41	40	19
Reduce employer contributions (level of payment for benefits)	32	50	18
Change number of insured services	12	44	44
Offer flexible benefits	7	45	17

Source: Adapted from Herzlinger and Schwartz, 1985, p. 77.

Table 6. Frequency of Use of Cost Containment Approaches.

Coordination of benefits	94%
Coalition membership	74
Second surgical opinion	61
Health promotion	50
Benefit redesign	49
Utilization review	35
Preferred provider organizations	3

Source: Handel, 1984, p. 56.

the promotion of physical activity and the control of cholesterol levels. The impact of weight control and stress management programs on health and cost containment is less certain. These approaches seek the health promotion goals of better employee health, lower medical costs, decreased absenteeism, and higher work productivity.*

Smoking Cessation Programs. Smoking is the largest single preventable cause of illness and premature death in the United States. Smokers are also more likely to be absent from work than nonsmokers. Research has indicated that men who smoke lose 33 percent more workdays than men who have never smoked. And, not only is the effect of smoking hazardous to smokers, recent studies

*Statistics in this section were obtained primarily from Herzlinger and Calkins (1986).

have suggested that passive inhalation of smoke significantly increases the risk of acquiring smoking-related illnesses.

Treatment evidence shows that about 20 to 30 percent of participants in smoking cessation programs succeed in quitting and remain nonsmokers twelve months later. Although the economic benefits of such programs may be long term, one large company has estimated that its smoking control program has reduced health insurance payments by $73 per employee per year.

Alcoholism Assistance Programs. Alcoholism accounted for $9.4 billion in health care spending in 1983. Alcoholism results in a higher level of performance and safety problems. In addition, a study of seven railroad companies found that problem drinkers had almost twice the number of absences as other workers.

Treatment success rates as high as 90 percent have been reported for an established corporate employee assistance program. This program, sponsored by the New York Telephone Company, includes hospitalization, detoxification, and referral for psychological counseling. In similar studies, Illinois Bell reported a 52 percent decline in sickness and disability days for those who participated in an alcoholism rehabilitation program, and Kennecott Copper found a 48 percent decrease in hospital costs and a 50 percent decline in absenteeism for former problem drinkers during the first year after their participation in a rehabilitation program.

Hypertension Control Programs. The effects of smoking and alcoholism programs on medical expenses are more immediate compared with hypertension (high blood pressure) control programs, which are more likely to be effective in reducing longer-term medical expenses. In a study of union employees, hypertensive workers had 14 percent more disability days than other employees in the year preceding the initiation of the control program. A study conducted by Massachusetts Mutual found similar results. Absenteeism was 18 percent higher for hypertensive workers in the year preceding program initiation.

Exercise Programs. Statistics reveal that only 35 percent of adults ages 18–65 participate regularly in an exercise program, but workplace programs can significantly increase the amount of regular exercise in which employees participate.

Several studies have shown decreased use of health services and/or decreased health care expenditures after introduction of a workplace exercise program. Prudential Insurance Company reported a 46 percent decline in health care expenditures for participants in the company's program during the year after enrollment. In another study, Control Data Corporation found that employees who reported exercising regularly had lower annual health costs ($321.01) versus those not exercising regularly ($436.92). Tenneco Inc. achieved similar results from its employee fitness program. During the first year of its operation, health care claims averaged $562 and $639 among men and women exercisers, respectively, as compared with the average $1,004 and $1,536 incurred by nonexercising men and women employees.

In a program for 80,000 employees begun in 1973, the New York Telephone Company estimated an accrued benefit of $2.7 million in 1980 through risk reduction health promotion programs in smoking cessation, fitness, hypertension control, alcohol abuse, breast cancer screening, and related activities (Handel, 1984). Other successful programs are reported by Lockheed Aircraft Corporation, Canada Life Assurance Company, Kimberly-Clark Corporation, and Johnson and Johnson.

Studies have also shown decreases in absenteeism as a result of exercise programs. Prudential reported a 20 percent reduction in disability days during the first year after the company's program was established. Not only are costs reduced or avoided by such programs, but workers report increased productivity on the job after workout sessions in workplace programs. Despite these encouraging reports, not all firms embrace the "wellness" concept. The reasons for this reluctance are discussed later.

Cholesterol Reduction Programs. Elevated blood cholesterol is a risk factor for three of the ten leading causes of death in the United States, including two of the top three cardiovascular diseases and stroke. It is believed that cholesterol acts in conjunction with other risk factors, such as smoking and hypertension, to increase the incidence of coronary heart disease. However, no firm data exist so far to indicate the effect of reductions in blood cholesterol on medical expenses or absenteeism.

Weight Control Programs. Among adults ages 20-74, 13 percent of males and 23 percent of females are defined as obese. Obesity refers to a body weight 120 percent or more of ideal. Corporate programs have had little success in achieving significant and sustained weight reduction. Attrition rates for such programs often exceed 50 percent, and the average weight loss among persons completing a typical program is ten pounds or less.

Stress Management Programs. Although stress is a risk factor in three of the ten leading causes of death, there is little consistent evidence of the beneficial effect of stress management programs. There is some evidence that such programs may decrease the frequency of use of health services by employees with chronic anxiety, but the impact on absenteeism is inconclusive.

Despite the lack of evidence to support stress management programs from the perspective of health care cost containment, recent reports indicate a growing trend in stress-related workers' compensation claims. Should this trend continue, employers may reconsider stress management programs as one option for reducing their exposure to compensation claims.

Tying Health Costs to Employee Behavior. Research on the effectiveness of health and fitness programs is likely to stir debate among employers, insurers, regulators, and employees. For example, some insurance regulators are considering new rules that would require insurers to build into their programs economic incentives for healthy life-styles. If insurance premiums are pegged to employee behavior, it is estimated that costs could rise or fall by 20 percent or more, depending on employee fitness patterns. At least one major insurer, Prudential Insurance Company of America, already has plans to market group insurance tied to employee health habits. Some insurance regulators indicate plans to require insurers to offer economic incentives for good health habits to obtain state certification.

Although studies show significant relationships between health practices and health claim costs, adoption of health-contingent insurance premiums raises serious legal questions. In particular, employees may view employer data collection related to off-the-job health habits as an invasion of privacy. And, as some compensation consultants point out, verification of employee behavior could be nearly impossible.

To offset potential employee concern, employers could reward health-conscious employees by sharing cost savings, by underwriting memberships in health clubs or wellness centers, or by increasing their benefits. Nevertheless, many employers may be reluctant to "get involved" in employees' personal lives. In the interim, health promotion, with its incumbent cost savings, may be the most effective strategy.

Employer Reluctance. The reasons employers are reluctant to use health promotion programs are not well known. It is possible that options other than health promotion are embraced because it is perceived that wellness activities may not produce a visible result in a short time. Despite the successes reported earlier, it is likely to be some time before the plan sponsor realizes any sizable financial rewards from initiation of a program. Thus, there is a high degree of uncertainty surrounding potential benefits to the employer. In fact, the early years of the program may be burdened by the cost of innovation and implementation.

To overcome some of these concerns that serve as barriers to implementation, it may be advantageous in the initial years of a program to limit activities to those sponsored by voluntary community organizations that require little expenditure by the plan sponsor or participant. Following a plan similar to that adopted by IBM, many companies have successfully developed programs utilizing local "Y's," community health centers, community colleges, local hospitals, United Way agencies, and other voluntary organizations.

Another possible reason for employer reluctance is the risk of liability for injuries or heart attacks. Although liability is a genuine concern, many contend the risks are minimal. First, a corporate fitness program would be part of the job and the employer should be protected by workers' compensation or private liability insurance (Association for Fitness in Business, 1987). Second, as Dr. Kenneth Cooper notes, any fitness program must include a good physical examination in advance of any physical activity. This examination should include resting and stress electrocardiograms. Additionally, good supervision in the form of a full-time, on-site fitness director trained in exercise physiology can further minimize injury and risk.

Summary

As a result of their cost containment initiatives, employers feel that they have had a substantial impact on health care costs. An Equitable Life Assurance Society survey revealed that employers estimated their 1985 health care costs per employee would be 16 to

18 percent lower as a result of changes made over the prior three years (Employers' Health Costs Savings Letter, 1986). However, there is reason to believe that health care costs will require continued attention by management. First, although health care cost increases have slowed, so has the general rate of inflation. If the Consumer Price Index should exhibit resurgence, one could expect health care costs to increase even faster. Second, some of the forces responsible for the upward trend in health care costs are unlikely to be influenced by traditional cost containment strategies. These include population growth, the aging of the population, rising input prices, and technological innovation and diffusion. Finally, some strategies may have already achieved their maximum effects. For example, after several years in which the average length of a hospital stay declined, the average stay increased by 2 percent in 1986. Thus, some strategies may provide smaller savings in the future.

Employers agree that successful health care cost containment programs must contain a variety of mechanisms. No single approach is a panacea. The "best" option or combination of options for a given organization can be determined only by examining several factors within the specific work environment and health history. Among these are

- The claims experience of the employee group (for example, usage levels and rates, types of services used by employees)
- Demographics of the work force (for example, future demand patterns and levels)
- Local health care environment (for example, availability of alternative service organizations, occupancy rates, employer-provider relations)
- Impact of benefit changes on the employer's ability to attract and retain the type of work force desired (for example, health benefits offered by other area employers, magnitude of changes proposed)
- Administrative feasibility (for example, size of work force, staff qualifications)
- Expected yield versus costs of change

It is also apparent that health care cost initiatives should not be considered apart from other organizational and human resources policies and goals. Although a significant concern, cost containment is only one aspect of an employer's total reward system. Without careful analysis, efforts to control costs can decrease the attractiveness of an organization as an employer. Health care benefits are also hygiene factors. Therefore, changes that lower benefit levels can adversely affect morale and induce turnover (depending on alternative employment opportunities in the surrounding community). Thus, cost containment should be only one consideration in any decision to alter service levels or payment schedules.

As noted at the beginning of this chapter, health care cost containment has been of growing concern for well over a decade. Despite an improving economy, its significance is unlikely to decrease over the next decade. Employers can be expected to devote increased attention and a more professionally qualified staff to its analysis and management. Technological advances, demographic trends, and a more highly competitive business environment will require it. Moreover, many attorneys contend that it is virtually obligatory for employee benefit plan administrators, acting in a fiduciary capacity, to become more involved in cost containment (Gertner, 1983). Only through such responsible action can benefit programs be broadened to meet employee needs and expectations and can employer costs be maintained at a level that permits the organization to remain competitive and profitable.

5

Comparable Worth:
The Issue of Job Value

Women, although they constitute a growing proportion of the work force, remain concentrated in a relatively few, low-paying job categories. Statistical comparisons of wage data continue to show a significant and continuing disparity between men and women. Consequently, comparable worth has emerged as a major equal opportunity issue. In this chapter we discuss the historical development of the issue, present arguments for each side, and outline the actions business can take to minimize the risks of potential litigation.

Although the term *comparable worth* means different things to different people, basically it means paying men and women similar wages for different jobs judged to be of "equal value" to the employer. In many instances, comparable worth is confused or used interchangeably with the well-accepted and legally mandated doctrine of equal pay for the same or closely related jobs. Comparable worth, however, relates jobs that are dissimilar in their content (for example, the office worker and the craftsman) and contends that individuals who perform jobs that require similar skill, effort, and responsibility under similar work conditions should be equally compensated.

Although the concept of comparable worth emerged after passage of the Civil Rights Act of 1964, it did not originate with the act. Title VII of the Civil Rights Act makes it unlawful for any employer to discriminate on the basis of sex in determining the amount of wages or compensation paid or to be paid to employees. However, nowhere in this act, or the earlier Equal Pay Act of 1963, was comparable worth mentioned or its essence discussed. Rather, the comparable worth issue appears to have emerged from statistical interpretations of wage data that continue to show a consistent disparity between men and women (Bell, 1985) and concentrations of women in low-paying jobs.

Bureau of Labor Statistics data indicate that in 1985 women working full time had median earnings of $268 per week for the first quarter, 66 percent of the $404 earned by men. And despite the increasing proportion of women in the work force, about one-fourth of all women employed today are found in three job categories: secretarial/clerical, retail sales, and food preparation and service. The wages for these and similar "female jobs" (for example, librarian, nurse) are the focus of the comparable worth debate (see Table 7).

A Brief History

Although comparable worth was catapulted into the fore-front of personnel and political debates by a federal district court decision in 1983 against the state of Washington, the debate

Table 7. Percentage Female of Traditional "Women's" Occupations, 1979 and 1986.

Occupation	1979	1986
Secretaries	98.8	99.2
Registered nurses	94.6	92.7
Bank tellers	91.5	91.7
Phone operators	90.8	97.7
Child-care workers	88.9	97.7
Bookkeepers/auditing clerks	88.1	93.0
Waiters/waitresses	82.7	78.7
Cashiers	77.7	79.8
Health technicians	71.6	65.1
Elementary schoolteachers	60.9	81.9
Social workers	60.6	60.0

Source: U.S. Census Bureau, September 1987.

between equal pay for equal work and equal pay for work of comparable worth is embedded in America's legislative and judicial history. Most people believe that comparable worth originated with the Equal Pay Act of 1963 and the Civil Rights Act of 1964. However, some of the decisions of the National War Labor Board, established to control wage increases and prevent inflation during World War II, have been cited as precedent for examining the value of "women's jobs" in determining if discrimination has occurred (Williams and McDowell, 1980).

National War Labor Board. In November 1942, the National War Labor Board issued General Order No. 16, which provided that employers could make adjustments that "equalize the wage or salary rates paid to females with the rates paid to males for comparable quality and quantity of work on the same or similar operations" without approval of the board (National War Labor Board Termination Report, 1945, Vol. 1, p. 290).

Several basic precedents pertaining to compensation for women were established by the board. These can be summarized as follows:

- Women should receive the same rates of pay as men when working in the same jobs, interchangeable jobs, or jobs that do not differ significantly in measurable job content unless other factors prevail (for example, differences in quantity or quality of performance or differentially higher costs resulting from the employment of women).
- Rates of pay for jobs that historically have been performed by women and that differ measurably from jobs performed by men are presumed to be correct in relation to men's rates, especially where they are of long standing and have been accepted in collective bargaining.
- The preceding presumption can be overcome by affirmative evidence of intraplant inequity resulting from a comparison of the content of the jobs in question with the content of the jobs performed by men.
- Whenever possible, inequities should be worked out through collective bargaining in good faith.

When wage inequities were suggested, the board could reaffirm traditional pay rates (especially if such rates were established through collective bargaining), remand the issue for further negotiations, or suggest/order the conduct of a job evaluation to establish the worth of a job on the basis of content irrespective of sex.

For the most part, sex-related pay issues considered by the board followed an "equal pay for equal work" doctrine. When comparisons of dissimilar tasks were requested, the board generally presumed that existing wage rates were correct if wage disparities were evident historically or had been established through collective bargaining.

On one occasion, when provided the opportunity to determine if women's wages should be adjusted on the basis of job evaluation conducted by two employers, the board chose not to engage itself in making comparisons between dissimilar jobs. Rather, it recognized the difficulties incumbent in making such determinations, acknowledged the task to be beyond its capabilities, and elected to accept evaluations performed by the employers (General Electric Company and Westinghouse Electric Corporation, 28 War Laboratory Report 666, 1945).

Equal Pay Act of 1963. The legislative history of the Equal Pay Act indicates the intent of Congress to continue the National War Labor Board's position, that is, to avoid becoming bogged down in the restructuring of existing wage systems (Williams and McDowell, 1980). Although initial forms of the law considered in 1962 by the House of Representatives would have prohibited employers from paying different wages for "work of comparable character on jobs the performance of which requires comparable skills," Congress appeared deliberate in its ultimate rejection of an approach that would have allowed findings of discrimination for jobs that were "comparable."

Representative Goodell, the sponsor of H.R. 6060 (the final House version of the Equal Pay Act), commented during debate on the bill that "when the House changed the word 'comparable' to 'equal,' the clear intention was to narrow the whole concept. We went from 'comparable' to 'equal' meaning that the jobs involved should be virtually identical" (see 109 *Congressional Record* 9197).

The Equal Pay Act states the following:

> No employer having employees subject to any provisions of this section shall discriminate within any establishment in which such employees are employed, between employees on the basis of sex by paying wages to employees in such establishment at a rate at which he pays wages to employees of the opposite sex in such establishment for equal work on jobs the performance of which requires equal skill, effort and responsibility, and which are performed under similar working conditions, except where such payment is made pursuant to (i) a seniority system; (ii) a merit system; (iii) a system which measures earnings by quantity of or quality of production; or (iv) a differential based on any other factor other than sex: Provided, That an employer who is paying a wage rate differential in violation of this subsection shall not, in order to comply with the provisions of this subsection, reduce the wage rate of any employee [Fair Labor Standards Act, 29 U.S.C. 206(d)(1)(1970)].

Thus, with limited exceptions, for wage discrimination based on sex to exist, an employer must be shown to pay different wages to employees of opposite sex for equal work on jobs the performance of which requires equal skill, effort, and responsibility (and which are performed under similar working conditions within the same establishment).

The courts have established, however, that to prove a violation it is not necessary that the jobs be absolutely equal. Such an interpretation would allow employers to circumvent the intent of the law by establishing unique pay and job classifications for various jobs. Rather, the courts have held that discrimination can be proven if the jobs are "substantially equal" in job content or function (Williams, 1984).

Civil Rights Act of 1964. Title VII of the Civil Rights Act of 1964 is a much broader statute than the Equal Pay Act. It simply prevents employers from discriminating on the basis of "race, color, religion, sex, or national origin." The original version of the bill, which ultimately became the Civil Rights Act, was intended to protect the rights of blacks and other minorities. It was not until later in the House debate that an amendment incorporating sex discrimination was included in the bill.

As with the Equal Pay Act, certain employment practices were excluded from its provision. These included compensation systems based on a bona fide seniority system, a merit system, or a system that measures earnings by quantity or quality of production.

The section of the act that excludes the employment practices just identified also contains a more specific provision, referred to as the Bennett amendment, which exempts compensation claims from Title VII coverage if the employer's compensation system is "authorized" by the Equal Pay Act. Specifically, the Bennett amendment states that "It shall not be unlawful employment practice under this title for any employer to differentiate upon the basis of sex in determining the amount of wages or compensation paid or to be paid to employees of such employer if such differentiation is authorized by the provisions of section 6(d) of the Fair Labor Standards Act of 1938, as amended," that is, the Equal Pay Act (Williams and McDowell, 1980). Thus, the Bennett amendment appears to provide that discrimination in compensation based on sex does not violate Title VII unless it also violates the Equal Pay Act.

Emerging Case Law

Early court decisions related to sex discrimination held consistently that Congress rejected the "comparable worth" concept and mandated that standing legislation should not be applied by judges to enforce their own conceptions of economic worth. And, emerging case law appeared to specify that the wage discrimination requirements of the Equal Pay Act and Title VII must be read *in pari materia* ("in harmony"), and that a person charging wage discrimination on the basis of sex has the same burden of proof under either statute.

In 1982, however, the courts made a significant departure from the above position. In *The County of Washington* v. *Gunther*

(452 U.S. 161(1981)), the Supreme Court held that broader protections contained in Title VII of the Civil Rights Act could include legal challenges to rates of pay for dissimilar jobs when discrimination was claimed as the reason for the disparity. Although the Gunther ruling has paved the way for placing unequal work claims under an adverse impact doctrine, the Court did not embrace comparable worth as an appropriate response in such instances. The decision demonstrated that employers cannot automatically rule out comparable worth challenges on the basis of discrimination; however, it did not establish the kinds of standards to be applied in such cases.

A year later, the federal district court for the state of Washington ruled in *AFSCME* v. *State of Washington* (578 F. Supp. 846 (W. D. Wash. 1983)) that the state had deliberately underpaid women in female-dominated state jobs compared with employees in male-dominated state jobs. The public employees' union charged that the state had failed to implement recommendations made in its (the state's) own study completed ten years earlier. The state of Washington study identified significant sex-based pay discrepancies and established a special fund to reduce the disparity over time. The union contended that the funds were never used.

Although the state of Washington case spurred the enthusiasm of comparable worth advocates, the victory was short-lived. In 1985, the Ninth U.S. Circuit Court of Appeals in San Francisco overturned the decision, ruling that a wage gap, by itself, does not show that the state intentionally discriminated against women (770 F. 2d 1401 (9th Cir. 1985)). In reversing the nation's first comparable worth ruling, the three-judge appeals panel said that employers can use prevailing market conditions in setting wages and need not follow surveys they commission.

That same year, however, a Seventh Circuit Court ruled (*Ende* v. *Regency University*, 757 F. 2d 176 (1985)) that a university was justified in adopting a salary equalization plan to increase the pay of female faculty members. When the plan was challenged by the male faculty, the court ruled it was legal to raise the salaries of past victims of bias to the amount they would have received had the discrimination not been present.

Despite a general lack of success in the federal courts, the comparable worth movement has sustained its momentum. Comparable worth studies are on the agendas of thirty-six state legislatures, and at least sixteen states have enacted some form of comparable worth legislation (Rynes, Rosen, and Mahoney, 1985). Public employee unions are making gender-based pay gaps a major negotiating and contract issue. Also giving hope to comparable worth advocates was the release in 1984 by the General Accounting Office (GAO) of guidelines for performing studies of pay equity in federal job classifications. A number of pay equity proposals based on the GAO recommendations are presently in legislative limbo. State and local pay equity initiatives are presented at the end of this chapter.

The Cases For and Against Comparable Worth

Those who would substitute "comparable worth" as the standard for wage determination maintain (Milkovich, 1980) that "women have historically been 'crowded' into certain occupations through discriminatory practices in society; the labor market reflects this crowding and thus the employment discrimination that caused the crowding; and if the labor market is discriminating, so too are pay systems based on market comparisons."

Most of the evidence used in support of these propositions is statistical. For example, testimony presented before a 1984 congressional hearing contrasted monthly salaries for government workers in various job classifications. Jobs paying higher wages were found to be held almost exclusively by men. Lower-paying jobs were dominated by women. At a more aggregate level, proponents of comparable worth note that an "earnings gap" exists between the median earnings of women and men. Historically, that gap suggests that full-time, year-round workers who are female earn about 60 percent as much as their male counterparts. Although more recent (1986) census data indicate that the earnings gap has narrowed to 30 cents on the dollar, these continuing statistical discrepancies are considered by some as sufficient evidence that society and contemporary compensation systems discriminate against women.

Studies aimed at determining the degree of earnings differences attributable to wage discrimination conclude that the portion of the earnings gap not attributable to work productivity factors ranges from 12 to 70 percent (Sawhill, 1973). A major factor that appears to explain non-productivity-related differences in wages between men and women is the employee's occupation. Proponents of comparable worth argue that occupational explanations for differences in earnings ignore the effects of employment discrimination. Oaxaca (1973), for example, asserts that men and women do not have equal access to occupations because of traditional, stereotyped employment practices. This unequal access, it is asserted, contributes to the overcrowding of women in certain occupations, results in wage discrimination, and masks the discriminatory effects of hiring and promotion practices.

Opponents of comparable worth contend the concept rests on three extraordinary propositions (Seligman, 1984): (1) pay relationships established by supply and demand in job markets are frequently inequitable and discriminatory; (2) it is possible to compare different jobs that are dissimilar and establish some "right" relationship between them; and (3) the government, therefore, must intervene to ensure that pay relationships are correct.

With regard to the first proposition, those opposed to comparable worth suggest that male–female pay differences are the result of several factors, not merely discriminatory labor market practices. The potential determinants of male–female pay differences are presented in Figure 2. Consequently, allegations of wage discrimination require rigorous statistical examination rather than simple comparisons of pay differences. Michael and Judith Finn, for example, in U.S. Senate hearings on the Equal Rights Amendment (1984), note that the statistic used to derive the wage gap (that is, annual earnings of full-time employees) does not mean the same thing for men and women. Collectively, male full-time employees work more hours (more jobs, longer hours in principal jobs) than female full-time employees. When these differences are accounted for, it is estimated that women earn approximately 73 percent of what is earned by men rather than the 60 percent more commonly cited. They also note that in every occupational group the earnings gap between men and women is greater among the self-employed than it is among wage and salary workers. This, they conclude,

Figure 2. Possible Determinants of Female/Male Pay Differences.

suggests that something other than employer discrimination is causing the earnings gap.

Subject to such statistical scrutiny, critics of comparable worth contend that much of the difference in wages between men and women can be explained by patterns of lifetime labor force participation. Single, never-married men and women exhibit the smallest earnings differentials as well as the smallest differences in lifetime labor force participation. The widest lifetime labor force participation differences exist among the married, spouse-present individuals, the group also exhibiting the widest wage differentials. In short, opponents of comparable worth claim that gender-based wage differentials are related to differences in lifetime labor force participation. Those with the highest labor market experience also have the highest wages, whereas those with the least work longevity earn the least. Even the most primitive models that link lifetime labor force participation to earnings explain nearly 50 percent of the gender-based differences in earnings. Using statistical specifications that more accurately reflect the impact of expected intermittency on initial schooling and job choices for women, some researchers contend that close to 100 percent of the wage gap can be explained (Polachek, 1984).

In a further argument against a discrimination explanation of gender-based wage differences, Polachek (1979) contends that the incentives to enter various occupations differ between men and women. The incentive for women, he asserts, is to enter those occupations with the smallest earnings losses for absences from the labor force over the life cycle as a result of childbearing and rearing. Thus, they are segregated into occupations characterized by a relatively slow rate of skill deterioration with successive absences from the labor force. These tend to be lower-paying occupations.

With regard to evaluating and establishing a "right relationship" between jobs, most opponents of comparable worth perceive this task as unsound theoretically and immense from a practical perspective. First, comprehensive evaluation would require the adoption of a common set of evaluation criteria (values). Whether common approaches to job evaluation could produce results acceptable to both critics and advocates of comparable worth is questionable. Second, current job evaluation practices link internal pay practices to market rates. Thus, use of job evaluation in its conventional form would perpetuate any existing gender-based wage discrimination. Avoiding the use of market rates would require the implementation of a standard, uniform approach to job evaluation and predetermined wage conversion factors, a task that again requires a convergence of values.

Further, to assume the uniform implementation of such an approach, enabling legislation would be required mandating a practice that is not now common. Moreover, the legislation would have to be comprehensive to avoid problems associated with the subjectivity of the job evaluation process (see the next section for a brief summary of job evaluation). This involvement would necessarily be continuing, as changes in external conditions would require internal adjustments in pay-setting practices. Naturally, critics of comparable worth strongly oppose such intervention in private enterprise decision making.

As noted earlier, however, governmental inroads are already apparent. In 1984, the General Accounting Office released guidelines for conducting studies of pay equity in the federal government, and the proposed Pay Equity Act of 1985 sought the Equal Employment Opportunity Commission's release of job classification guidelines. Critics of comparable worth contend that present statutory guidance is adequate to meet the challenge of sex-based wage discrimination, and has been proven to be reasonable and workable. Barriers that once prevented women from having equal access to jobs have been broken down. Further, they note, the courts have continued to rule against governmental involvement in rate-setting practices. In *Kohne* v. *Imco Container Co.*, the court found that "Congress did not intend to put either the Secretary of Labor or the courts in the business of evaluating jobs and in determining what constitutes a proper differential for unequal work. . . . Sufficient remedies exist under Title VII to deal with discriminatory hiring and promotional practices, without the courts becoming embroiled in determinations of how an employer's work force ought to be paid" (*Kohne* v. *Imco Container Co.*, 1979, 480 F. Supp. at 1039).

Job Evaluation

The debate on comparable worth focuses on the process of job evaluation. Typically, this process involves the following steps:

1. Job analysis is performed to determine job dimensions and characteristics. The result of this analysis is a job description, or statement of duties, responsibilities, and job conditions.
2. Compensable factors are chosen to represent what the organization wishes to reward. This might include job knowledge required and level of accountability, among others.
3. Job descriptions are evaluated with respect to the compensable factors.

4. A hierarchy of jobs is determined based on the degree to which factors are exhibited in each job.
5. Job evaluation results are compared with current or market wages.

Although different methods of job evaluation exist, the "point system" is by far the most commonly used method in the United States, probably because it combines the apparent precision of quantification with a simplicity that makes the results relatively easy to explain to employees. Under the point system, compensable factors are weighted as to the degree of importance the organization ascribes to them. Then, each factor is subdivided into degrees that define the relative amount of that factor that may be evidenced in a job. To obtain a total point score for a job, the proper degree of every factor is assessed, and the corresponding points are summed. The point total corresponds to a predetermined labor or salary grade which, in turn, specifies a particular wage or salary range.

Adoption of a system of job evaluation, however, does not automatically ensure the absence of discrimination in pay practices. First, as noted earlier, current practices link evaluations to market rates. Beyond this, all methods of job evaluation are inherently subjective. Perhaps the most subjective are the ranking systems that incorporate global comparisons of jobs. And the more subjective the evaluation process, the greater the opportunity for gender-based bias. For example, judgments may be strongly influenced by present wage rates—rates that potentially present patterns of discrimination.

Nevertheless, even point-based systems retain opportunities for discrimination. Job evaluation consultants inevitably differ among themselves about what factors to measure and what weights to assign the different factors. For example, a system that weights physical factors heavily will undoubtedly favor men. Less obvious, perhaps are gender-biased interpretations of the degree to which certain factors (for example, accountability) are present in a job. In the *County of Washington* v. *Gunther,* two independent consultants conducted evaluations that produced substantially different results. When the scores generated by each system were used to rank-order jobs, differences on the order of 2.9 rankings were noted

(Seligman, 1984). The two methods also produced gender-based differences.

Employer Options

Given the current status of the comparable worth debate, what course of action should employers pursue? Several comprehensive sets of guidelines have been proposed by those intimately involved in the debate.

Alvin Bellak, a general partner of Hay Associates, the leading firm of compensation consultants in the United States, states the position of his firm (Bellak, 1984):

1. Each pay structure should be positioned against the appropriate competitive labor market.
2. All jobs covered by a single pay structure should be priced in proportion to their measured job content without regard to the ability, performance, potential, education, sex, color, or any other characteristic of the job holder.
3. Variations in actual pay among job holders within or beyond the resultant pay range for jobs of a given size should be based *only* on truly business-relevant factors such as individual merit, qualifications, seniority, or individually negotiated differentials.

More specifically, Bellak (1984) offers ten operational guidelines for employers:

1. Base the compensation system upon clear and complete definitions of specific jobs. These jobs must be so designed and defined as to not restrict participation for any protected class unless one can demonstrate a necessary and irrefutable occupational requirement.
2. Identify the extent to which each job or job family or occupational family is dominated by a

protected class. The common definition of "dominated" is 70 percent or more. Where domination exists, determine whether it stems from business necessity or is simply a matter of custom, convenience, or indifference. In the latter instances, we recommend actions to reduce or remove the domination. One well-known attorney has gone so far as to suggest that when openings in male-dominated jobs appear, not only should the openings be posted, but that female employees be specifically invited to apply; rejection of the invitation by a female should be recorded in her own hand. This sounds extreme to us. More suitable actions to balance the work force might include focused external recruiting, in-company training, or subsidized external training.

3. Where many employees hold the "same" job, whether this job is dominated by a protected class or not, test for "equal pay" for "equal work." This is the law. It would also be prudent to test for equal pay in jobs that are very similar, although not equal, and where one or more are dominated by a protected class. At least one federal district court has found illegal discrimination in such an instance without using job measurement or task analysis.

4. Where the organization says that it has no job evaluation plan and that it uses a strictly market-pricing system, do the descriptions of grades or job families suggest or indicate some de facto form of job measurement? For example, slotting jobs that could not be market priced into the pay scale could be labeled "whole job ranking," a technique recognized in all the text books as a specific method of job evaluation. Because it is a crude method, it would be particularly difficult to explain and defend.

5. Test the job evaluation process to determine if the results are repeatable as, for example, by committees with various combinations of knowledgeable members. Where protected class job domination is common, involve members of such classes in the job evaluation process.

6. Identify specific labor markets from which current and prospective jobholders are typically drawn. If a protected class dominates the labor markets that are used as a basis for job pricing, make sure that there are no reasonable alternatives.

7. Set typical or midpoint or single rate pay for each job in relation to job size on the same basis as for all other jobs that are drawn from the same labor market.

8. Test "any" compensation procedures that produce significantly different pay within a single pay structure for jobs of similar size. To the extent that any aspect of the administration of the compensation program produces unsupportable adverse effects for protected classes, change it. This would include the performance appraisal program, the size and frequency of merit awards, the level of starting pay in the range, and so forth.

9. Document and publicize the compensation program internally. If the program is sound, there is nothing to hide.

10. Perhaps above all, make sure that all jobs are open to all qualified applicants. An affirmative action program, combined with a well-conceived and supportable compensation program, is the certain route to the elimination of pay discrimination.

To ensure that pay practices, once established, remain free of sex bias, other compensation professionals recommend that companies audit on a regular basis the impact of pay practices on men's and women's salaries. Management should examine any statistically significant disparities to ensure that factors other than sex account for the differences. For smaller populations, the same result can be obtained by examining the distribution of men and women within set salary bands. However, because of the court's findings in *AFSCME* v. *State of Washington,* Sara Armstrong, director of employee compensation for ITT, recommends that companies avoid big, companywide pay equity studies (Willis, 1986b). Such studies, she contends, may serve simply to prove the plaintiff's case in a lawsuit brought by employees or a union. Should a firm choose to conduct a companywide survey, she suggests it be prepared to act on the results quickly. A more judicious approach, she suggests, would involve small-scale studies, perhaps by department. A company can then analyze compensation rates in each area, decide what action is required, and implement any necessary adjustments quickly. To avoid problems of this type involving self-audits, another company concluded that an investigation of its pay practices should be initiated by the legal department to protect the study's findings.

Such specific actions are prudent to ensure that legal requirements that could place the company at risk are met. However, they do not address underlying issues. To address these issues and reduce the likelihood of more stringent comparable worth legislation, employers should examine their employment practices in several related human resources areas that tend to perpetuate the salary gap between sexes. Such an examination might include the full range of recruitment, selection, and promotion policies. Efforts to increase female representation in nontraditional job categories should also be considered, along with additional training efforts to upgrade the capabilities of female employees. RJR–Nabisco, for example, has attempted to place women in jobs previously held only by men (for example, yard lift operators, machinists, truck drivers). More recently, it has been suggested that employer provision of child-care benefits would extend the ability of women to remain active in the labor market, thereby reducing longevity-related sources of discrimination. Forward-looking companies may also consider initiating preemployment awareness programs in conjunction with high schools, vocational schools, and community colleges to familiarize students with the full range of career options and the requirements for entry into each.

Employers should also recognize that the process of working toward fair and equitable compensation practices may be nearly as important as the actual pay system itself. Thus, organizations may wish to increase their communications about how pay rates and ranges are established. They may also wish to establish credible procedures for resolving complaints or questions about pay-related matters. Good faith efforts to address problems of internal disparity and work toward their elimination will not obviate the possibility of a lawsuit. But, on the basis of case law to date, such efforts can reduce an employer's liability if a complaint reaches the courts.

Finally, recognizing that comparable worth is also a political phenomenon, employers may consider lobbying efforts and educational campaigns to present the measurement problems associated with determining a job's worth, as well as the possible economic, legal, and administrative complications that may arise from applying comparable worth principles to pay administration (Rynes, Rosen, and Mahoney, 1985).

Summary

Given the current status of comparable worth, employers can make one of four basic responses: (1) ignore the issue, (2) do the minimum required by law, (3) take positive action to identify and redress pay inequities, or (4) actively address underlying social and political causes of wage inequity.

Pursuit of the first alternative runs the risk of violation of the law. Even though comparable worth is not the law of the land, equal pay for equal work is. And, uninformed actions can only serve to enhance the likelihood of sex-based discrimination and further government intervention.

With regard to the second alternative, it is difficult to determine what the "minimum" required by law is. Unless management takes positive action to determine if sex-based wage inequities are present, there can be no assurance that discrimination does not exist. Therefore, management must be proactive in its posture, following the guidelines suggested earlier in this chapter, to merely ensure compliance with the law. This would include, for example, auditing for sex-based pay differences and reviewing job analysis and job evaluation programs for indications of male-female bias.

It is with the final level of response that employers truly have a choice. The potential for serious litigation can probably be minimized without efforts to address underlying social and political causes of wage inequities between the sexes through recruitment, cross-training, and promotion practices; however, these actions also provide significant benefits to the firm. First, such actions improve the morale of female employees, potentially improving their retention and productivity. Second, enhancing the opportunities for women to move into nontraditional occupations can improve the internal labor pool for these positions. Recent labor force trends suggest that employers who ignore the growing role of women in work may experience a shortage of qualified employees later this century. Third, visible efforts to ensure improved opportunities for women and provide pay levels based on comparable worth principles can be helpful in enhancing an employer's ability to attract qualified female applicants. These benefits cannot be regarded as inconsequential. As Grider and Shurden (1987) conclude, for some employers comparable worth may be an impending storm, but those who are more forward looking can use it as an opportunity to reexamine their personnel practices and revitalize the human resources department.

Appendix: Initiatives in State Pay Equity Legislation

State	Year	Description
Alaska	1980	Adds specific comparable worth (CW) language to fair employment practices (FEP) law.
California	1981	Establishes CW as policy for state workers. Requires annual reports.
	1983	Prohibits local government ordinances or policies that preclude consideration of CW. Creates commission on status of women. Adds specific CW language to FEP law.
Connecticut	1979	Pilot study for state workers.
	1981	Full job evaluation (JE) study for state workers.
	1983	AFSCME negotiates pay equity increases for clerical workers.
	1987	Amends state CW legislation to include employees in collective bargaining units. Appropriates money for salary adjustments resulting from JE process.
Hawaii	1981	(Resolution) Urges employers to adopt CW policies.
	1982	Requires report and recommendations on CW for state employees.
	1983	AFSCME wins pay equity increases for nurses through arbitration.
	1984	Authorizes CW study.
	1985	Adopts House resolution requesting all employers to adopt CW principles.
	1986	Authorizes pay equity study of state and county civil service employees in certain occupations.
Idaho	1977	Provides for JE study on state employees.
Illinois	1982	Requires pilot CW study for civil service.
	1983	Requires comprehensive JE study for civil service. Includes CW standard in state equal pay act. AFSCME wins pay equity increases for word-processing operators through arbitration.
Iowa	1983	Establishes CW policy. Requires JE study of civil service. Appropriates $150,000 for study.
	1984	Establishes pay grade system based on CW. Appropriates funds for salary adjustments and implementation.
Kentucky	1982	Allocates $14,000 for JE study.
Massachusetts	1983	Requires JE study of civil service. Appropriates $75,000 for study.
	1984	Establishes committee to study CW in state service.
Michigan	1982	Amends wage and hour law to prohibit wage secrecy policies.

State	Year	Description
Minnesota	1982	Establishes CW policy and process for civil service.
	1983	Appropriates $21.8 million for CW increases.
	1984	Requires political subdivisions to establish equitable compensation relationships among its employees.
Missouri	1983	Requires report and recommendations on CW for civil service. Establishes CW policy.
Montana	1983	Requires "work toward goal of establishing equal pay for comparable worth," study, and annual report.
Nebraska	1978	Requires preliminary civil service study.
Nevada	1983	Requires preliminary civil service study.
New Jersey	1984	Establishes task force to study civil service. Appropriates $150,000.
	1985	Accepts interim CW task force report proposing pay increases for certain employees. Introduces implementing legislation.
New Mexico	1983	Appropriates $3.3 million in salary increases to lowest paid state workers.
North Carolina	1984	Authorizes pay equity study for classified employees.
	1985	Repeals 1984 law providing for study of CW and development of a job evaluation and pay system.
North Dakota	1987	Directs study of feasibility and desirability of CW legislation.
Oregon	1983	Requires JE/CW study for civil service. Appropriates $300,000 for study.
	1987	Requires each branch of state government to adopt method of determining comparability of the value of work. Creates Pay Equity Adjustment Fund.
Pennsylvania	1983	Adds CW language to FEP law.
Rhode Island	1984	Authorizes commission to study pay equity in state employment.
Utah	1985	Authorizes study of CW for state employees.
Virginia	1984	Requires research of CW.
Washington	1977	Requires biennial update of 1974 JE study that had not yet been implemented.
	1983	Establishes CW policy for civil service and sets up a 10-year implementation plan. Appropriates $1.5 million for salary increases to lowest paid workers.
	1985	Appropriates nearly $46 million for CW implementation.

State	Year	Description
West Virginia	1984	Creates Task Force on Public Employee Pay Equity to develop point factor evaluation system.
Wisconsin	1977	Establishes CW policy for civil service.
	1984	Creates task force on CW to review current pay systems and develop job evaluation methods.
	1985	Appropriates money for CW implementation.
Wyoming	1985	Funds an evaluation of state job classification system based on CW principles.

Sources: (1) Rothchild, N. "Overview of Pay Initiatives, 1974–1984." In *Comparable Worth: Issue for the 80's.* Vol. 1. (2) A consultation of the U.S. Commission on Civil Rights, 1984, pp. 127–128. (3) U.S. Department of Labor, *Monthly Labor Review*, January 1985, January 1986, January 1987, January 1988.

PART THREE

The Changing
Employment Environment

During the last twenty-five years, few areas of human resources management have been subjected to as much turbulence as the employment function. Beginning with the Civil Rights Act of 1964, both private and public organizations have been continuously pressured to change long-observed employment practices. Human resources professionals must be prepared to identify the sources of pressure and to adopt effective organizational responses.

The employment function is defined as the recruitment, selection, and maintenance of a work force for the effective and efficient performance of the organization's mission. To carry out this function, the employment manager must respond to forces of change from several different aspects of the firm's operating environment. These forces are frequently categorized as economic, technological, social/cultural, and legal/political.

Examples of how each type of force has previously had an impact on employment readily come to mind. Among the memorable economic forces, the double-digit inflation and high unemployment of the late 1970s and early 1980s have had a lasting effect on salary expectations and the value of a job. Technological factors have brought about fundamental changes in the way many jobs are performed and require people with new and different kinds of training and skills. Social and cultural forces have included the change in the expectations of women and their demands for a different role in the workplace. Finally, forces in the legal and political environment have brought legislation such as the Civil Rights Act and have forced changes in numerous hiring and record-keeping practices.

Even as managers have responded to these forces, new forces have added new pressures for change. One dominant force has been generated by the low growth in productivity this country has experienced since the mid 1970s. The lack of productivity has come at a time when many of our international competitors have made great strides in improving productivity. As a consequence, the United States has lost its dominant competitive position in many international and domestic markets. The impact of this poor competitive position has been and continues to be felt throughout the economy. The large number of business failures, retrenchments, mergers, and acquisitions are testimony to the profound changes American industry is undergoing.

A major consequence of these turbulent times has been the need for many firms, including many of America's leading firms, to significantly reduce employment levels. Organizations must decide how they will approach employment stability. They are faced with choices ranging from simply going with the flow of business activity and adjusting the rates of hiring and termination to business requirements *to* actively seeking and adopting methods that buffer the effects of erratic business activity. Chapter Six explores the pressures that force organizations into these choices and the measures necessary to cope with these pressures. Although the focus is on steps that can reduce or eliminate layoffs, practical advice is offered on methods to most effectively accomplish work force reductions.

The social and legal/political environments exert pressures for change in the long-established practices related to a firm's right to terminate personnel. Based on English common law and generally referred to as "employment-at-will," an absolute right to terminate employees for any reason has long been enjoyed by employers. Recently, however, this practice has been increasingly challenged in the courts. On the basis of several different legal theories, the courts have denied employers the right to continue this practice.

Chapter Seven discusses employment-at-will, beginning

with its history and its importance to business organizations. The discussion continues with an analysis of the legal foundations for exceptions to established common law principles and the implications for preserving traditional employment-at-will rights. Finally, advice is provided that may help employment professionals protect these rights for the benefit of both the company and the employee.

6

Organizational Downsizing: Managing the Restructuring Process

A harsh reality of the 1980s has been the use of work force reductions to control costs. In industry after industry companies have taken actions to reduce the size of their work forces. From such heavy industries as the steel industry, which faces intense foreign competition, to high-tech firms that face sagging markets, to healthy firms merging with one another, a common fact of life is the need to meet business requirements with a smaller work force.

The Office of Technological Assessment found that 11.5 million jobs were lost in the United States from 1979 to 1984 because of plant relocations and closings (Adler, 1987). Another study estimated that in 1986 more than 1,000,000 jobs were lost in midsized and major companies (Cook, 1987b). In 1986 and early 1987, as a result of business restructuring and its merger with RCA, General Electric terminated more than 100,000 persons through a variety of reduction strategies. AT&T cut 10 percent of its work force of 322,000, including more than 11,500 management jobs, in an effort to save $1 billion annually. Kodak made similar cuts in its 129,000-person work force in an attempt to produce an annual savings of $500,000 (Russell, 1987).

Although the reasons for reducing the size of the work force are as varied as the firms making the reductions, the reasons most commonly cited for the increase in layoffs and other downsizing activities are foreign competition, deregulation, mergers and acquisitions, increasing costs, changing technology, the shift from a manufacturing to a service economy, shifts and cutbacks in government spending, and simply poor management. With no abatement in most of these forces on the horizon, the downsizing trend is sure to continue. If the Firestone and General Motors examples are any indication, many firms with long histories of retrenchment and downsizing have not made the turnarounds necessary to make them competitive in industries in which they were once dominant.

What is most surprising about these work force reductions is that most have occurred during the longest period of business expansion since World War II and at a time of generally decreasing unemployment. Today's work force reductions are substantially different in character from most previous work force reductions in this country. Downsizing and restructuring activities have been employed by companies previously thought to be immune to large reductions. For the first time in more than a generation, it is not just the rank-and-file hourly workers, but employees at all levels, who are being displaced. For example, both Du Pont and IBM have significantly reduced the layers of management through attrition, hiring freezes, early retirements, and reassignments. Joseph Coates, a Washington, D.C., analyst, estimated that by the end of 1986 almost 75 percent of the Fortune 500 companies had undergone a reorganization in which 1,000 or more workers were cut (O'Connor, 1986).

As the trends that spawned these layoffs continue, more displacements and different patterns of employment can be expected. It is becoming increasingly important that top management consider the impact of business decisions on human resources and that they take action to reorganize the work force to face the increasingly competitive environment. "Restructuring for Competitive Advantage" was the theme of the 58th Annual American Management Association Human Resources conference in 1987. Although the conference made clear that every part of an organization must contribute to its revitalization, human resources should be at the forefront of the effort.

Work force reduction is referred to by a variety of names in the human resources literature, including "downsizing," "cutback," "layoff," "demassing," "restructuring," and "reorganization." Although most writers use these labels interchangeably, some attempt to distinguish the terms. Tomasko (1987) makes a distinction between downsizing and demassing. He refers to downsizing as a strategy with several objectives, including improved communication, faster response times, clearer definition of accountability, and, in general, improvement in productivity. He regards demassing as a strategy the sole objective of which is quick reduction in the size of the work force. Regardless of the specific purpose of the reduction, such activity has important legal and human resources management challenges that affect a firm's ability to successfully carry out work force reductions.

Decisions to close plants or to demass or downsize organizations are never easy and are not taken lightly. The high costs associated with such reductions must be considered along with the benefits. Some of these costs are

- Increased unemployment taxes that sometimes are equal to the benefits received by the unemployed person
- Severance pay and benefits
- Retirement or voluntary resignation incentives
- Administrative costs such as outprocessing, benefit maintenance, and conversion
- Outplacement programs to help former employees get new jobs
- Increased costs for hiring personnel in the future
- Loss of skills required to continue the company's work
- Damage to morale of remaining employees
- Lawsuits by disgruntled employees
- Aid to local communities impacted by plant closings
- The threat of state and federal legislation on plant closings and layoffs

In many cases, however, only through such reductions can a firm gain the necessary competitive strength to survive.

This chapter addresses two different approaches to work force reductions related to Tomasko's definitions of downsizing and demassing. One strategy addresses maintenance of a lean organization to gain and preserve a competitive position; the other strategy deals with the need for an immediate work force reduction. The two strategies are not mutually exclusive, but address somewhat different situations.

Avoiding Work Force Reductions

Because of the high costs associated with personnel cutbacks, employers naturally prefer to avoid such measures if alternatives are available. Through effective human resources utilization, it is often possible to avoid or delay the reduction of the work force. Alternatives to work force reduction are available to organizations that anticipate changes in their human resources requirements and take action well in advance of the changes. These alternatives add to the stability of the work force and reduce the long-term costs of maintaining a qualified work force.

The contrast between Texas Instruments and Motorola during the downturn in the semiconductor industry in the late 1970s illustrates the benefits of maintaining a policy of employment security to the greatest extent possible. Texas Instruments laid off large numbers of its workers in response to low semiconductor sales. Motorola, on the other hand, went to great lengths to maintain the work force intact throughout the slump. When sales began to turn around, Texas Instruments was forced to hire new workers to replace those who were dismissed earlier. It was, of course, necessary to train the new workers in production and quality techniques; during this time, Texas Instruments experienced low production rates as well as problems with quality control. In contrast, Motorola, with its work force still largely in place, surpassed Texas Instruments as the country's largest semiconductor manufacturer, a position it still enjoys.

Keeping the Organization Lean

Much has been said and written about the need to maintain a "lean" work force and to reduce organizational "fat." But the simple fact is that one of the most important human resources-originated steps that can be taken to lessen the probability of a work force reduction is monitoring the organization to minimize the size of the work force required for a given level of sales. Keeping the organization lean starts with an analysis of two aspects of organizational structure—span of control and hierarchical levels or layers of management. If tight control is maintained over these structural dimensions, the tendency of organizations to get fat as they prosper can be curbed. Organizations with reputations for running lean, such as Federal Express, closely monitor work force statistics such as the ratio of direct and indirect staff to each $1,000,000 in sales. For example, Federal Express reported only 2.1 staff employees per $1,000,000 in sales compared with the national average of about 5 as reported in an A. T. Kearney survey in 1984 (Wagel, 1987b). Clearly this gives Federal Express a competitive advantage over its rivals in the express mail/package delivery business.

The figures at Federal Express are no accident. They are the result of a conscious campaign to control organizational size, which includes an awareness program, study of other companies, monitoring of corporate processes such as selection, compensation, an incentive system to reward nonmanagement personnel for their achievements, careful review of all requests for additional manpower, and frequent evaluation of new positions or changes for effectiveness. The campaign is further supported by the company's performance reward system which provides powerful incentives to maintain high levels of profit performance (Wagel, 1987b).

Organizations must also seek alternative means to accomplish more work without increasing the work force. One or more methods should be used, especially during peak periods of relatively short duration, to add human resources hours without direct additions to the company's payroll.

Overtime. One way to increase the level of output without increasing the employment roll is through increased use of overtime. A 5 to 10 percent increase in labor hours can be attained in this manner without severely impacting employee morale or adversely affecting quality or safety.

Subcontracting. A second method is subcontracting. Subcontracting work to another company increases the capacity to produce without adding facilities or human resources. This method is especially effective when the need to increase output is of limited or uncertain duration. It may not be as effective, however, in service industries where the use of regular employees may provide advantages that cannot be attained through subcontracting. Also, it is sometimes difficult to find noncompeting firms capable of supplying the required services.

Leased Employees. In this variation of subcontracting that has recently been widely accepted in a number of fields, individual workers are contracted for varying periods. Like the highly advertised clerical help available through temporary agencies, companies can contract for a computer programmer for six months, a year, or longer. Similarly, designers, engineers, production workers, accountants, and even salesworkers can be hired. These persons are not part of the using company's employment roll so there is little cost associated with discontinuation of their services. For professional positions, salary costs may be higher, but there are no long-term costs such as medical coverage or retirement.

In many cases, organizations have been able to obtain production workers for less than half of previous in-house rates. According to a study conducted by Paine Webber, Inc., reported in *Business Week* (Pollack and Bernstein, 1986), subcontractors now represent 7.5 percent of the work force in the steel industry (up from 3 percent in the mid 1970s). USX (formerly U.S. Steel) has been very aggressive in the use of this strategy and has reduced the number of in-house labor hours required to make a ton of steel by 20 percent. (This was one of the major issues at stake in the six-month strike by the United Steel Workers union in 1986-1987.) The use of subcontracted labor gives an organization flexibility in changing the size of the work force. Employment can be reduced without the high costs of supplemental unemployment benefits—up to 85 percent of normal wages for as long as two years. Neither will the company be required to provide medical benefits under the rules of the Consolidated Omnibus Reconciliation Budget Act of 1986 (CORBA).

Using Retirees. Another approach that has proven effective when relatively few workers with specific skills are needed for limited duration is the rehire of retirees. The company does not have to retrain or introduce the person to the company's systems. The retiree benefits from the extra income, as long as the amount is within the earning guidelines established by the Social Security Administration for workers in prescribed age categories. Several companies have been forced into this solution because of poor planning of their work force reductions.

Accelerated Personnel Development. An approach that ties in well with human resources planning strategies is accelerated development of exceptional personnel. In this approach, qualified persons are given broader responsibilities at an earlier than normal stage in their careers. One variation of this approach is to "seed" high-potential technical employees throughout the company as supervisors. The knowledge base of the company is diffused and can take root and grow.

Alternatives to Downsizing

In poor times, some organizations adopt strategies that improve business to such an extent that reductions in employment are not necessary. The steps that may have been taken to keep the work force small can be reversed. For example, if work has been subcontracted to other firms to avoid an increase in the employment roll, it can be recalled and performed in house, thus saving jobs that may have been eliminated because of lower production requirements. Likewise, if contract employees have been hired, they rather than regular employees can be terminated.

Attrition. Natural attrition should be used to maximum advantage well in advance of an expected need to reduce the work force. By the use of a hiring freeze, attrition through retirements, deaths, voluntary quits, terminations for cause, and so on, the roll can be gradually reduced over time. Care must be taken in these situations to ensure that the required skills are maintained within the organization. During a necessary hiring freeze, attrition may be higher than normal as people become nervous about losing their jobs (especially if the company has a history of work force reductions). In many cases the most capable people leave first because their skills are the most likely to be demanded by other employers. As an example, in early 1987, IBM made plans to save $500 million by reducing its work force by 40,000 over a three-year period through attrition and 5,000 early retirements. However, the plans call for the continued hiring of 1,500 people in critical areas and 1,000 new college graduates each year (versus 6,000 per year in 1983).

Work Sharing. A step sometimes taken as a last resort before layoffs and terminations is work sharing. Employees work a reduced number of hours. For example, four workers may share three jobs, so that each works 30 hours per week for a total of 120 hours; normally, three workers would work 40 hours per week for a total of 120 hours. Work sharing spreads the burden of reduced earnings over a larger segment of the work force. It also provides the employer with a greater degree of control over the work force. Hewlett–Packard, for example, used this method in the early 1970s during a downturn in the electronics industry. In their plan, known as the "nine-day fortnight," workers were given every other Friday off without pay in lieu of a 10 percent reduction in the work force. In similar circumstances in 1982, Motorola reduced the number of hours worked (and paid for) by 10 percent (Feuer, 1985).

Options for Downsizing

As the collective bargaining agreement negotiated between the company and its unionized employees governs the provisions for layoffs and terminations, the procedures for work force reductions are fairly well established at the time the contract goes into effect for this segment of the work force. As a result, the options for the unionized work force may be limited. The remainder of this chapter focuses primarily on the nonunion work force.

Regardless of the causes, two basic strategies are used to achieve a work force reduction: (1) voluntary methods, which include early retirements and voluntary resignations, and (2) involuntary methods, which include layoffs and terminations. Each strategy has its own advantages and limitations.

Voluntary Retirements and Resignations

The use of incentives to induce employees to leave the organization has gained popularity recently as an alternative to layoffs and terminations. These methods, any and all of which are known as the "golden handshake," are often used by large, well-established companies with attractive pension plans or with business segments that are still sufficiently profitable to fund buyout programs.

Early Retirement. Typically, employees are offered full retirement at an earlier age than would normally be possible under the retirement plan. Employees may also be offered cash incentives or payments to supplement their retirement income until they become eligible for Social Security at age 62. Exxon, Du Pont, 3M, and IBM have used such plans to help reduce their work forces.

Voluntary Resignation. Programs to induce workers below retirement age to resign are used less often than early retirement programs but offer an alternative for companies with many young workers who would not be eligible for company retirement benefits unless the plans were badly distorted. The methods used to compute the amount of incentive vary greatly. In two recent examples, one company offered 5 percent of the employee's salary for each year worked and another company offered to pay 50 percent of the employee's salary for two years.

Incentives are offered in the hope that enough people take advantage of the opportunity to leave early, making layoffs and terminations unnecessary. It is difficult, however, to predict the response to these inducements. Sometimes the plans are too successful. In 1985, Du Pont offered an early retirement plan to its employees. Responses were at almost twice the expected rate. The company lost many people with critical skills in key areas. To offset the loss, the company was forced to hire some retirees as special consultants until other employees could be trained to carry out the work (Adler, 1987).

Problems with Voluntary Programs

Voluntary reduction programs have raised a number of thorny legal issues, several of which arise from the Age Discrimination in Employment Act (AEDA). As interpreted by the Equal Employment Opportunity Commission (EEOC) and the courts AEDA permits company retirement plans to include provisions for early retirement at a certain age and that age may be considered in determining benefits. For example, a plan that offered a $10,000 incentive for retirement at age 55 with a reduction of $500 for each year past 55 until age 60 and a $1,500 reduction annually for each year past 60 was found valid despite its differential treatment of persons of different ages. The court concluded that given the purpose of the early retirement program, it was appropriate to create a sliding scale of benefits.

By far, however, the most troublesome issue has been the "voluntariness" of early retirement programs. The essential question is, When is a voluntary retirement plan not voluntary? The 1978 amendments to AEDA prohibited the involuntary retirement of anyone under age 70. Additional amendments in 1982 removed the age ceiling altogether (with the exception of senior executives in policymaking positions—defined as being eligible for an annual pension in excess of $44,000). The courts have found in several cases that employers' actions in conducting early retirement programs constituted an involuntary retirement of some of the plan's participants. *Reardon* v. *Sharon Steel* (no. 83-2112, slip op. (W.D. Pa., Feb. 5, 1985)) and *Allen* v. *Colgate-Palmolive Co.* (539 F. Supp. 57 (S.D. N.Y. 1981)) are typical of forced retirement programs. The courts found that the employer's plans were involuntary because they required employees to choose among an early retirement program, a layoff, and a demotion.

Another problem occurs when the company offering early retirement also has a severance plan for which employees electing early retirement might also be eligible. In some cases employers have denied severance benefits to those who elected early retirement. Although the companies have argued that the decision not to award severance pay was based on retirement eligibility, not age, the court found that the distinction between age and retirement eligibility was too fine to deny the severance benefits (for example, *EEOC* v. *Borden's Incorporated* (618 F. Supp. 115 (N.D. Ohio 1985)).

Whether voluntary resignation or early retirement is used, employers should seek protection against future age discrimination suits by requiring employees to sign a written release acknowledging the voluntary nature of their choice. In the release, early retirees waive their rights to claim age discrimination as it was their option to retire. It is also prudent to have retiring employees waive rights to reemployment so that the employee may not later apply for work and claim age (or other) discrimination if not rehired. This waiver is required because the EEOC, in an opinion letter dated December 13, 1983, stated that employees accepting early retirement incentives "may not be refused consideration for rehire merely because of their status as retirees." The waiver should have the following provisions indicated to afford a high level of protection against subsequent claims.

- The release of claims should be limited to the specific claims of greatest interest, for example, age (AEDA) and other types of discrimination (Title VII) and constructive discharge.
- The portion of the release relating to the fact that the employee is giving up the right to bring a suit should be in simple language and in bold type.
- Employees should be allowed time to study the waiver before signing it; there should be enough time for the employee to contact an attorney.
- A statement should be included that asserts that the type of settlement is for administrative convenience and does not preclude the negotiation of an individual settlement.

When a severance pay plan is used in conjunction with either a voluntary or an involuntary reduction plan, managers should be aware that such plans are governed by the Employee Retirement Income Security Act (ERISA) and therefore must meet certain standards for fairness and equity. The courts have found that the act applies whether the severance plan is formal or informal (*Donovan* v. *Dillingham,* 688 F. 2d 1367 (11th Cir. 1982)) or published or unpublished (*Blau* v. *Del Monte Corporation,* 748 F. 2d 348 (1984)). The result of these rulings has been that companies have had to extend severance benefits in situations where they had not planned to do so. Employers have been found to have a fiduciary duty to act in the interest of the employees to the extent that a firm may not change the plan in anticipation of a work force reduction if such changes would materially affect the payments the discharged worker would receive (*Dependahl* v. *Falstaff Brewing Corporation,* 491 F. Supp. 1188 (E.D. Mo. 1981)). This does not mean that employers may not change the provisions of a plan; however, such changes must be made at a time when no actions are being contemplated that would invoke the provisions of the severance plan (Dowdle and Eide, 1987).

Involuntary Reduction Plans

When voluntary methods of reducing the roll do not meet the reduction objectives, involuntary means must be used. The decision now is who to lay off or terminate. The most commonly used methods are based on either seniority or performance. As was seen in the case of Du Pont's voluntary retirement program, however, it is important for companies to maintain control over who leaves the organization. To the extent that seniority and voluntary programs are relied on, the firm loses control over which skills leave the organization. The most common and most sensible alternative to seniority systems is job performance. If performance evaluations are objective and fair, they will be accepted by employees as a legitimate criterion. If the evaluations are perceived as unfair, the whole layoff/termination process will be seen as unfair. This greatly increases the likelihood of challenge of a termination in court.

Seniority. Frequently the most convenient and the most objective method of deciding who to lay off is a seniority system. For union-eligible employees, layoffs and recalls are almost always based on company seniority. When layoffs are necessary, inverse seniority is used to determine who goes (the last to be hired is the first to be laid off). Conversely, when recalls occur, the first hired (last laid off) is the first to be recalled.

Both Title VII and AEDA explicitly provide protection for employers whose actions are based on a bona fide seniority system. The seniority system tends to favor older workers rather than discriminate against them. On the other hand, seniority-based layoff and termination plans tend to have a negative effect on women and minorities because they are frequently the least senior members of the work force. Nevertheless, the courts have upheld the use of inverse seniority layoff plans (for example, *Teamsters* v. *U.S.*, 431 U.S. 324 (1977), and *Croker* v. *Boeing Co.*, 437 F. Supp. 1138

(E.D. Pa. 1977)) even though they have an adverse impact on protected groups. In fact, a recent Supreme Court ruling [*Wygant v. Jackson Board of Education*, 54 U.S.L.W. 4479 (U.S. May 20, 1986 (No. 84-1340))] stated that minorities could not be protected from a layoff by the laying off of more senior whites to achieve the school district's Affirmative Action Plan goals.

Performance. With an established performance evaluation system, the process of determining who is to be terminated is relatively straightforward. The poorest performers are laid off or terminated. The courts have consistently supported terminations based on acceptable and consistently applied performance evaluation systems. (Chapter Seven discusses the requirements for an acceptable performance evaluation.) In the case of *Surrisi* v. *Conwed Corporation* (636 F. 2d 1116 (6th Cir. 1980)), the court found no evidence of age discrimination even though Surrisi was in the protected age class and was terminated while a younger person kept a similar job.

For organizations without such systems, the process is more difficult; however, the payoff for being able to control the composition of the future work force is high enough to make the investment of time and effort to create a performance appraisal system worthwhile. A number of companies have even designed and instituted performance evaluation systems expressly for the purpose of determining who should be laid off.

In most cases, neither seniority- nor performance-based reduction plans can be applied across the whole organization to achieve the desired reductions because not all areas of the company require the same level of staff cuts. Although this does not stop some organizations from adopting across-the-board cuts, prudent companies recognize the need for differential cuts. In these situations, first specific subdivisions of the organization may be targeted for cuts and then either seniority- or performance-based plans put into effect. In other cases, certain jobs may be identified for elimination and the incumbents terminated. Care must be exercised that only lawful criteria are used in establishing which jobs should be eliminated. The criteria must reflect sound business judgment, and must not mask other reasons such as age or sex.

Handling the Work Force Reduction

Once it has been determined that a layoff or termination program is required, many questions still remain that will affect the ultimate success of the process: timing, notification process, benefits to be offered, administration of outprocessing, outplacement assistance, provision of public information, and morale of employees who remain with the company.

Timing

There is never a good time for a work force reduction, but some times are worse than others. For most companies the reduction can be made within a time range varying from a month or two to as long as six to eight months, depending on the likelihood of a change in the business picture. Obviously, it is best to avoid the end of the year—from the end of November to mid-January. Most people need their income to pay Christmas expenses; also, hiring activity (for full-time jobs) is lowest at this time. Any special local factors should also be considered in the choice of time.

How far in advance should the announcement of pending layoffs be made? If announcements are made too far in advance, the company may lose control over who stays with the firm. Many employees begin to look elsewhere "just in case" and the better qualified ones are likely to find other employment. Although the roll may be reduced to an acceptable level, the people leaving may be those the company wanted (or needed) to keep. Knowledge of a pending layoff may also have a detrimental effect on productivity. Some workers will seek to maximize personal benefit, figuring that they will soon be gone and the company "owes it to them." Others may try to take advantage of the situation to make questionable claims on workers' compensation programs.

In some cases productivity may actually be increased as workers are motivated to save their jobs. Unless low productivity is the company's real problem, however, this will have little or no effect on the need for a work force reduction, especially in the short run. And, if the reduction is still made after the employees have worked harder, there will be real resentment against the company.

Policies should already be in place to cover the benefits laid off or terminated employees will receive. Information about these benefits should be made available to affected workers as soon as they are notified of their termination. A detailed breakdown of any vested retirement, savings, or stock plans should also be made available as soon as feasible. Within a few days of termination, the former employee should know where he or she stands in relation to all entitlements. If such information can be provided at the time of the notification, it would be even better.

Notification

How an employee is notified of a termination can have a significant impact on his or her acceptance of the situation, his or her ability to deal with the emotions in the situation, and the likelihood of a legal challenge to the termination. The news should come from the employee's immediate supervisor. This person most strongly represents the "company" to the employee. The supervisor would not be as impersonal as "someone from personnel" who is frequently the alternative when supervisors are not used.

This is a tough job for the manager. It is not easy to tell a person you hired and with whom you have established a strong working relationship that he or she is no longer employed by the company. But it is even harder for the employee to hear it from someone else. Managers should, at a minimum, have instructions on what to say in the termination meeting. It would be preferable if they were trained to conduct such a meeting.

If managers must take part in the termination announcement, it is proper that they also have input into who is to be terminated. Unless managers are made part of the evaluation and selection process, they will not be committed to the program, and this will be hard to hide during the termination interview. Managers up and down the line must be convinced of the necessity for a reduction if it is to be handled effectively.

A problem exists, however, in having managers all the way down the line aware of the timing of the reduction because they may leak the news. Another problem surfaces when managers talk too much with employees after terminating them, as careful wording may be required to ensure compliance with policy and to preserve legal protections. Note these helpful instructions for managers who must terminate employees:

1. The termination interview should be held in a private location.
2. The manager should be direct and to the point.
3. The employee should be told the reason for the reduction in the work force; but not the reason that the particular employee was selected for termination.
4. Employees should be told that several factors were considered in selecting those for termination, including continuing job skill requirements, performance, and seniority.
5. The manager should not permit the employee to argue about the termination; the employee should be told that the decision has been reviewed by senior management and that it is final (this should be true).
6. The manager should be able to tell the employee what happens next—when outprocessing will take place and what special benefits will be offered (for example, outplacement assistance, severance pay, or other help in making the transition).
7. Managers should encourage employees to take advantage of any assistance programs offered by the company. Employees often feel that they can do everything on their own or that they do not want anything to do with the company; but most greatly overestimate their ability to write a good resumé and to make job contacts quickly.
8. Boxes or bags for carrying personal belongings should be available so that on top of everything else people do not have to worry about their belongings; temporary storage should be provided while the person outprocesses.

Outprocessing

The smooth administration of outprocessing requires a great deal of advanced planning. Most companies have an established procedure that is used when any employee leaves the organization. This procedure normally ensures that all company property has been returned or accounted for; the employee has left an address to which any required correspondence, for example, W-2 forms, can be forwarded; the employee has information and forms required to make conversions on medical and life insurance coverage; the employee knows how any benefit plans will be affected and knows how to take appropriate actions to exercise rights under the plans; the employee knows how to file for unemployment insurance; and if a security clearance has been granted, the employee has completed all required debriefing forms.

The employee should be given a written statement that summarizes all benefits and required actions (with appropriate deadlines). The employee should be required to acknowledge receipt of this information by signing and returning a copy of the statement. This will help to protect the company if a question is later raised about eligibility for benefit programs. Employees cannot say that they were not told about benefit plan requirements.

The number of employees affected determines the type of facility and the schedule required to accomplish the reduction in the least amount of time. If the number of employees laid off/ terminated at any one location is large, a schedule will be required to coordinate the outprocessing. The schedule should require that all affected persons within a given department or division be scheduled for outprocessing at about the same time. If the numbers and facilities will accommodate, people should be processed in relatively small groups (up to 50). This makes it less likely that people will feel as if they were treated as cattle.

Outplacement Assistance

Outplacement consists of a variety of services to help employees to find another job. Almost all large firms use some type of outplacement service to help their employees make this often difficult transition. Several essential questions must be answered with respect to outplacement assistance: Under what conditions will it be offered? Who will be eligible? Who will conduct it? What services will be offered? How will contacts with employees and outplacement organizations be handled after the employee terminates?

Outplacement can be used for one person or for thousands of people. The following discussion focuses on situations in which a substantial number of persons are affected by termination. When terminating only one or relatively few individuals, a company has more latitude and can offer unique outplacement plans tailored to the individual. In large-scale reductions, such freedom is not practical.

Gelb (1986) offers three primary reasons why companies offer outplacement services. First, outplacement is offered for humanitarian reasons; it helps to uphold employee morale and preserve a favorable public image of the company as a humane place to work. Second, if severance benefits are of the "bridge" type, that is, they end when the employee has a new job, then it is in the financial interest of the company to shorten the time the employee is out of work. Third, by offering help and perhaps reducing the search time, the employee is less likely to be "bitter" and to seek redress through a lawsuit for wrongful discharge.

If one or more of the following conditions exists, outplacement should be considered:

1. Large-scale reductions are planned and there will be a significant impact on the local, regional, and national economy.
2. The company is already the center of public attention, for example, because of a merger or acquisition, troubled industry, or widely held stock.
3. The skills of terminated employees are in low demand and a long job search is likely. If retraining and refocusing of career objectives are appropriate, outplacement may make this more apparent to employees and speed the transition process.

Who Provides Outplacement Services?

Once the decision is made to offer outplacement assistance, two questions remain: Who will provide the services? What services should be provided? A large organization may be capable of providing most, if not all, of the services itself. Obviously, it is much less expensive for an organization to provide its own outplacement services than to hire an outside firm. However, there are several arguments against using in-house services. First, the credibility of the outplacement program must be considered. The organization must have a training department (usually the employment department) that can work with the other human resources staff to provide an outplacement program that is meaningful to and gains the respect of the terminated employees. For organizations with little experience with such terminations this may be difficult. If the layoff is large, providing in-house outplacement services may overtax the company's resources and jeopardize its productivity. Second, there may not be sufficient time for a credible program to be developed in-house.

Outside firms, if selected carefully, can provide a high level of credibility and can often provide service on very short notice. Most, especially the larger outplacement specialty firms, are willing to work with a company to provide a combination of inside- and outside-provided services. In the Chevron/Gulf merger, two outside firms were used to provide some of the services and to train company employees to provide some services. Who got which service depended on a number of factors including location, organizational level, and whether the separation was under a voluntary or an involuntary plan.

Texas Instruments, among others, divided the in-house and outside consultant responsibilities based on the stages of the outplacement process. The outside firm provided training on the job-search process, while Texas Instruments provided clerical services, job listings, individual counseling, and other associated support services. In this case, the company believed that it was more capable of helping its own employees to find work in the specialty fields associated with the electronics industry.

Another reason to choose an outside firm is that training sessions are less likely to turn into "gripe sessions" about the employer and how the employees are treated. The outside provider can allow time for employees to vent their feelings, which may be useful in the transition, but these sessions will not become the focus of the program. In many cases, employees from different companies may be mixed in a group session so that there is even less possibility that the session will focus on a specific company.

Other Factors

Whether the outplacement assistance is provided from the company itself or from outside the company, the location where these services are provided is important. Job-search training and other services should be provided away from the workplace. This serves to reinforce the separation from the company so that employees do not feel that it might be possible to return to work. It keeps employees from disrupting the work of others. Not having to see the terminated employees at the workplace helps to maintain the morale of other employees.

If the decision is made to use an outside outplacement firm, basically two options are available: (1) a national firm and (2) a smaller local firm. National firms offer the advantage of greater credibility based on broader exposure and publicity. However, it is unlikely that many people outside the human resources field are aware of outplacement firms so national reputation may not be very important. The national firm's reputation may serve as a reference but not as a guarantee of quality. The best way to learn what kind of service you can expect is to talk with other companies that have used the outplacement firm. The most important factor is the skill of the counselor the firm employs. If the number of employees eligible for outplacement is large, many different counselors will be required. Therefore, it is important that the outplacement firm have many qualified counselors. This is, of course, difficult for local firms to achieve.

A number of placement firms have recently entered the outplacement field as well. One would be well advised to select these with caution. There exists a potential conflict of interest if those in the outplacement program were to be considering employment with a client of the placement firm.

Very important in selection of the firm is the "chemistry" or "comfort level" between the manager making the selection and the representatives of the outplacement firm. If the outplacement firm's other clients rate the representatives highly and the firm seems capable of meeting the hiring company's needs, then it probably is a good choice. Statistics on the number of placements a firm is able to help people make are unreliable and subject to interpretation. Therefore, it may be better to go with what feels right.

What Services to Provide

Two activities are involved in getting a job: (1) developing the job-search strategy and (2) implementing the strategy. In developing the strategy, individual objectives must be outlined, key strengths and weaknesses in abilities and skills must be identified, and companies in which these abilities and skills are in demand and in which individual objectives can be met must be found. In addition, the job seeker must prepare a resumé and learn how to interview effectively. The outside outplacement firm can instruct terminated employees in all these areas to ensure that they have a good chance of securing career-enhancing jobs. Instruction in how to prepare an attractive resumé and cover letter is not enough. Much more is involved in a successful transition than just getting a job.

To implement the strategy, the target companies must be identified and the resumé and cover letters must be typed, printed, and mailed. It is also important to have someone to talk with about search tactics and to bolster spirits. These services can be provided by either the firm terminating the employee or the outplacement firm.

Summary

This chapter has presented a view of the changing nature of layoffs in America today. With many of the country's largest and most profitable firms using work force reductions as a tool for controlling costs, it is beneficial for managers to be aware of the problems and costs associated with work force reduction plans and how to carry them out effectively. Layoffs and other reductions are no longer procedures that the "other guy" uses; any organization may need to use them.

Managers can prepare for the changing environment by being proactive in their approach to management of the work force. Through more thoughtful human resources planning, the most serious problems of reorganization and reduction can be minimized or eliminated. Planning begins with efforts to maintain the organization at a size consistent with its mission requirements—to keep the organization lean. The demassing or downsizing program, if necessary, can be carried out in a manner by which the organization's image as a good place to work is preserved, a qualified work force is maintained, and the dignity of those who must leave the organization is protected.

7

Employment-at-Will:
Balancing Employer
and Employee Rights

In the absence of a contract, the ability of an employer or employee to unilaterally terminate the employment relationship has long been viewed by both parties as a fundamental right. Employees have been free to leave and employers have been free to discharge employees for any reason and at any time. After more than 100 years of working under this common law rule of employment-at-will, the absolute right of employers to terminate employees has recently been challenged on a number of grounds and this right now faces serious erosion.

The employment-at-will concept serves as the basis for an employment relationship in which the two parties are not specifically bound by a contract. Although many employment relationships, such as those between a union and a company or between a teacher and school system, are governed by a contract, more than 75 percent of all employment relationships are employment-at-will relationships.

Some may argue that employment-at-will is unfair because it gives too much power to employers; however, the courts have until very recently supported employers' rights to terminate at will. In one of the earliest confirmations of this right, the judge in *Payne* v. *Western & Atlantic R.R. Co.* (Tenn. 507, 519–520 (1884)) ruled that employees could be discharged "for good cause, for no cause, or for cause morally wrong."

In this country, despite many challenges, the right to terminate at will has prevailed. However, in many other countries including Great Britain, where our common law had its beginnings, more strenuous restrictions have been imposed on employers. For example, a national law in Great Britain requires that a "progressive" discipline procedure be followed prior to dismissal and prohibits any form of "unfair" discharge. Other leading economic nations such as Japan, Germany, and Sweden require that employees be dismissed only for "just cause." Most of these countries also require some form of "due process" before an employee can be dismissed. Although the trend to place greater restrictions on employers' rights to terminate employees has taken a long time to develop in this country, recent events have greatly accelerated the movement.

Sources of Erosion

Three factors have contributed to the erosion of employment-at-will rights. The first limitations appeared as the labor unions grew in size and strength after passage of the National Labor Relations Act (NLRA) in 1935. This act was followed in the 1960s by various state and federal civil rights statutes that prohibited certain employment practices and sought to create fairness in employment and termination processes. The latest, and potentially most wide-ranging, limitations on employment-at-will have arisen from the application of legal principles not previously applied to employment cases. Each source of limitations is discussed here.

Unions. After passage of the NLRA, unions gained important rights and powers including the requirement that employers bargain with unions. The act also provided for the enforcement of collective bargaining agreements through the National Labor Relations Board. The number of agreements increased dramatically over the next decade. Most agreements now contain clauses that require that union employees be dismissed only for "just cause." Under the terms of these agreements, an employee who feels that he or she has been dismissed unfairly has a right to appeal through a grievance and arbitration process. In the final step of the process, the arbitrator is empowered to determine whether the dismissal was for just cause and to reinstate an employee improperly discharged.

Although the "just cause" provision applies only to those collective bargaining agreements that include such language, it has become widely expected that any dismissal should be subject to the just cause test. Many companies have either formally or informally adopted just cause as the criterion for dismissal even though they are not obligated to do so for those employees not covered by a collective bargaining agreement containing this provision.

Civil Rights. State and federal civil rights legislation, especially Title VII of the 1964 Civil Rights Act, has done much in the last twenty years to erode the unlimited right to discharge employees. Although many different statutes have been applied to the employment relationship, the intent is clear and now well understood. An employee cannot be discharged solely on the basis of sex, race, color, religion, national origin, age, union activity, or, in some cases, handicap or sexual orientation.

Wrongful Discharge. Recently, however, employees challenging their dismissal on grounds other than civil rights violations or enforcement of express contract provisions have won reinstatement and/or punitive damage judgments on the basis of being "wrongfully discharged." In California alone, between October 1979 and January 1984, fifty-one cases went to trial. Employees won 70 percent of the cases, with an average jury award of almost $180,000 (Holley and Walters, 1987). Recently, both the number of employees winning suits and the size of the awards have been increasing. For cases tried in California from 1982 to 1986, plaintiffs still won 70 percent of the cases, but the awards averaged $652,100 and several individual awards exceeded $2,000,000 (Gould, 1988). California is not unique in the increased use of wrongful discharge as a cause of action. Courts in Michigan, Illinois, and Ohio have also accepted some wrongful discharge arguments. The increased willingness of the courts to make exceptions to the traditional employment-at-will doctrine has led labor unions to increase demands for more legislation to protect employee rights (Gould, 1988).

At the same time that employers' rights to terminate are being challenged, many organizations face increasing pressure to improve productivity. Greater emphasis is being placed on dismissing poor performers and those with skills inappropriate to achieve improved productivity. Fulmer (1986) cites several studies indicating that managers are increasingly willing to fire employees as a means of dealing with incompetent workers or reducing the work force. Many companies, however, feel powerless to use this method in the face of the potential legal liabilities that may be incurred if such terminations are deemed "wrongful."

The purpose of this chapter is to explore how organizations can preserve their rights to terminate at will. It examines the bases on which discharged employees have won lawsuits, how companies can avoid actions that enable an employee to show wrongful discharge, and how to terminate with a minimum risk of future liability.

Bases for Wrongful Discharge Claims

A plaintiff (discharged employee) can seek redress for an unlawful termination through one of three means. First, the plaintiff may claim that a violation of a collective bargaining agreement has occurred. Second, the plaintiff may claim that one of the "fairness" statutes has been violated. Third, the plaintiff may seek a specific exception to the employment-at-will doctrine.

Employees seeking redress for alleged wrongful discharge under one of the fairness statutes have more than twenty years of court decisions and legislation on which to base their arguments. Although still evolving, these theories of recovery are based on some form of discrimination, are limited in their scope, and apply only to well-defined groups of individuals. These types present relatively fewer problems to personnel managers today than employment-at-will issues.

The third basis for challenging the principle of employment-at-will presents most of the unresolved questions facing personnel managers and is the primary focus of the rest of this chapter. The types of claims on which the courts have made exceptions to the employment-at-will doctrine can be grouped into two broad categories: contract claims and tort claims.

Contract Claims. In contract claims, the plaintiff attempts to establish (1) that the employer has through its actions made an implied contract with or a legally enforceable promise to the employee, (2) that the employee has acted reasonably in accepting the promise, and (3) that the employer through its termination of the employee has breached the promise. The determination that an implied contract existed has generally been based on oral representations made to an employee during the recruitment process, in written company information such as policy and procedure statements or employee handbooks, or through a firm's practices over a period.

In one of the early cases to establish an exception to the employment-at-will doctrine, the court found that the employer had told the employee that he would "be with the company as long as he did his job" (*Toussaint* v. *Blue Cross and Blue Shield of Michigan,* 292 N.W. 2d 880 (Michigan, 1980)). The court also found that the company's employee handbook stated that the "policy" of the company was to release employees only for just cause.

In this case, the court found that an implied contract existed even though there was no evidence that the parties had mutually agreed that the statements would establish a contract, that neither party had signed the policy statements, that the statements could be unilaterally changed by the employer, and that no reference to these statements was made in the preemployment interview process.

Courts have also found that many typical personnel practices may form the basis for an implied contract. For example, longevity of employment, granting of pay raises and promotions to employees, lack of criticism of work performances, assurances of continued employment, and policy and procedures prohibiting terminations except for good cause (Robbins and Norwood, 1986) may be interpreted by the courts as a form of contract between the parties.

Shortly after the finding in the *Toussaint* case in Michigan, the California Appeals Court returned a case to a lower court for hearing on the basis that an implied contract may have been established as a result of the employer's actions over the duration of the employee's tenure with the company. The company had regularly commended and promoted the employee and there was no evidence of direct criticism of the employee's work. The court continued the appeal in spite of an explicit provision of the state labor code permitting the at-will termination of a noncontractual employment relationship.

Closely related to the implied contract exception to the employment-at-will doctrine is the concept of promissory estoppel, which has been used in several courts, notably in California and Ohio. This exception is based on the legal theory that when an inducement (promise) of such magnitude has been offered, the promisor (employer) should be precluded (estopped) from withdrawing it from an employee who has been reasonably led to act in anticipation of fulfillment of the promise.

The Ohio Court of Appeals found in the case of *Jones* v. *East Center for Community Mental Health, Inc.* (19 Ohio App. 3d 19 (1984)) that the employment manual did not mention that the employer retained the right to terminate "at will" nor did it state that the statements in the manual held no legal significance. Accordingly, the court said, "the promises contained therein are quite likely to create expectations of benefit and lead the employees to some form of action or forbearance in reliance on those promises." In continuing its argument, the court said that an employer should not be allowed to make high-sounding promises of fair treatment to obtain loyal service from employees and then be allowed to disaffirm the promises and rely on an employment-at-will doctrine for dismissing these same employees.

It seems clear from these cases and similar ones that have followed in their wake that the courts are setting limits on employment-at-will and holding employers to a standard of "fairness" in dealing with employees. In fact, in several cases the courts have explicitly applied a standard of good faith and fair dealing in determining that employees had been wrongfully discharged. For example, in *Fortune* v. *National Cash Register Co.* (364 N.E. 2d 1251 (1977)) the court held that the employer had breached the contract (implied) when it terminated a long-term employee rather than pay him the large sales commission he had earned under the company's sales incentive system.

Tort Claims. The second type of claim that a discharged employee might make is a tort claim. A tort is an injury or wrong committed against a person or that person's property. In claiming a wrongful discharge tort, the employee asserts that the discharge is injurious to the employee and violates "public policy." Findings of wrongful discharge under tort law have been made (1) by employees who refused to violate a criminal law, (2) by employees who exercised a legal right, (3) by employees who complied with a legal duty, or (4) where the discharge would violate the public policy.

Peterman v. *International Brotherhood of Teamsters, Warehousemen, and Helpers of America, Local 396* (344 P 2d 25 (1959)) is an example of the first category. In this case, Peterman claimed wrongful discharge because he was terminated for refusing to commit perjury. The court held that "public policy . . . would be seriously impaired if it were held that one could be discharged by reason of his refusal to commit perjury."

The courts have found dismissal of an employee for exercising a legal right such as filing a workman's compensation claim or complying with a legal duty (for example, serving on a jury or cooperating with agencies empowered to conduct investigations of business practices) to be inconsistent with public policy. In such cases, the courts have reasoned that specific legislation has been enacted to protect the public interest. Allowing an employee to be discharged for exercising rights designed to protect the public would undermine established public policy.

There are marked differences in and considerable debate over how union and nonunion employees can pursue remedies for alleged wrongful discharge. With few exceptions, the courts have restricted employees working under a collective bargaining agreement to remedies available under the agreement's grievance arbitration process and have generally not allowed discharged employees to collect punitive damages as nonunion employees have been allowed. The courts have upheld the preemption of the labor contract and processes established by the NLRB. The exceptions have generally been of the "public policy" type discussed later (compare Robbins and Norwood, 1986; Taldone, 1986).

Establishing Effective Human Resources Practices

Given changing employee expectations of the employment relationship and the increased willingness of the courts to uphold employee challenges to dismissals, how does a company protect its right to manage its own affairs and make terminations when required without a large risk of a court challenge?

Although the law in all fifty states and the District of Columbia still presumes the employer's right to terminate at will and requires that the employee prove that a wrongful discharge has occurred, judges and especially juries are likely to hold little sympathy for the employer in such cases. There seems to be a bias in favor of the "little guy" in the awards of many juries today. This bias is seen not only in wrongful discharge cases but in malpractice, personal injury, and a variety of other cases that pit businesses against individuals in the courtroom. To convince judges and jurors that a discharge was not "wrongful," a company must be able to demonstrate that it acted in a fair and reasonable manner. The firm's ability to do so depends on the human resources policies and practices that have been established to manage the employment relationship.

Two avenues are open to firms that desire to maintain defensible terminations. On the one hand firms may close the chinks in their defenses by never promising permanent employment, requiring employees to sign statements acknowledging the firm's right to terminate at will, and including in all literature disclaimers about the permanency of employment. Although many firms have adopted this legalistic approach, it may, at best, provide only limited protection against contract-type claims for wrongful discharge and almost no protection against tort claims.

The other avenue combines a legalistic approach with a management style that emphasizes fairness and termination only for just cause. By establishing practices based on good faith and fair dealing, firms are more likely to win favor with judges and juries and to shift the weight to the plaintiff to prove that the termination was not reasonable in the circumstances. Another reason for the low probability of success of the legalistic approach when used alone is the belief, held by many, that if the business community does not do a better job of meeting the rising expectations of its employees for fairer treatment then the federal government will (Horton, 1984). Just as Congress stepped in with the Norris–LaGuardia Act to protect workers from being forced to sign "yellow-dog" employment contracts prohibiting them from joining unions, Congress may act to limit the rights of employers to terminate at will. It is in the long-term interest of employers to police themselves in this area through the establishment of sound human resources practices before legislation such as that which established the EEOC, OSHA, and ERISA is enacted to protect employees from "wrongful" discharge.

Five areas require attention in establishing a complete system to safeguard the rights of both employers and employees: (1) staffing, (2) orientation and training, (3) performance appraisal, (4) grievance procedure, and (5) dismissal procedure.

Staffing. Protection of discharge rights begins with the company's staffing process and a job candidate's introduction to the organization. The staffing process consists of recruiting, selection, and placement. In the recruiting step, care must be taken that no promises, either written or oral, are made that the firm does not intend to honor. Do not, for example, discuss "permanent" employment. When discussing "career" opportunities, discuss what others who have stayed with the organization have done, but make it clear that no one is guaranteed a job for any specific length of time or until retirement. The employment application should include a disclaimer that the employment relationship is subject to termination at any time, with or without notice, by either the employer or the employee.

Human resources specialists usually have no trouble staying within these guidelines; however, line managers involved in the interviewing process tend to get carried away with what the company can or will offer in terms of "career" opportunities. It is advisable to provide training for these managers not only in basic interviewing techniques but in how to keep the interview legal from both discrimination and employment-at-will perspectives. It should be made clear to both job candidates and line managers that only authorized personnel (usually from the human resources division) can make offers of employment and discuss the terms of employment. The offer of employment should be in writing and should include a disclaimer similar to that used on the application.

To select and place a job candidate properly, a great deal must be known about both the candidate and the job requirements to ensure a productive match. This process can be enhanced if detailed position descriptions and job specifications are available and if the job candidate is given a "realistic job preview" (Wanous, 1980). The realistic job preview shows the "bad" aspects of the job along with the good. Wanous has found that although some job candidates may not join an organization because of negative information learned on the job interview, those who do join are likely to fit better and to stay longer. The better the fit between the candidate and the job, the lower the probability that the employee will have to be terminated for unsatisfactory job performance.

Orientation and Training. To ensure satisfactory job performance, it is important to establish appropriate performance expectations for new employees, preferably in the initial orientation and training. The supervisor plays a major role in this process. It is important that supervisors be trained to set realistic expectations of good performance, not just adequate performance. Performance expectations should reflect the firm's policies and practices with respect to all aspects of employee performance including attendance, conflict of interest, and ethics, not just day-to-day work activities.

One means often used to convey information and expectations to employees is the employee handbook. Many firms use these handbooks as a primary communication technique to ensure that all employees operate on the same basis. Other firms are reluctant to use an employee handbook because they fear being held responsible by a court of law for promises contained in the handbook. (As discussed earlier, courts have relied on statements contained in employee handbooks for determining whether a contract exists between employee and employer.) Should a company have an employee handbook?

Although handbooks are associated with possible legal problems, they also have many positive benefits. Handbooks give employers an opportunity to establish a common set of operating rules, to build an image, to establish expectations about the employment relationship, to solve many routine problems before they arise, and to provide a symbol of security for the employee (Coombe, 1986). It would be irresponsible for management to discard these benefits for fear of a legal action based on policies established in the handbook. Handbooks *should not contain* statements (promises) that the employer does not intend to keep. It is poor management practice to disregard established policies and practices when making decisions. In many of the cases decided in favor of the employee, the employer had violated its own policies and practices when making the termination that led to the suit. In the *Toussaint* case, for example, the employer did not follow the rules outlined in the handbook in dismissing the employee. If employers wish to maintain their employment-at-will rights, they must consistently follow their own policies in making termination decisions.

Should an employer decide to use an employee handbook, it is important that care be exercised in its writing. As with the job application and offer letter, the language in the handbook must be purged of any statement that might later be interpreted as a contract. For example, the term *regular employment* should be used rather than *permanent employment.*

Under reasons for discharge, the term *for cause* should be avoided. This term has been interpreted widely by various courts and is fraught with ambiguity. It is better to list the offenses that can result in discharge and to include a statement that the firm reserves the right to discharge at any time for any reason.

Statements that suggest "job security" should also be avoided. Employees have frequently used discussions of careers, career paths, and job security as the basis for a claim that a contract for employment exists and that the employer violated this contract when it failed to follow a "due process" procedure in discharging the employee.

A specific disclaimer denying that the document constitutes a contract should also be included. Several court cases including *Edwards* v. *Citibank N.A.* (425 N.Y.S. 2d 327 (N.Y. Sup. Ct. 1980)) and *Novosel* v. *Sears, Roebuck & Co.* (495 F. Supp. 344 (E.D. Mich. 1980)) have found that a disclaimer prevents employees from reasonably relying on the statements of the handbook as promises in a contract with the employer.

Performance Appraisal. One of the most important facets of a program to protect against wrongful discharge suits is an effective performance appraisal system. Through performance appraisal the employer can let employees know where they stand so that they are not surprised when they are terminated for poor performance. Although performance appraisal is more fully discussed in Chapter Eight, key points relating to employment-at-will are addressed here.

There are five elements to a successful performance appraisal system. First, employees should know how they will be evaluated. Standards for evaluation should be based on relevant job dimensions as determined by job analysis or as set with the input of the employees as in management-by-objective systems.

Second, managers should be thoroughly trained to use the system. Training should provide information on selection of relevant rating dimensions, standards for rating categories, completion of the evaluation form, and so on. The training should stress the link between performance appraisal and ability of the firm to discharge employees. If performance shortcomings are not adequately addressed through the appraisal process, the firm's ability to terminate an employee later may be jeopardized.

Third, narrative statements should be included along with the checklists used for rating. Narrative comments more completely document performance than a checklist.

Fourth, the employee should receive direct feedback. The evaluation should be discussed with the employee so that the employee has an opportunity to correct shortcomings and achieve an acceptable level of performance. The employee should also be given the opportunity to respond to the evaluation and be required to sign the evaluation to acknowledge its receipt (whether or not he or she agrees with the evaluation).

Fifth, the system should provide for someone, usually the rater's superior, to review the evaluation. A review made by someone who does not interact daily with the employee will help to ensure the fairness of the ratings. This will also result in fewer arguments over the adequacy of the ratings and their intent.

Grievance Procedure. Companies can also establish fairness in their human resources policies by providing the means to resolve employee problems. Most union contracts provide such a means in the grievance arbitration process. Many organizations also provide procedures for nonunion workers based on union grievance procedures. An alternative to the grievance procedure is the ombudsman. The ombudsman is a person set apart from the managerial hierarchy (frequently reporting directly to the president or vice-president for human resources) who is given broad powers to investigate employee complaints.

Under either system, the employee is given the opportunity to complain to someone who can take a disinterested perspective on the problem. Grievance handling procedures slow the discharge down so that emotions can be defused and objective decisions can be made. These processes help to ensure compliance with all company policies, and also assure the company that there is consistency among various units of the organization.

Termination Procedures. The procedures used to terminate an employee can also substantially affect the likelihood of a challenge to the termination. As Ewing (1983) points out, the courts have never denied the right to dismiss an employee for "just cause." Therefore, it is essential that there exists a well-established procedure leading to a termination and that the procedure is followed. If the steps outlined earlier are followed, the employer should have a well-documented case for dismissal, because it has shown that the employee was given the opportunity to improve performance, or that because of the seriousness of the offense no second chance should be given, and that the termination is consistent with previous treatment for similar situations.

The actual termination process is similar to that discussed in Chapter Five. Several differences should be noted, however. Fulmer (1986) offers the following guidelines:

- Make the discussion fairly brief and private.
- Be straightforward and firm, yet tactful.
- Give all information concerning severance pay and the status of benefits and coverage.
- Tell the employee how long he or she has to leave the organization.

- If possible (and appropriate) try to stress some of the employee's good qualities and skills.
- Explain how inquiries from other firms seeking references will be handled.

Follow-Up. What happens after a termination may, in some cases, affect the defensibility of the termination. Employees who are fired for cause generally do not have a right to collect unemployment compensation. The first occasion on which an outside party may judge the appropriateness of the termination may be when the terminated employee files for unemployment benefits. If the employee is awarded benefits, it means that the examiner has determined that the employee is unemployed through no fault of his or her own; that is, he or she was not discharged for "just cause." The firm then has two choices. First, it may do nothing, permitting the employee to collect benefits, and hope that the employee is satisfied and the matter ended. Second, the firm may contest the examiner's decision and attempt to demonstrate that the discharge was in fact for "cause." Contesting the decision and losing could leave the firm open to a claim of wrongful discharge, but it would also provide an opportunity to assess the strength of a possible suit brought against the company by the employee (Dube, 1986).

Unemployment compensation claims hearings may provide an early indication of the employee's intent with respect to challenging the dismissal. In some jurisdictions, the finding by a state court on the presence or absence of "just cause" in an unemployment claims proceeding may bar a further suit by the losing party. Obviously, the unemployment claims process should be treated seriously and every effort should be made to provide the examiners with straightforward and honest answers to inquiries about the circumstances surrounding the employee's dismissal.

Summary

The ability of employers to freely dismiss employees has been profoundly altered by recent judicial opinions in a number of important court cases. Although the many cases challenging the employment-at-will relationship have occurred in only a few states, there is evidence that more jurisdictions are adopting some of the principles leading to decisions of wrongful discharge. In addition, there is a growing expectation by employees that they have a fundamental interest in and a right to a job. These factors are increasing the pressures on judges and legislators to place restrictions on employers. To help stem the erosion of their rights, employers must be more proactive in safeguarding their rights. To do this, they should pay greater attention to "fair dealing" and take steps to notify employees of the actual terms and conditions of employment. Employers should modify job application forms, job offer letters, and employee handbooks so that they clarify the employers' rights, and should also change performance appraisal systems and termination procedures so that they are fairer and prepare the employee for the possibility of termination if performance does not meet the required standards. Additionally, an appeal process based on the grievance/arbitration process used to settle disagreements between unions and management may be effective in dealing with dissatisfied employees without resorting to a lawsuit to settle a disagreement over termination. Whatever methods are chosen, however, it is clear that employers can no longer be passive with respect to their rights.

PART FOUR

Employee Performance and Productivity

The era of price recovery—passing along price increases for material, labor, energy, and capital to customers—has come to an end. The reluctant and unsuccessful attempts by corporations to confront this fact are well known. From U.S. Steel to Osborne Computers, from the farm equipment industry to the textile industry, liquidations and reductions in force bear grim testimony to the fact that America's capacity to compete in both global and domestic markets has been severely challenged. The often painful shift from price recovery to alternative strategies for maintaining a viable position in the marketplace is now a necessity, however.

Although substitutions of capital for labor in some instances will contribute to ongoing efforts to resolve American industry's competitive crisis, much of the gain in productivity will have to come from the people who staff our organizations at all levels. Obtaining these increases in people productivity will require increased attention to and proficiency in managing people for performance. As performance is determined primarily by a person's motivation, skills, and understanding of what is to be accomplished, managers must concentrate on those activities that enable employees to perform to job requirements and not conform to organizational rules. For example, managers will have to spend more time selecting, evaluating, and coaching than in the past. They will have to recognize that these matters are not solely personnel functions but management functions in which various human resources staff professionals can provide assistance.

Managers must make some strategic adjustments as well. As the demographics of the work force change and as advances in technology continue to modify the way in which work is accomplished, management must make a substantial commitment to retraining. As the work force continues to mature, management must think in more strategic terms about their people as investments in human capital. And people can continue to yield a positive return to the organization if their skills are realigned to meet changing technological conditions, and their motivation to contribute is sustained by enlightened management practices that allow for more participation and challenge.

Maintaining employee commitment and contribution is not a slogan for the present either. As fewer and less well educated young adults enter the labor force, the more adept and reliable workers with years of valuable experience will be needed to sustain operations. Retraining, therefore, will become an increasingly important component of an organization's productivity plan. Extending an employee's career will require one of two options— renewal or repositioning. Renewal is the adaption of existing skills to new conditions; the employee is retained in his or her basic field or line of work. Repositioning, on the other hand, applies to employees who must qualify for positions in other fields; often the repositioned employee is employed by a different company in a different industry.

Chapter Eight is a comprehensive assessment of performance management practices in industry. It also provides a useful framework to critique organizational practices designed to enhance employee performance and productivity. Chapter Nine focuses on the growing need to retrain large segments of the work force. It concludes with a strategy for career development that incorporates retraining as a planned phase of development.

8

Performance
Management Methods:
Enhancing Employee Productivity

Other chapters in this book address issues only recently of concern to human resources managers; however, performance management has a long history. Historically, in management theory and practice, periods of attention to technical improvements or changes in organizational design and structure have been followed by periods of increased attention to the human side of work performance. Examples of technical improvements include scientific management; management science; and automation, robotics, and microcomputers. Efforts to improve through design or structural changes have included decentralization of decision making, matrix organizations, and functional specialization. Efforts to improve the human aspect of work have included the human relations and participatory leadership movements, task design/job enrichment, and management-by-objectives.

Once again, changes in the legal, cultural, and competitive environments have pressured business and public organizations to pay more attention to employee performance. Organization after organization has found that it is not enough to have the latest manufacturing technology, the newest computer systems, and the perfect competitive strategy if the work force does not productively utilize these tools to the organization's advantage.

Traditionally, organizations have managed individual performance throughout the organization in rather fragmented ways. Attention has been given to the establishment of regulations to control behavior, to the training of management in coaching and motivating skills, to participatory or joint decision making, to incentive pay schemes, and to any number of plans that encourage the desired performance. Perhaps more than any other method, management has put their faith in performance evaluation and appraisal methods to elicit the performance they sought. But for a host of reasons these and many other plans have failed to fully satisfy management's demands for improved performance.

This chapter examines some environmental influences that have forced management to search again for new methods to increase individual and organizational performance. Problems with previous attempts to improve performance, especially performance appraisal methods, are discussed, and an alternative view of performance management that may be the key to future organizational success is suggested.

Environmental Forces Affecting Performance Management

An organization's operating environment can be characterized by the forces that act on it from different segments of the environment. These segments have been classified in different ways but usually four major categories of forces are recognized in the operating environment:

Economic

Competition
Low productivity growth
Shift to service economy

Social/Cultural

Older work force
Well-educated work force
High career expectations

Technological
Information systems
Knowledge work
Computer-aided manufacturing

Legal/Political
"Fairness" legislation
Employment-at-will

Economic Forces. Forces in the economic environment are pressuring management to increase the efficiency of business operations. One often-cited force is the heightened level of competition experienced by many U.S. firms. Foreign competition for many manufactured goods is putting the squeeze on many industries. From steel and automobiles to electronics and computer components to shoes and clothing, American firms are experiencing unprecedented competition from overseas. This competition has forced many U.S. firms into bankruptcy or severely scaled-down operations. The survivors have been forced to find new ways of doing business and to improve the efficiency of their operations.

One of the chief reasons for the dramatic inroads of foreign manufacturers into American markets has been the low rate of productivity growth experienced by U.S. firms. Several of our primary competitors, notably Japan, have enjoyed productivity growth more than twice our average for much of the last decade. Other factors contributing to increased competition include the low wage rates, the greater attention to quality/value concerns of the American consumer, and significant manufacturing and technological innovations (for example, "just-in-time" manufacturing and VCR technology) in most competitor countries.

Simultaneously with the increase in competition, and partially as a result of this competition, the nature of the U.S. economy has undergone a significant shift. Although manufacturing industries have diminished, service industries have flourished. As a consequence, today there are more workers in service-related jobs than in manufacturing jobs. This change in the type of work that people do has had a profound effect on work and the relationship between people and their work. In the past, for the majority of jobs performance was determined in large part by the technology of the manufacturing process, whereas today performance is more directly determined by the individual. This shift places a premium on regulating the performance of every person in the organization, as individual performance is no longer tied to the pace of the manufacturing process.

Technological Forces. Changes in technology have also had a large impact on performance management. The shift to a service economy from a manufacturing economy has resulted in a different kind of work force. For example, computer and related electronic logic technology has had an effect on almost every job and has created a new worker—the knowledge worker. Knowledge workers have as their primary responsibility the processing and utilization of information. This type of work is significantly different from the typical work of the past; hence its management requires new approaches.

Even on the factory floor, things have changed with the advent of computer-aided manufacturing. Some manufacturing jobs now require greater skill and technical knowledge. Others require minimal skill; these jobs have become routine because the skilled aspects of the work are performed by a computer or computer-controlled machinery. Each case presents its own challenges for managing and encouraging performance.

Social and Cultural Forces. A number of social and cultural forces have increased the requirements that must be met by performance management systems. As in so many other aspects of our society the "baby boom" is having a pronounced effect on performance management. The baby boomers are the most highly educated age group in the history of the country. By age thirty, more than 40 percent had attended college. This high level of education led members of this group to have high career aspirations, and for many, these expectations have come true.

Members of the baby boom, particularly the cohort from the first half of the boom (1946–1953), enjoyed unprecedented success in climbing the organizational ladder because of the rapid growth of business and government during the 1960s and 1970s as they entered the work force. This period of rapid growth has ended, however, and this group and those who follow them are faced with the prospect of slow advancement (that is, many years in the same job).

Keeping this group satisfied, motivated, and committed is a formidable task.

Legal and Political Forces. Several state and federal laws as well as court interpretations of previous law and common law have also pressured employers to accurately evaluate and document individual performance. Most notable among the legislative acts affecting performance management has been Title VII of the Civil Rights Act of 1964. Interpretation of the act's provisions by federal agencies and subsequent support by the Supreme Court (for example, *Griggs* v. *Duke Power Company*, 401 U.S. (1971), 3, EPD 8137) have firmly established the need to relate selection processes to job performance. To determine on-the-job performance, a validated performance appraisal system is required. As a result, today organizations spend much more time and effort in developing appraisal systems that meet the standards required by the act.

Another reason for conducting performance appraisals relates to a company's right to terminate personnel. As discussed in Chapter Seven, rights can be protected by several methods, including a performance appraisal system that lets people know where they stand. If performance is unsatisfactory, individuals are provided the feedback with which they can correct performance deficiencies, thus eliminating the need to terminate. The performance appraisal serves as a notice to the employee, provides a record of the organization's attempts to correct performance, and demonstrates fair treatment of the employee. It will help the firm to establish in court, if necessary, that it was justified in terminating the employee.

Although far from exhaustive, the aforementioned reasons clearly demonstrate why organizations should be concerned about performance management. To date, however, too few organizations have treated performance management thoroughly and systematically. Most organizations have sought to solve performance management problems with performance appraisal systems. In most cases, they have found not a solution but more problems.

Relationship Between Performance Management and Performance Appraisal

Although performance management and performance appraisal are often confused or considered different names for the same process, they are in fact two very different processes (Guinn, 1987). Performance management is concerned with the total process of directing, encouraging, and controlling human resources productivity in the organization. Performance appraisal, on the other hand, is concerned only with the evaluation of performance. The information gained in the evaluation of an individual's performance is used for administrative purposes such as salary administration, promotion, and termination. Although the performance appraisal can be used as a tool in developing individual capabilities through feedback and identification of training needs, its usefulness in this role is limited.

Development of an individual's capabilities is more appropriately undertaken by performance management. Rather than a once-in-a-while event, performance management is an ongoing process. It is more than filling out appraisal forms and discussing past performance with an employee. Performance management is a continuing process that includes a number of basic managerial activities. Before analyzing performance management in depth, we should gain a perspective on the problems of performance appraisal as an improvement technique.

Problems with Performance Appraisal

No figures are available that show how much it costs U.S. firms to operate their performance appraisal systems. However, there can be little doubt that the price tag is high when one considers the activities required. Costs are incurred in developing the system, in training managers to use the system, in allocating time to managers to prepare the appraisal and to managers and employees to participate in the appraisal interview, and in filing and maintaining appraisal records. But just what are business and government getting for the money? Not much, according to several recent criticisms of performance appraisal (for example, Geis, 1987; Kane and Freeman, 1986, 1987; Lefton, 1986).

Some of the problems in performance appraisal are intrinsic to the process and can only be minimized, not eliminated. Other problems are extrinsic to the process and can be eliminated through proper planning and implementation. Lefton (1986) identifies four intrinsic problems. First, fundamentally, appraisals represent a potential confrontation between rater and ratee, as each has different interests and perspectives in the situation. Second, people are reluctant to take a judgmental role (McGregor, 1957). Third, the appraisal situation is emotionally charged. Each party has to defend past actions and decisions to protect self-esteem and ego. Fourth, appraisals by their nature deal with very complex issues involving motivation, personality, communication, and values. This makes it very difficult for managers to deal with all the behavioral situations that arise in connection with an appraisal.

The extrinsic problems arise because performance appraisal is not viewed as a part of a total system of performance management. Rather, performance appraisal is viewed as a separate, formal event occurring at a fixed interval (usually a year). The focus is usually on accurate completion of the forms, not on motivating and developing people. Managers become the center of action, not the employee. As a consequence, managers fail to adequately involve employees in the process. Because of their fear of creating an emotional or confrontational situation, managers fail to probe deeply to find the cause of performance problems, fail to address tough issues, fail to use all the data available, and ignore the need to treat each person according to his or her own personal needs.

Programs that are a part of total performance management, such as goal setting, interim reviews and coaching, training needs identification, and career planning, are seen as distinct from performance appraisal. People place a lower value on these programs than on performance appraisal because they are not an expected part of the appraisal process and "are not on the form." Too frequently, managers believe that these issues have been taken care of once the performance appraisal is completed. The major criticisms leveled at methods designed to overcome some of the shortcomings of performance appraisal as means to manage performance are aimed at one specific technique: management-by-objectives (MBO). Although numerous complaints have been made against MBO, the one of most concern in this discussion is the charge that MBO places too much emphasis on short-term achievement and cost-related measures such as sales, waste reduction, or units produced and too little attention on the behaviors required to achieve the desired performance (Latham and Wexley, 1981, p. 127).

Over the years, American firms have adopted a number of shortsighted strategies that have left them in a vulnerable position in international competition. These strategies, which stress near-term profits, cater to Wall Street, advocate low risk taking, and emphasize numbers rather than creativity, are blamed on performance management systems that emphasize these factors (compare Hayes and Abernathy, 1980; Zucker and others, 1982). Companies are still dealing with the consequences of the unintended decisions to pursue these directions.

A major reason for this emphasis on the short term is the need to make periodic evaluations of performance for the purpose of certain personnel decisions (for example, pay increases, promotions, terminations). Because it is difficult to wait five years to evaluate the outcome of a project, shorter time spans are chosen. The result is that objectives are set in relation to the time frame required to make these decisions even though they may have little relationship to the desired long-term objectives.

A fundamental cause of performance appraisal problems is that formal performance appraisal systems are generally asked to fulfill two different purposes: (1) The performance appraisal is used to document information used for administrative decision making. (2) The information is used to improve individual performance (Meyer, Kay, and French, 1965). Many appraisal systems focus on the first purpose, administration, rather than on the second, developing people to be better performers.

Recent legislation and judicial decisions are increasingly holding organizations accountable for the consequences of their personnel decisions. The only sure way to defend such challenges is through documentation of the circumstances affecting the decision. For example, in a decision to promote an employee to a higher position, the employer should be able to show how the candidate's performance compared with that of another employee. This establishes that the basis for promotion is actual job performance, not race, sex, religion, and so on.

When used for human resources development the information gathered about job performance serves as the basis for redirecting current behavior and for identifying training and development needs to provide a skill base to improve current performance and prepare an individual for future performance requirements.

Most organizations do not feel that they can invest the time and effort required to produce two essentially different performance reviews. Accordingly, a compromise solution must be found that can adequately deal with both purposes. This is seldom done. Many explanations of why most performance appraisal systems fail to accomplish the developmental purposes have been given. Those offered by Geis (1987) are typical: poorly defined performance standards, emphasis on maintaining equity rather than distinguishing among performers, forcing ratings into a specific distribution, an annual rather than an ongoing process, and inflexibility to change with changing conditions.

Another consideration in the design of a performance appraisal system is the need to fulfill the legal requirements imposed on the process. Based on an extensive review of recent court decisions, Romberg (1987) found support for performance appraisal systems with the following characteristics:

- Has a proportional impact on protected classes
- Is developed from a systematic job analysis
- Emphasizes work behaviors rather than personal traits
- Sets expected standards of performance
- Provides feedback on how well standards are attained
- Provides written instruction and training for raters
- Regularly updates job descriptions
- Requires written appraisals for future reference
- Forms the basis for personnel decisions

As employees have a higher stake in performance appraisal systems than in other personnel systems, employers would find it instructive to learn what factors employees feel contribute to a fair and accurate performance appraisal system. Landy, Barnes, and Murphy (1978) found that performance appraisal systems were viewed as fair and accurate when performance was evaluated frequently, supervisors were familiar with the employee's actual performance levels, supervisors and employees were in agreement on the requirements of important job duties, and supervisors set specific objectives with subordinates for performance improvement.

Performance Management

The challenge for the future lies in the capacity of organizations to move beyond performance appraisal as a primary focus of performance improvement activities to what is described here as performance management. Successful performance management depends on four activities: directing behavior, energizing and gaining commitment to action, controlling behavior, and rewarding desired behavior. Table 8 outlines the basic elements required to support a successful performance management system. Although some conceptual distinctions can be made among the four activities, in practice they are very closely related. For instance, even though some of the major rewards are not administered until the end of the cycle, the prospect of receiving rewards is a primary energizing factor. Likewise, the appraisal process supplies some of the information required for feedback in the controlling process.

Directing. Direction is a critical issue. Little organizational success can be achieved by energizing action and gaining commitment if the wrong direction has been chosen. It is clear from the earlier discussion on the shortsighted objectives in U.S. industry that performance management systems of the future must be aimed in more appropriate directions.

Direction is concerned with the *what* and *how* of performance management. The first step is identification of key results areas (KRAs) (Somers, Locke, and Tuttle, 1986). These are the performance areas that have the greatest impact on an individual's work accomplishments. Because a person cannot give equal attention to every facet of work behavior, it is necessary to focus on those areas that have the biggest payoff. The final step in directing is identifying and establishing the specific behaviors required to perform in the key results areas. Understanding these behaviors enables the performer to accomplish the necessary tasks efficiently with little additional guidance from a supervisor. This step outlines the *how* of performance; the preceding step identified the *what*.

Table 8. Performance Management Process.

Direct	Energize	Control	Reward
Key results areas	Set goals	Monitor	Evaluate
Performance indicators	Establish behavioral expectations	Provide feedback	Reinforce
Required behaviors		Redirect	
		Develop	

Note that in this element of performance management the focus is on identification of individual responsibilities and specific job behaviors associated with fulfilling these responsibilities.

Once the key results areas and specific job behaviors have been identified, specific indicators of performance must be established. These performance indicators serve to measure progress toward desired ends and provide the foundation for feedback and redirection in the goal and control systems to be established in the next step. Performance indicators should provide an unambiguous means to monitor job behaviors and goal attainment.

Energizing. Energizing is motivating people to work in the desired direction and gaining their commitment to maintain motivation over time. Two factors have consistently been linked to high performance motivation: goal setting (for example, Meyer, Kay, and French, 1965; Latham and Yukl, 1975) and participation (Nemeroff and Wexley, 1977; Greller, 1975). It is for these reasons that MBO-based performance appraisal systems have so frequently been prescribed. However, although some observers have pointed out potentially serious flaws in MBO-based appraisal systems (for example, Kane and Freeman, 1986, 1987), others have found these systems to be highly effective when design and implementation are tailored for specific situations (for example, Carroll, 1986). How then does one obtain the advantages that MBO offers in providing a means to set goals and foster employee participation at the same time?

Kane and Freeman (1986, 1987) argue that the major problems associated with MBO do not arise from the techniques themselves but from their application to performance appraisal systems. What is required is a way to combine the useful features of MBO with a performance appraisal method that does not negate them. Such a method is outlined in the following discussion of other elements of a performance management system.

Controlling. Controlling is the activity most often associated with performance management because it encompasses the function of the performance appraisal process. It is concerned with monitoring and measuring work behavior to ensure compliance with the task requirements specified in the direction component. Performance that is not on target is redirected by emphasizing specific goals and associated behaviors or through training and development, if the behavioral skills are not sufficiently strong to permit accurate performance.

It is not unusual, however, for attempts to control performance to sabotage a firm's efforts to accomplish other performance management activities. Too often, measurement becomes an end in itself. Organizations lose sight of the direction they should pursue and focus only on certain measurable aspects of performance, for example, the attention to near-term results and numerical objectives discussed earlier. This issue is aptly summed up in an old adage: "You get what you measure." To the extent that what is being measured is inappropriate to the long-term interest of the organization, the organization will suffer.

Even though many managers know that they are not measuring "real" performance, they commit themselves to attaining high marks on the selected performance indicators, because their own rewards are usually tied to the results. If measures of performance are vague or not acceptable to employees, the system will eventually fail. Employees will tend to perform only toward their personal goals rather than toward organizational goals.

Rewarding. The final element in the performance management process is rewarding. Rewards are used to reinforce utilization of appropriate behaviors and to attain desired results. Before rewards can be administered, performance must be evaluated, and the performance of the individual must be compared with that of others in the organization. These personnel decisions are made on the basis of information gathered through performance appraisal systems.

Latham and Wexley (1981; see also Lawler, 1971; Mobley, 1974) outline five reasons for linking pay and performance. First, it is an objective means for allocating rewards. Second, it reinforces employee efforts and enhances employee motivation. Third, it emphasizes the importance of the appraisal process and increases the perception that pay is distributed in an equitable manner. Fourth, performance-contingent pay communicates to the employee the value the company places on his or her services. Fifth, most people want to be paid on the basis of their performance.

Nevertheless, problems have long plagued the attempt to manage performance through reward systems (compare Meyer, 1975). If pay is to influence performance, several conditions must be met (compare Lawler, 1971; Mobley, 1974). First, pay must be contingent on performance. That is, the amount of pay must vary directly with the level of performance. Second, receipt of pay must occur soon after performance. Third, pay must be perceived as being equitable with the amount of effort expended and with the amount of pay received by others performing similar work at a similar level. Fourth, pay must be in a sufficient amount to make a noticeable difference in spendable income (Jespersen, 1987).

The hottest items on the agenda of most compensation professionals today is "pay-for-performance" systems. After decades of thinking (hoping?) they had systems that rewarded workers in relation to their performance, organizations now realize that most plans fall well short of this objective. These plans never achieve the intended results because most organizations limit the amount of money allocated to the "merit budget." With a limited budget, managers usually try to ensure that everybody gets something. They try to distribute what is left to the better performers but too often there is no reliable way to tell who the better performers really are. As a consequence, the higher rewards are distributed on a variety of bases including seniority, age, job assignment, sex, and race. Today, a major activity of managers is devising new ways to justify allocation of the budget in his or her preferred manner.

Suggestions for a Performance Management System

From the foregoing analysis, a performance appraisal system that can serve both administrative and performance management purposes begins to come into focus. Such a system should handle both objectives and behaviors, be relatively simple to administer, provide information for both administrative and developmental uses, have high participation, be based on a sound job analysis, and be compatible with the performance management objectives of the organization.

It is important that specific objectives be included in the performance management process. Objectives clarify what is to be done. However, attainment of objectives cannot be the sole criterion by which people are appraised, as it is subject to influences not under the control of the particular employee. Other standards of performance must be established. These standards are the job behaviors required to achieve the objectives. Job behaviors tend to be more stable than objectives over time and are under the direct control of an individual. It is the things that people do that must be influenced to attain the desired objectives. The challenge to the system designer is to distinguish between objectives and behavior and to emphasize behavior rather than objectives.

To help distinguish between objectives and behaviors, Kane and Freeman (1987) suggest that a matrix be used to conceptualize an individual's expected job performance. Job behaviors are plotted on one dimension of the matrix and planned objectives are plotted on the other. From the matrix one can then readily identify the behaviors that are prerequisites to achievement of a specific objective. Exhibit 4 is an example of such a matrix.

The horizontal axis tracks the objectives to be accomplished in a particular job. The vertical axis displays the behaviors generally required on the job. An "×" indicates that a particular behavior is required to accomplish a given objective. Conceptualizing a job in this manner enables both the rater and the ratee to focus on the aspects of the job over which the ratee has control, behaviors, and at the same time to remain mindful of the objectives toward which the employee's behavior should be directed.

Several different approaches to performance management have been detailed in the recent literature on performance appraisal. Guinn (1987) offers an example of the typical performance management cycle approach. It is a three-step process for making performance management a year-long process, not a year-end one. The

Exhibit 4. Behavior/Objective Matrix.

		Behaviors			
		1	2	3	4
O b j e c t i v e s	A	×		×	×
	B		×	×	
	C	×		×	

Source: Adapted from Kane and Freeman (1987).

steps are planning, managing, and appraising. The key elements of the cycle are listed in Table 9.

In the first step, performance planning, performance targets are established through discussion between subordinate and manager. At the same time, the job behaviors expected to lead to these objectives are identified and discussed along with the basis for measuring performance on both objectives and behaviors.

The first step provides the direction and the initial energization of behavior. The second step, managing, is the key to providing control and making the process continuous. The behaviors established in the first step must be monitored to ensure that they are directed toward the established objectives or toward new objectives if conditions change during the year and the old objectives are no longer operational. Behaviors that are aimed in the appropriate direction are reenergized through reinforcement and encouragement. Behaviors that are not aimed in the desired direction are redirected through coaching. When new skills and behaviors are required, it is especially important that reinforcement and coaching take place frequently to maintain direction and motivation.

Performance appraisal, the final step in the cycle, is differentiated from the day-to-day performance management process by its formality and the written record of the meeting. If coaching and

Table 9. The Performance Management Cycle.

Planning	*Managing*	*Appraising*
Establish performance targets	Monitor behavior and objectives	Formal meeting of employee and manager
Identify job behaviors	Reinforce desired behaviors and objective attainment	Written record
Identify basis for measuring performance		Focus on future and employee's development
Provide direction, initial energizing of behavior	Redirect inappropriate behaviors	
	Provide control	Provide for replanning and new objective establishment

reinforcement have been regular features of the performance management process, then the formal performance appraisal should be straightforward and without surprises. The performance appraisal gives the two parties an opportunity to temporarily withdraw from day-to-day concerns and focus on long-term career development needs. The manager should take advantage of this opportunity to work with subordinates to increase commitment to the organization.

The performance management cycle is reinitiated at the conclusion of the performance appraisal with plans for the next period. Just as in the initial planning period, the focus is on the subordinate's objectives and required behaviors. These factors provide the basis for the next appraisal.

Merck and Company, Inc., the international pharmaceutical firm, recently made a number of changes in its human resources systems including redesign of the appraisal system (Wagel, 1987a). The new system incorporated many of the factors discussed here. The system emphasizes both objectives and the behaviors required to attain them. For managers, the system includes a separate section on rating performance.

The Merck system was designed, in part, in response to a need to distinguish more clearly among the various levels of performance in the salary administration system (Wagel, 1987a). Accordingly, the system uses five rating categories ranging from "not adequate" to "exceptional." Each category is associated with an expected distribution of ratings. The distributions for the five categories are 2, 8, 70, 15, and 5 percent from the lowest to the highest performance category, respectively. A sixth category, "progressing," is used for persons new to a position. The salary administration system includes specific guidelines for determining the raise to be given for each category and position within a given salary range. A primary objective of the system is to provide higher increases for exceptional performers to reinforce good performance. The distributions of rewards completes the loop in the performance management cycle by encouraging employees to strive for better performance to receive high rewards.

The Merck plan is indicative of the emerging trend of tying pay to performance. General Motors (GM) provides another example of a firm actively moving toward a pay-for-performance system. In 1985 it placed 15,000 employees in twelve divisions on a merit pay system. The system was expanded in 1986 to include an additional 110,000 employees (Kanter, 1987). A revised plan was put into effect in early 1988 that covers low-level managers, clerical workers, and other white-collar workers (Schlesinger, 1988).

The GM plan uses a forced distribution system after finding in the previous system that the majority received the system's two top rankings. The new system has four categories; the top category represents 10 percent of the employees, the next 25 percent, the next 55 percent, and the bottom category is made up of the lowest 10 percent. Although assignment of the employees to the groups is up to the individual departments or offices, differences between the categories are strictly enforced.

In addition to this merit system, GM has instituted a special recognition award program to administer lump-sum awards to high performers. Recognition awards are used to encourage "team" performance to foster a higher level of cooperation within a department. GM also has a spontaneous reward program that permits managers to distribute such rewards as theater tickets or trips for a specific performance such as an outstanding report or an unusually good idea (Schlesinger, 1988).

Summary

Competitiveness—international and domestic—is becoming increasingly critical to the success of American businesses. A key

element in improving competitiveness is managing the performance of the work force. This chapter has revealed a number of
weaknesses in current efforts to manage performance, placing
special emphasis on the problems of traditional performance
appraisal methods. Successful performance management begins
with the recognition that it is an ongoing process, not a sporadic
event. All four elements of performance management—directing,
energizing, controlling, and rewarding—must be present to ensure
an adequate performance management system.

These elements are carried out in a cycle of plan, manage,
and appraise. The planning portion of the cycle includes the
direction and initial energization of behavior. In this phase, the
behaviors required to achieve specific performance criteria are
identified and the employee's commitment to them is attained. In
the managing portion of the cycle, much of the real work is done.
Supervisors must work with their subordinates through coaching
and on-the-job training to develop the skills and motivation
necessary to achieve the desired performance. Finally, in the
appraising phase, performance is evaluated and rewards are
distributed based on the person's (and the organization's) performance. Rewards reinforce specific behaviors if they are identified in
the appraisals and reenergize behavior for the next period. There are
no simple solutions or shortcuts to high performance. Only
carefully conceived and thoughtfully implemented programs will
be successful.

9

Retraining:
Realigning Skills
to Meet Changing Job Demands

For the past two decades in this country, the workplace has experienced great turbulence. Much of it can be attributed to a variety of complex and volatile issues that have transformed work organizations into more open and adaptive units of economic activity. The major events responsible for this rapid and pervasive change include the following:

- *Changing demographics in the labor markets.* People over sixty-five will constitute almost one-third of the work force by 1990; the participation rate of women in the labor force will climb to 58 percent; both the level of education and the functional illiteracy rate will increase by 1990, as 18 percent of all workers will have college degrees and 23 million adults will be functionally illiterate (Galagan, 1987). Exacerbating these conditions is the fact that total labor force growth will slow from the 1.3 percent projected for 1984–1990 to 1.0 percent between 1990 and 1995 (Semarad, 1987).
- *An accelerating pace of technology and competition.* New technologies are creating new industries, products, and processes; as resources are shifted to accommodate these changes, structural imbalances are created between skills available in the labor force and skills demanded by the new technologies; as

manufacturing strategies shift from price recovery to productivity in the face of growing competition from domestic and foreign producers, investments in human capital will simultaneously grow and become more selective.

In terms of the demographics, movement into and out of the labor force is predicted to decline. Older and more experienced workers, therefore, will increase as a proportion of the work force. In terms of literacy and education, the work force will become more bimodal. Functional illiteracy will place more demands on organizations to provide remedial training in basic learning skills as well as job skills training. For the well educated, the major challenge will be avoiding job obsolescence as changes in technology transform the nature and structure of current jobs. Because of these trends, retraining is and will continue to be a major policy issue confronting human resources managers.

The emphasis on retraining acknowledges the special need to develop policies and programs designed for current employees and former workers who have been displaced from their jobs. The content and pace of retraining programs may differ significantly from the content and pace of entry-level training programs. For experienced employees with proven learning capabilities, the key policy issue is often overcoming resistance to change by providing psychological as well as technological support in developing new skills. For displaced workers who have demonstrated good work habits and a willingness to learn, the key policy issue is often upgrading basic skills to meet more complex job requirements created by new or expanding technologies.

To meet the demands for retraining, human resources managers will have to work closely and continuously with managers in other functional areas to realign the fit between available skills and changing job requirements. In accomplishing this goal, managers will need to mix two key strategies: repositioning of displaced workers and renewal of in-place workers. Each strategy responds to a different situation, yet each is a logical target for retraining.

In succeeding sections of this chapter the causes and consequences of job displacement and job obsolescence are discussed and evaluated. Subsequently, the factors that determine the success or failure of retraining programs designed to contend with each situation are discussed in detail.

Causes of Job Displacement and Obsolescence

A Congressional Budget Office (CBO) study estimates that between 1.6 and 1.9 million workers lost their jobs in early 1983 because of declining industries or declining occupations (Condon, 1984). Of those with at least three years' tenure in a job who were displaced between January 1981 and 1986, about half, or 2.55 million, worked in manufacturing. Of the operators, fabricators, and laborers, fewer than 67 percent were able to find new jobs (Horvath, 1987). This situation, although somewhat improved over that of the early 1980s, suggests a continuing need to identify and monitor the causes of job displacement to reduce the social and economic disruptions resulting from them.

Emerging Demographic Trends. As noted previously, the work force is becoming more diverse and less typical than that of previous generations. The proportion of women in the labor force in 1987, for example, is estimated at 42 percent; in 1947, it was 27.4 percent. The increasing presence of women in the work force represents both a change in expectations and a change in the work environment. Women are advancing steadily into higher paying professional and technical positions. Their increasing presence here broadens and enriches the pool of talent from which employers can draw to meet new business opportunities. Women are also advancing into lower skilled positions. As automation changes the character of certain jobs, men are vacating them for more challenging and better paying jobs. Women who are less well educated and, perhaps, less confident than women in technical and professional positions tend to fill the void. In the insurance industry, for example, no-fault insurance laws and increased automation have taken much of the decision-making authority away from insurance adjustors. As men have migrated out of these positions, women have taken their place for the most part. For the large numbers of women in these situations, job displacement is a growing threat.

Minorities are becoming a greater proportion of the work

force too. In 1982, minorities represented 12.8 percent of the labor force; in 1995, they are expected to represent 14.5 percent of the labor force. As minority representation increases, the problems of displacement for minorities are likely to intensify. The 1986 survey of plant closings and reductions in employment levels conducted by the Employment and Training Administration noted in its findings, for example, that after displacement, reemployment was more difficult for black and Hispanic workers. The survey reported that about 36 percent of black men and 28 percent of Hispanic men who had been displaced were unemployed as of January 1986 compared with only 17 percent of white men (Horvath, 1987).

Another major demographic change confronting employers is the increased percentage of older employees in the work force. Demographers predict that by 1990, almost 33 percent of the work force will be 65 years old or older (Galagan, 1987). Although an older work force provides more experience to employers, it also poses some potential problems in terms of adaptability. A survey of personnel managers conducted by Yankelovich, Skelly and White in 1986 reported that older workers were seen as productive in their current jobs but resistant to new technologies and the consequent restructuring of jobs (Bové, 1987). If employers ignore or mismanage this situation, labor shortages and inefficiencies will result at a time when the demand for a reliable and resourceful pool of labor is increasing.

These demographic trends in the workplace signal a major change in the composition of the work force. The change is troublesome, moreover, because of its consequences for meeting the new skill requirements demanded by changing technologies.

Impact of New Technologies. Emerging technologies—machines and processes—simultaneously create new opportunities for employment and conditions for unemployment or job displacement. A recent review of the circumstances causing displacement notes that more than 35 million workers may be affected by technological changes in work content and processes (Bracker and Pearson, 1986). The effect of the changes is pervasive. Semiskilled and skilled operatives in manufacturing are no more vulnerable to the changes than service workers. Higher paid workers in knowledge-intensive professions like engineering are increasingly at risk too. A study of

2,500 engineers in the electronic and aerospace industries, for example, noted that individual performance peaked between ages thirty-one and thirty-five and declined steadily thereafter (Dalton and Thompson, 1971). Finally, administrators and managers incur the indirect effects of changing technologies. As rank-and-file employees are eliminated or reclassified and repositioned elsewhere, administrative and managerial positions are reduced as well to create more efficient and less costly operations.

A key issue among skilled operatives in manufacturing is their ability to learn and apply the functional skills needed to implement the new technologies successfully. Antecedent or enabling skills, therefore, must be addressed before managers can focus on the operational or performing skills associated with the actual implementation of new technologies. For example, more sophisticated machines performing standard milling operations are now numerically controlled by computer. Numerically controlled machines produce higher degrees of accuracy in meeting exacting tolerances for machined parts and subassemblies. The economic benefits to the organization resulting from this application of new technology are self-evident. To realize this advantage, however, machine operators need the conceptual and, in some cases, computational skills to operate the numerically controlled machines. Math skills are the antecedent or enabling skills needed to excercise the operational or performing skills required of the new technology.

More sophisticated technologies are not the sole determinant of displacement, but they are the major one. Consequently, human resources managers need to review their policies and practices carefully to assess the likely impact that technology will have on job displacement. In general, as technological change accelerates and proliferates while employee skills and knowledge languish by comparison, human resources managers will need to become more proactive in devising adjustment strategies. To be successful in this effort, they will have to address a variety of policy issues, including the economic implications of investing in human capital through retraining versus exporting jobs to foreign producers; the social implications of investing in human capital, especially as such investments affect minorities whose increasing presence in the labor force makes them more visible to politicians and legislators; and the political implications of including or excluding agencies of government, labor unions, and educational institutions as programs are developed to retrain displaced workers.

Complicating any analysis of the policy issues is the fact that the pace of technological change varies by industry and, to a large extent, by plant or facility within industries. Companies whose competitive position and financial resources are strong are far more likely to investigate and implement new technologies that are expensive and complicated. Weaker companies, however, tend to choose cost-cutting measures in the short term to preserve operating margins. One of the most expedient measures to cut costs, unfortunately, is to reduce the roll through involuntary layoffs. Industries that are quite knowledge intensive and heavily dependent on technological advantage to establish or maintain competitive position are also more apt to pursue and adopt new technologies. Human resources managers and top management need to consider these matters, therefore, as they coordinate the economic, social, and political implications of specific policy initiatives.

Finally, for any retraining effort to succeed in reducing the number of displaced workers, or those about to be displaced, it must be derived from a conceptual framework that encourages flexibility in its employees. This means that retraining cannot focus narrowly on operative skills such as data entry, programming, and information retrieval. It must include a complementary focus on basic skills that include higher competencies in reading comprehension, numerical analysis, and, in many cases, greater proficiency in both deductive and inductive reasoning. Reasoning skills will become increasingly important to troubleshoot the more sophisticated and complicated work flow systems that will evolve as we move into the twenty-first century.

Retraining: Issues to Consider

Retraining may be conducted for current employees who will be displaced in the near term because of the consolidation of operations and the consequent restructuring of jobs. It may also be conducted for those who are unemployed and recognize that without new skills they have little opportunity of being reemployed as skilled workers. From a policy perspective, these are closely related issues.

A Shift in Demand: The Opportunities and the Threats. Once an employee becomes displaced, the sense of mutual commitment between employer and employee diminishes. The incentives that may exist to extend a retraining program to former employees are few and frequently insufficient to encourage employer commitment. Several legislative initiatives such as the National Training Incentives Act initiated by Congresswoman Nancy Johnson (R-Conn.) and the Education and Training Partnership Act cosponsored by Senators Edward M. Kennedy (D-Mass.) and Dan Quayle (R-Ind.) have attempted to focus more attention on and provide more support to workers already unemployed. Their costs have proved to be very high, however, and their benefits seem to accrue, if at all, to those least involved in financing the efforts. Current programs, therefore, tend to focus more narrowly on current employees whose aptitude for new skills is high and whose personal qualities tend to merit special consideration. The intent of these programs obviously is to renew those employees who are most likely to succeed in adapting to new job demands and to retain these employees within the organization for the long term.

Restricting efforts to retrain only those members of the current work force who are most likely to adapt successfully and quickly to new technologies, however, may prove inadequate over the long haul. Employment growth predictions by major occupational groups indicate that with the exception of operatives in occupations other than transportation and private household workers, job growth has been strong since 1972. Table 10 summarizes this trend.

Strong job growth combined with lagging efforts at retraining in the craft and kindred worker occupational classification could produce disastrous results for industry. Harley Shaiken, a labor economist at the University of California at San Diego, claims that in ten years industry may have so few people who know how to repair machinery, cut precision metal parts, or build an airplane engine from scratch that American industry will not be able to function (Mitchell, 1987).

Table 10. Employment by Major Occupational Group, 1972–1986
(numbers in thousands).

| | | | 1972–1986 | |
| | | | Absolute | Percent |
Occupation	1972	1986	Change	Change
Total	82,153	109,597	27,444	+33.4
Professional, technical, and kindred[a]	11,538	18,532	6,994	+60.6
Managers and administrators	8,081	11,385	3,304	+40.9
Salesworkers[b]	5,383	10,935	5,552	+103.1
Clerical and kindred workers[b]	14,329	20,055	5,726	+40.0
Craft and kindred workers	10,867	13,405	2,538	+23.4
Operatives, except transport	10,388	8,892	–1,496	–14.4
Transport operatives	3,223	3,583	360	+11.2
Laborers, except farm	4,242	4,685	443	+10.4
Farmers and farm laborers[c]	3,077	3,444	367	+11.9
Service workers, except household	9,584	13,699	4,115	+42.9
Private household workers	1,442	981	–461	–32.0

[a]To improve the comparability of these data, we include accountants with professional occupations rather than with managers for 1986.

[b]For 1986, cashiers are included with clerical workers rather than with salesworkers.

[c]The 1986 figures include forestry and fishery occupations.

Source: These data are from the Current Population survey. The data are on a "person" concept and, therefore, count each individual only once, even if he or she is a multiple jobholder. The occupational classification in the household survey was changed in 1983 so that strictly comparable data are not available for 1983 forward. The table was reproduced from "Technological Change and Employment: Some Results from BLS Research," by Jerome A. Mark, *Monthly Labor Review, 110,* 4 (April 1987), p. 27.

To some, Shaiken's assertion may sound too hyperbolic. However, critical shortages in skilled trade occupations have already been noted in some labor markets. Electric Boat, a division of General Dynamics, had some 300 positions open for machinists, pipe fitters, and welders in late 1987. The company's inability to fill the positions caused concern among top management that production schedules would slip.

Exacerbating the problem over the long haul is the decline in enrollment in apprenticeship progams. The Machinists Union estimated that apprenticeship positions dwindled by 45 percent to some 12,000 from 1982 to 1987. Government surveys report similar declines in apprenticeship programs for pipe fitters (down 30 percent to 11,200 since 1979) and for bricklayers (down 53 percent to 4,000 since 1979). The causes for the declines vary. The reasons cited most often include poor pay and working conditions and demands for higher academic achievement to contend with the more sophisticated equipment and tools used in the job (Mitchell, 1987). These conditions strengthen the argument for industry to increase its efforts to retrain employees in declining occupations to meet the demands for skills in occupations that are growing.

IBM, among others, has developed policies to accommodate major shifts in the balance between skills available and skills in demand. In response to declining sales precipitated in part by competitive pressures stemming from changing technologies, IBM had to cut thousands of production, staff, and managerial jobs. After absorbing some of the reductions through early retirements and normal attrition, IBM concentrated on retraining to complete the reductions in the targeted areas. Some 3,700 employees were retrained as programmers, and an additional 4,600 became sales agents or customer consultants (Bernstein, 1988).

Ultimately, it seems that decisions to retrain those confronting job displacement in the near term are made primarily on utilitarian and practical grounds. Specifically, employers consider a mix of financial criteria and work requirements. Of course, legal requirements are complied with and gross displays of social insensitivity are avoided by all but the most inept employers. With a possible few exceptions, however, economic factors drive the decision-making process.

Comparison of Costs and Benefits. The U.S. Department of Labor estimated a $5 to $10 billion increase in capital expenditures for automation and technical advancements by employers during 1986–1987 (Opalka and Williams, 1987). Much of this investment in new technology required corresponding increases in investments in human capital through retraining. If retraining is to be postured as an investment and not as a sunk cost or "donation" in the name of corporate social responsibility, however, the economic benefits of the retraining effort should exceed their costs.

Participants in a White House conference on productivity

concluded that layoffs and roll reductions typically cost more than employers realize. Direct and indirect costs include severance pay and short-term continuation of some benefits, additional administrative and legal fees, outplacement costs, and increases in unemployment insurance. The conference participants also noted that productivity generally declined among organizations whose rolls were being reduced (Opalka and Williams, 1987).

In another study conducted by GTE Communications Systems, the costs involved in retraining existing workers were found to be lower than the costs associated with hiring new employees. The direct and indirect costs of hiring an employee, training that person to reach an acceptable level of job proficiency, and laying off an existing employee whose skills were obsolete were compared with the costs of retraining the targeted worker. In three of four job classifications, GTE concluded that retraining was decisively cheaper. In the fourth classification, the difference was less than 1,200 dollars (Saporito, 1987). Although these data are not conclusive, they do indicate that retraining can be a less expensive approach to contending with obsolete skills than firing and hiring.

The Xerox Reprographics Business Group found the cost of retraining to be more advantageous than firing and rehiring too. In cooperation with the Rochester Institute of Technology (RIT), they developed a program to retrain experienced exempt employees from other technical specialties to become electronic and computer engineers. Xerox diverted funds programmed for relocation and severance payments to the retraining program. Wayland Hicks, president of the Reprographics Business Group, considers the program a success for two reasons. First, it contributed to the professional growth and long-term contribution potential of some good employees. Second, it gave Xerox a stronger pool of critical talent in areas needing more technical skills at that time (Morano and Deets, 1985).

In many cases, retraining is demonstrably less expensive than replacing workers. It is not an inexpensive proposition, however. The Chicago Commons Association, a city-funded program to retrain displaced workers, reports a cost of $5,100 per trainee to train screw machine operators. Chicago's Mayor's Office of Employment and Training cites a per trainee cost of $2,333 for occupations in emerging service industries (Goozner, 1987). These data suggest that retraining for industrial trade skills is expensive in absolute terms. Proponents of these programs contend that they are necessary because they prepare people for occupations in which the continuing demand for qualified people is high. In meeting this demand, these programs also contribute to a more stable work force. A joint study of the Organization and Strategy Information Service (OASIS) of Hay Management Consultants, the Strategic Planning Institute, and the University of Michigan has observed that in manufacturing especially, a stable and experienced work force is generally a more productive work force (Opalka and Williams, 1987).

As noted previously, the effort to retrain existing workers must include an effort to reeducate them as well. The problem of functional illiteracy is large and will continue to exacerbate the problems of lost productivity until reeducation is accepted as part of the total responsibility to retrain workers. At an electronics product plant, for example, the introduction of automated storage and retrieval technology was delayed because only 10 percent of the workers involved in the change passed the qualifying test for retraining. Poor language comprehension and mathematical computation skills were the primary cause of the workers' difficulty (Helfgott, 1988). The transaction and application costs of undereducated and inadequately prepared workers can present significant liabilities to employers also. The Business Council for Effective Literacy in New York, for example, cites an insurance clerk who mistakenly paid a claimant $2,200 on a $22 settlement because she did not understand the concept of decimals; a steel mill worker who misordered $1 million in parts because he could not read instructions; and a feed lot laborer who misread a label and killed a pen of cattle by giving them poison instead of feed. One estimate of the cost to industry, in terms of lost productivity and remedial training, of poorly educated workers is $25 billion annually (Simpson, 1987).

The evidence on the costs of retraining versus the benefits suggests that the benefits clearly exceed the costs in most instances. Although some of the retraining effort for most organizations will include a mix of remedial and reclassification objectives, the data still support the investment in retraining as the less expensive alternative to preparing the work force for today's requirements and tomorrow's opportunities. Financing this investment requires cooperation and commitment from different sources.

Cooperative Efforts to Fund Retraining. Funding for retraining programs comes from many sources. At the federal level, several programs are available to employers. To obtain the funds, however, recipients must comply with a set of conditions and constraints. Presumably, these conditions and constraints ensure that the funds are properly used and directed at retraining programs that feed growing occupations. Of course, some applicants for these funds and informed observers dispute these contentions. Gary Orfield, professor of political science at the University of Chicago and author of several studies of Illinois and Chicago job training programs, contends that laws such as the Job Training Partnership Act are biased against expensive and long-term training even when such training is needed. He argues that many government-funded programs emphasize placement and low-cost training at the expense of skill development (Goozner, 1987).

Orfield's observations and experiences point to one of the major concerns that employers have in cooperating with outside agencies, especially governmental agencies, to conduct large-scale retraining efforts. This concern might best be presented as an example of the phenomenon described as goal displacement. In the case of bias against expensive and long-term programs noted by Orfield, the goal of providing skills and competencies to retrainees for long-term employability becomes displaced by that of operating low-cost programs that allow for quick placements. The concern, of course, is that low-cost, quick placement goals may produce short-term results that fail to address the longer-term need for a more stable and productive work force. Over the long term, therefore, replacement costs could escalate as a growing population of displaced workers is periodically recycled through low-cost, quick placement training programs.

Although governmental sources of funding are sometimes seen as overly restrictive and shortsighted, they will continue to be a major and important source of money. National Semiconductor Corporation relied heavily on funding from Title VII of the Comprehensive Employment and Training Act's (CETA) Private Sector Initiative Program to retrain thirty of its employees. Those retrained were being prepared for future job demands to meet changing technological requirements (Raitt, 1982).

Cooperative efforts among employers, employees, and unions are providing substantial financial support too. In 1984, for example, General Motors was contributing $6.7 million a month into a special fund for retraining at the local level. The fund has financed the retraining of workers who were candidates for displacement through layoff. These workers received training in the repair and operation of robots and computers as well as instruction to upgrade their language and math skills. Ford Motor Company and the United Auto Workers Union are jointly sponsoring a training and education program open to all of Ford's 109,000 hourly employees. The program, operating since 1984, is envisioned as a long-term effort to adapt its work force to changes in the demand for skilled labor ("New Blueprints in the Drive for Job Security," 1984).

Individual training accounts (ITAs) represent another approach to cooperative funding. The concept requires employers and employees to pay equal amounts into a training fund until some predetermined amount is reached. At this point, the employee is free to draw on the fund to pay training expenses and, in some plans, to defray job search or relocation costs. For workers confronting a situation in which displacement seems inevitable— perhaps even desirable—ITAs have much appeal. ITAs pose some problems as well, however. Unions, for example, may look askance at a program that could force migration from union jobs in one location to nonunion jobs in another location. Small businesses would receive little, if any, benefit from ITAs as they seldom buy experienced talent in most technical skill occupations. More often than not, they lose homegrown talent to larger organizations offering more attractive compensation and advancement opportunities.

For many organizations, the costs of retraining to reposition displaced workers will discourage employers from making the effort. Public programs report that retraining costs per displaced employee range from $2,333 to $5,100 for machinists in Chicago (Goozner, 1987) and averaged $3,500 in California in 1985 (O'Connell and Hoerr, 1985). Without financial incentives and tax inducements, private industry is unlikely to offer broad-based support for repositioning strategies. Therefore, partnerships between industry and the public sector must be encouraged to meet the needs for repositioning displaced workers. One such partnership that offers much promise is California's Employment Training Panel (ETP).

California's ETP began in 1983 and has trained more than 50,000 employees for some 3,000 employers throughout the state. To fund the program, one-tenth of one percent of the unemployment insurance tax paid by employers is reallocated as an employment training tax. The ETP also limits participation to experienced workers who are either recently unemployed or who are about to be displaced from their jobs. To ensure that the program is paying for jobs and not just retraining, the company that hires and retrains a worker is reimbursed for training expenses only after the person has been on the job for ninety days. The program reports impressive results too. Of those who complete ETP training, 94 percent are hired for the job for which they were in training. And nearly 90 percent of these workers remain on the job ninety days or longer (O'Connell and Hoerr, 1985; Verespej, 1986). California's ETP seems to provide the elements that are necessary for success: joint government-industry participation; payments funded by reallocating existing tax liabilities, not creating new taxes; payments made for jobs needed by companies and not for training activities conducted by public agencies; training limited to experienced workers—people who have a demonstrated propensity to work and accept responsibility for adapting to changing job requirements.

A Comprehensive Strategy for Retraining

Meeting the retraining needs of today's organizations requires careful attention to what Thorstein Veblen described as the problem of "organizational psychosis," or doing well what no longer needs to be done at all. Recognizing and responding to the symptoms of organizational psychosis will be difficult, however, for the reasons discussed previously in this chapter. As the work force ages and the pool of entry-level employees diminishes, the tendency to hold on to what you do well, regardless of organizational needs, increases for most employees. Managers will need to consider the behavioral aspects of change, therefore, in planning for and implementing a comprehensive retraining effort. In particular, employers will need to consider carefully the situation confronting older workers and those production workers and professionals who are now in the "maturity phase" or peak contribution time frame of their careers.

Career Progression Cycle. In many respects, a normal career progresses in the same way a product does as it moves through the product life cycle. There is an entry and orientation phase where probationary expectations are encountered and, for most people, met satisfactorily. This initial phase is followed by a period of growth in which employees become more proficient in their functional responsibilities, and some progress into and through successively higher levels of management as well. At varying points in time, employees enter a maturity phase in which their potential to advance as managers or technical specialists becomes increasingly limited, yet their performance and productivity in their functional area of expertise are at their peak. Most employees remain in this phase several years. After an extended period in the maturity phase, employees begin to regress into a period of decline. Decline may result from physical or mental impairments that prevent employees from performing the full range of tasks required of the job as well as they were once performed. Decline may also result from changing technological conditions that make present skills obsolete. Figure 3 summarizes the concept of a career progression cycle.

The inertial quality of movement through the decline phase is natural and, in most cases, desirable. Because the changes in demographics and technology have created a need for a renewal phase, however, overcoming the inertia that leads to decline is now a matter of strategic significance to many employers. Specifically, top management needs to devise strategies that extend the maturity phase of workers. General Electric's Aerospace Electronic Department's Technical Renewal Program is a current example of such a strategy. In this program, engineers are retrained in new skills required of new systems. It is interesting to note, moreover, that half the engineers in the program are older than fifty (Maxwell, 1987).

Figure 3. Career Progression Cycle.

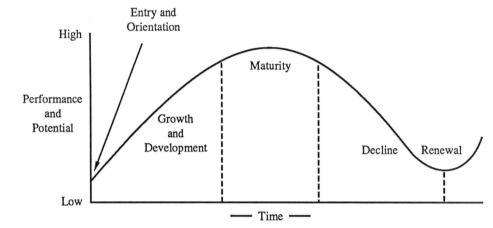

Figure 3 illustrates the concept of career progression in a general way. The actual slope and duration of any phase will vary with circumstances.

For those who achieve the highest levels of authority and responsibility in an organization, the growth and development phase may be longer than the maturity phase.

For those who enter into decline prematurely as a result of structured shifts in employment patterns brought on by technological obsolescence, renewall is possible through retraining.

For those who make significant career changes, more than one career progression cycle may apply over the course of a work life.

Source: The career progression cycle is adapted from the marketing concept of product life cycle and is analogous to paradigms developed by Hall (1976) and Schein (1978).

To serve a much more diverse group of talent and changing job needs, General Electric has established its Reemployment Center in Columbia, Maryland. The center has provided transitional help to employees displaced from their jobs by General Electric's decision to discontinue the production of microwave ovens. General Electric's programs accommodate both the need to renew for internal adaptation and the obligation to reposition for external adaptation.

Retraining: The Renewal Strategy. The renewal strategy

focuses on the need to "retrain-to-retain." It is confined largely to knowledge-intensive workers whose basic skills are compatible with the changing demands of evolving technologies. Renewal also incorporates qualitative factors such as dependability and cooperativeness into its selection criteria. Renewal is a highly selective approach, therefore, to minimize the time spent in "decline" and accelerate movement into a new phase of growth followed by a maturity phase in the new technology.

Advanced manufacturing technology (AMT), the incorporation of numerically controlled machines, robots, and laser optics, for example, into production processes, makes a compelling case for the renewal strategy. As manufacturing systems become more sophisticated and complex, occupational half-lives, the time in which one-half of a person's knowledge and skills become obsolete, are reduced substantially. Accompanying the reduction in occupational half-life is an ever-increasing need for better interpersonal and conceptual skills. The latter skills are needed to meet the increasing demands for integration as well as specialization required for AMT. A machine operator, for example, needs to integrate data, troubleshoot problems, and understand the relationships among increasingly integrated pieces of equipment. Operators must be able to think about the tasks of the job as a process of work that contributes to a larger process of manufacturing. The larger process of manufacturing includes integration of functional areas of responsibility like engineering, purchasing, production control, and material support with manufacturing activity. Renewal for AMT, therefore, includes not only the functional dimension of new process technology, but also the cross-functional dimension of integrating activities organizationwide to meet schedules, budgets, and quality specifications.

One of the clear implications of the renewal strategy is the need for a small proportion of the work force to be in training continuously. In fact, one executive for a machine tool company estimates that 15 percent of the company's engineering work force would be in training continuously. This requirement for continuous training would be necessary to support their new concept of "simultaneous engineering," whereby customers work with design and production engineers to transform concepts into machines

(Committee on the Effective Implementation . . . Technical Systems, 1986). Another implication of the renewal strategy is to integrate retraining requirements into a company's strategic plan for staffing. The rates of technological change will continue to accelerate; however, our capacity to absorb the changes will grow more slowly. Fred Steingmaker, chairman and chief executive of the management consulting firm A. T. Kearney, estimates that it will take five to ten years to complete the introduction of advanced technology into our plants and offices. Another five years will then be required to learn how to make the best overall use of that technology to compete successfully in tomorrow's markets. Retraining as a strategic response to technological change will have to become part of the staffing and assignment plans for operations. Although this concept seems to contradict prevailing attitudes of reducing manning levels to lower costs, it will prove to be cost-effective over the long term. AT&T, Control Data Corporation, and General Electric are a few of the companies who have recognized the continuing commitment to renewing their organizations through retraining.

Retraining: The Repositioning Strategy. Renewal will help many organizations extend the contributions of selected employees. As technological change places continuing demands on employers to retrain, and as the work force grows older as a result of changing demographics, renewal will become a necessary part of the strategic plan to compete successfully in world markets. Many organizations, however, will find it necessary to displace workers as structural and technological changes occur. A few large industrial companies have both recognized this condition and made a commitment to help reposition their displaced workers in jobs elsewhere. Of particular note are the efforts being made by Ford Motor Company, General Motors Corporation, and the General Electric Company. Ford and General Motors have helped retrain workers for positions in the aerospace industry on the West Coast, and General Electric, through its Reemployment Center in Columbia, Maryland, has worked to reposition its people displaced because of discontinued product lines (Verespej, 1986).

To manage these retraining efforts more effectively, employers may want to consider establishing an identifiable pool of

Figure 4. The Strategic Skill Pool Life Cycle.

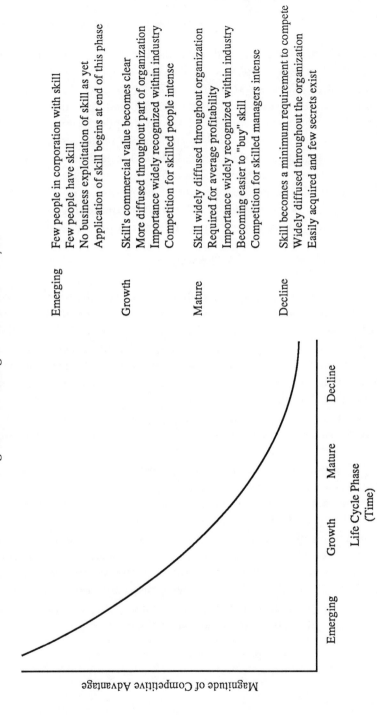

Emerging
Few people in corporation with skill
Few people have skill
No business exploitation of skill as yet
Application of skill begins at end of this phase

Growth
Skill's commercial value becomes clear
More diffused throughout part of organization
Importance widely recognized within industry
Competition for skilled people intense

Mature
Skill widely diffused throughout organization
Required for average profitability
Importance widely recognized within industry
Becoming easier to "buy" skill
Competition for skilled managers intense

Decline
Skill becomes a minimum requirement to compete
Widely diffused throughout the organization
Easily acquired and few secrets exist

Magnitude of Competitive Advantage

Emerging   Growth   Mature   Decline

Life Cycle Phase
(Time)

Source: Reprinted with the publisher's permission from "Strategic-Skills Pool and Competitive Advantage," by D. G. Naugle and G. A. Davies, *Business Horizons,* 1987, *30* (6), 41.

strategic skills. Strategic skills maintain the core technology of an organization and contribute to its competitive advantage in the marketplace (Naugle and Davies, 1987). As technology changes, the mix of strategic skills will likely change too. Anticipating these changes and the effect they will have on the pool of strategic skills will be a major responsibility of human resources managers. Maintaining the pool of strategic skills will contribute significantly to a company's competitive posture in the years to follow. Therefore, being able to develop emerging and growth skills (see Figure 4) to accommodate emerging and growth technologies should be a major policy objective for a company's retraining strategy.

Summary

Retraining focuses somewhat narrowly on the population of recently displaced workers and those still employed but facing either displacement or reclassification. Changing technologies and work force demographics are creating increasing pressure on employers to retrain. Older and more experienced workers will become more available to employers, whereas younger entry-level employees will decline in number and, for many, in ability to learn as well. In these circumstances, retraining becomes as significant a policy issue for human resources managers as entry-level training is.

Whether the appropriate retraining strategy emphasizes renewal or repositioning, employers are entering an age when retraining will be as normal an activity as training has been for entry-level employees. To maintain and, in some cases, increase the productivity of labor in work organizations, existing employees will be called on to adapt their skills to changing work conditions and, for some, to extend their careers to meet the continuing need for skilled and reliable workers. As governments and private employers recognize the magnitude and pervasiveness of this situation, more attention will be paid to this important issue.

PART FIVE

Emerging Challenges for
the Human Resources Manager

Up to now, we have discussed the trends and issues that presently affect organizations. There exist other forces that although affecting only a few firms today, may become of increasing concern within the next decade. It is important that firms be aware of these emerging forces and develop a strategy for anticipating issues to which they should respond with specific programs and policies. Chapter Ten discusses three issues that may be significant to human resources managers in the future. Chapter Eleven presents a way of thinking about factors in the environment that will enable human resources managers to better detect the emerging forces and to take effective action.

The recent increase in merger and acquisition activity has had an effect on firms of all sizes. This activity, as noted in Chapter Six, has led to numerous restructurings, layoffs, and other actions that affect the ultimate success of the merger. The effects of a merger go far beyond the initial realignment of organizational and financial structures to accommodate the current level of business. Mergers place great stress on the human systems in the organizations. Much of the strain is avoidable through effective planning. Chapter Ten discusses the problems most likely to be encountered in mergers and acquisitions and offers advice on how to increase the likelihood of successful organizational combinations.

The second issue to be addressed in Chapter Ten draws attention to the effect of demographic changes and other forces on future recruitment and staffing. Population dynamics accounts for a number of shifts in the availability and expectations of persons in the work force. These shifts challenge human resources managers to maintain an appropriate-sized work force with the requisite skills.

First the "baby boom" and then the "baby bust" play havoc with manpower requirements as surpluses and shortages of workers affect different industries at different times. Compounding the effect of demographic changes is the uneven demand for and development of persons with key skills required to be competitive in the domestic and global marketplaces. Meeting these challenges requires a knowledge of population trends and the planning of specific action on the basis of that knowledge.

The final issue covered in Chapter Ten, terrorism, is of concern to human resources managers seeking to protect employees in a hostile world. Terrorism can be defined as an unprovoked act of violence to attain a political end. Such an act may be perpetrated against a government, a firm and its employees, or the general public. Although we most often associate terrorism with the Middle East or Third World nations, it is becoming uncomfortably common in Europe and North America. Groups as well as individuals increasingly use violence to bring attention to their causes and achieve their objectives.

Unless they are operating in one of the world's known "hot spots," most firms give little thought to how terrorism might affect them. One of the chief problems is that one never knows what the next target will be. One day's headline may be about news reporters held hostage in the Middle East. The next day's may be about sabotage at a family planning clinic by "prolife" activists or at a mink ranch by animal rights activists. The current impact of terrorism on business and the ways in which firms can prepare to handle this growing problem in the future are examined in Chapter Ten.

Chapter Eleven presents a methodology for studying and evaluating forces in the external environment that provide a firm with the opportunity to increase competitiveness. Drawing on the literature of corporate strategic planning, this chapter presents a framework within which the environment is examined. The framework outlines a procedure for identifying important human resources issues to ensure that they are brought to the attention of appropriate decision makers in a timely manner. Suggestions for appropriate "issues management" are also presented.

10

Further Developing Issues: Mergers and Acquisitions, Employment Trends, and Terrorism

The preceding chapters have focused on a single issue. This chapter addresses three issues—mergers and acquisitions, emerging employment trends, and corporate terrorism. These issues are important to many organizations, but compared to other issues, they are likely to affect relatively fewer organizations in the immediate future. As with the other chapters, we identify the environmental forces creating the new challenges and provide insights into methods that could be used to meet the challenges. The discussion should alert line managers and human resources professionals to the importance of the issues, lead to a better understanding of how they may be affected in the future, and show them how to anticipate and cope with the problems arising from these developments.

Mergers and Acquisitions: Human Resources Implications

Over the past five years, merger and acquisition activity has had a significant impact on the American economy. Although the statistics are inexact, some sources report 1,500 mergers in 1983, 2,433 mergers in 1984, and 3,001 mergers in 1985 (Cook, 1987a). A Conference Board survey of nearly 600 major corporations found that 60 percent of these firms expect to be affected by merger, acquisition, or divestiture activity within the next three years (Sanderson and Schein, 1986). This section focuses on the effect that merger and acquisition activity has on employees. It recommends how to minimize the potential dysfunctional consequences associated with these activities and suggests how strategic advantages can be obtained by human resources planning.

Human Impact of Mergers and Acquisitions. Although mergers and acquisitions have mostly economic effects, they portend significant human costs as well. In many cases, takeovers result in employee displacement. Some critics of "merger mania" believe that recent corporate combinations cost the economy up to 1 percent in gross national product (GNP) in 1986 because of the loss of hundreds of thousands of jobs. A survey by the executive recruiting firm of Lamalie Associates shows that of 150 senior executives in the largest acquisition targets between 1982 and 1984, nearly half left within a year of the acquisition (Kanter and Seggerman, 1986). In the Wells Fargo acquisition of Crocker National Bank (1986), the largest merger in banking history, 1,600 managers were terminated on the day the deal was closed.

Though the prospect of job loss is a major source of employee stress, the psychological impact of mergers and acquisitions can be severe even for those who retain their jobs. Some feel guilt because they are still employed; other feel a sense of loss from the displacement of long-term colleagues. Many experience stress and anxiety, wondering about the potential for future job loss or diminished promotion opportunities. The impact is almost always a loss of productivity.

Because of the lack of attention to the human aspects of mergers and acquisitions, the financial and organizational benefits expected of the new combinations are frequently not realized. As many as one-half to two-thirds of all mergers and acquisitions ultimately fail ("Do Mergers Really Work," 1985). More importantly, it is estimated that one-third of all merger failures are caused by the faulty integration of diverse operations and culture (Shrivastava, 1986). Clearly, if the current wave of restructuring is to produce the desired economic results, the human resource aspects of mergers or acquisitions must receive greater attention from acquiring executives.

Managing Merger-Related Stress. The human resources objectives of a merger or acquisition are several. Naturally, many technical and legal details need to be resolved (for example, integration of organizational systems, assimilation of benefit plans). Although these aspects of organizational combination are important, this section focuses on more general concerns related to human expectations and performance. Specifically, human resources goals during a merger or acquisition typically involve (1) retaining highly qualified employees of both the acquiring and acquired organizations; (2) reducing the employee roll, as necessary, to achieve the desired efficiency in a manner that minimizes anxiety and other human costs; (3) minimizing the negative impact on productivity during the transition period; and (4) promoting integration of corporate cultures to achieve strategic advantage.

It appears that the key to achieving these objectives is effective communication. Nearly all writers addressing this topic emphasize the need for open communication throughout the entire merger or acquisition cycle. Shrivastava (1986) advocates communication with all stakeholders. It is apparent, however, that employees must be the central focus of communication efforts. Although this recommendation appears straightforward, organizations engaged in merger or acquisition activity are often concerned that various aspects of the negotiations may become public. Thus, communication objectives are often in conflict, and the benefits of openness must be weighed against the need for confidentiality. Nevertheless, failure to adequately address employee concerns and tensions can produce devastating organizational effects.

During the *planning stage* of a merger or acquisition, the possibility of job loss is a key stressor for nearly all employees. The most frequently publicized aspect of corporate restructuring is employee termination. According to Ivancevich, Schweiger, and Power (1987) three dimensions of communication should be considered: What information should be provided? What media should be used? How accurate should the information be? To the extent possible, management should inform employees whether the company is a target for a merger or acquisition and, if it is, how management plans to respond. Formal letters and memos to key managers and employees can be used to provide reasonable and accurate information. False promises, overly optimistic pronouncements, or otherwise uncertain information should be avoided. Communication should not go beyond what is known.

During the *in-play stage,* the identity of the acquiring firm and its intentions will become clearer and employees should be prepared for potential changes. If job loss is likely, employee protection plans should be considered. Employment contracts, benefits, thrift plans, severance pay, retirement plans, and job transfer and moving provisions should be explored. Many organizations are developing "poison pills" that include lucrative separation clauses to ward off potential hostile takeovers. Although these actions do not eliminate fears of job loss, they do reduce uncertainty regarding the personal impact of the intended merger or acquisition. Stress management training, individual counseling, and other professional help can also be beneficial.

At this stage, key executives and other high-potential employees should also be given specific assurances about their job security to avoid an unnecessary loss of talent.

During the *final stages* of a merger, many different organizational changes are possible. To handle these interventions effectively, many experts suggest the creation of a transition management team. In addition to its technical responsibilities, the team should ensure that all key stakeholders, especially key employee groups, are represented. This approach can help to reduce stress by giving affected employees some feeling of control over their future. Obviously, this approach is more likely to succeed when merger or acquisition negotiations fall within the "friendly" category.

Once the team is in place and its goal is clear, action should be swift; all potential channels of communication should be used to ensure that the actions are perceived as necessary and fair, given the firm's situation and objectives. How a company handles downstream activities, which may involve consolidation of units, layoffs, sale of business units, employee transfers, and so on, can have long-lasting effects on the employees who remain.

When the terms of a merger or acquisition have been finalized, employees should be informed formally, and preferably by the CEO, of impending actions and other information about the merger. Unfortunately, in most instances, employees are forced to secure information about their situation from newspapers, other external sources, and the rumor mill. Not only does this leave employees with continuing uncertainty, it creates resentment toward the employer for failing to be forthright with employees about their future.

Barrett (1973) suggests thirteen items of information that companies should disseminate to their stakeholders when a merger or acquisition is announced. Initially, he recommends seven areas:

1. Reasons for the merger/acquisition and its potential benefits
2. General facts about the acquiring company
3. Changes in the company name
4. Changes in organizational structure or key management positions
5. General plans for any reduction in roll
6. Plans for emphasizing or deemphasizing products the acquired company is making
7. Detailed changes in benefits and compensation (for example, insurance, retirement plans, sick leave)

Later, as the transition team moves into action, Barrett proposes the dissemination of six additional types of information:

8. Specific layoff targets and provisions for job loss (for example, severance pay, outplacement services)
9. Specific job and role changes
10. Changes in management and reporting relationship
11. Changes in personnel policies
12. Changes in career paths
13. General changes in other company policies

As Ivancevich, Schweiger, and Power (1987) note, an open, direct, and empathic communication plan, although perhaps not received joyfully, will be appreciated by most employees. The task of the acquiring organization during these several stages is to make acquired employees feel a part of the new organization. Unless employee identification and commitment can be generated early in the process, the full range of benefits anticipated from the combination of the two enterprises will not be realized.

Building an Integrated Culture. The primary problem in managing merged firms effectively is shaping their operations into an integrated unit (Shrivastava, 1986). Several types of integration are necessary. First, key procedures and processes must be integrated. This includes combination of the accounting systems and creation of a single legal entity. Another type of integration involves the creation of synergy by combining physical assets, production systems, product lines, and so on. But the most critical and difficult type of integration is cultural. Harold Clark, executive vice-president and head of human resources at J. Walter Thompson, agrees: "How do you motivate acquired people who have been loyal to one company culture in which they have grown up with a set of assumptions? Suddenly the assumptions are different and there is now a different corporate culture" (Sanderson and Schein, 1986).

Sales and Mirvis (1985) point out that cultural change imposed by the presence of a new dominant culture (the acquirer's) is a common source of anger and conflict. Accommodation to these cultural changes requires progression through a four-stage process: (1) awareness of the difference, (2) anger about the difference, (3) introspection, and (4) integration (Harris and Moran, 1979). A danger for merged organizations is employees who remain at the second stage. These employees are uninvolved or hostile or may even sabotage the organization.

Overcoming these potential problems requires attention to three specific integration tasks: coordination, control, and conflict resolution. Table 11 summarizes these key postmerger integration tasks (Shrivastava, 1986).

To achieve integration at the sociocultural level, several approaches can be pursued:

1.   Establish transition teams composed of key representatives from both organizations to manage various procedural and physical integration tasks. Such premerger "seeding," by involving managers who will be responsible for running the acquired business in acquisition analysis and developing

Table 11. Postmerger Integration Tasks.

Integration Area	Coordination	Control	Conflict Resolution
Procedural	Design accounting systems and procedures	Design management control system	Eliminate contradictory rules and procedures Rationalize systems
Physical	Encourage sharing of resources	Measure and manage the productivity of resources	Allocate resources Redeploy assets
Managerial and sociocultural	Establish integrator roles Change organizational structure	Design compensation and reward systems Allocate authority and responsibility	Stabilize power sharing

Source: Shrivastava, 1986, p. 67. Reprinted with permission from *Journal of Business Strategy,* copyright © Summer 1986, Warren, Gorham & Lamont Inc., 210 South St., Boston, Mass. 02111. All rights reserved.

operating plans for the postacquisition period, can facilitate the integration process.

2. Transfer personnel from the acquiring firm to the acquired firm, and vice versa. However, transfer of personnel per se does not result automatically in integration. When RJR acquired Del Monte and transferred its foods division to Del Monte's location in San Francisco, the RJR Food executives were perceived as cliquish. Frequently, other team-building interventions are necessary to reduce barriers inhibiting group collaboration.

3. Offer attractive early retirement packages to encourage upper-level management personnel likely to be opposed to the merger to leave the organization.

4. Develop projects and establish task forces that span organizational boundaries. A unique concept employing this approach is used by American Express for managing its diversified financial services operations (Koeth, 1985). James Robinson III, CEO and chairman, is committed to expanding the use of "one-enterprise" projects. These projects are bridges between

.company operations, resulting in cross-products and services developed by combining the expertise and resources of different operating units. Currently, American Express monitors about 120 projects. According to Robinson, these projects provide an opportunity to benefit from a broad spectrum of views, foster intracompany transfers, and develop in-house talent.

5.   Establish clear lines of authority between functional groups of the acquired firm and the parent company. This will help to eliminate turf battles and smooth the development of consolidated policies and operations.

6.   Provide new strategic leadership by quickly assuming control of all critical variables that influence performance and articulating a shared operating vision for the future (Bennigson, 1985). The use of superordinate goals provides unity of direction for operating units. In one successful merger, the CEO of a major communications company went to the headquarters of the acquired company to meet with the fifty top executives to lay out his strategy for the future. The executives of the acquired firm knew where they stood and were able to share in the CEO's vision for the combined company (Kanter and Seggerman, 1986).

   Many writers note that not all mergers and acquisitions require the same degree of integration and, hence, the same postmerger actions. For example, less integration is required when unrelated businesses are acquired than when similar operations are combined that draw on common resources, market related products, and/or use similar production processes. This was the case with ITT's acquisitions in the 1960s and 1970s. Only the integration of accounting functions for financial control was necessary.

   Lower levels of integration may also be the goal when small entrepreneurial companies are acquired by large bureaucratic firms. In this case, overintegration is likely to stifle the creativity and flexibility that made the entrepreneurial organization successful. This situation is exemplified in Exxon's acquisition of Vydec (Shrivastava, 1986). Promising the founder-entrepreneur a free rein and financial support, continued interference from Exxon managers and turf disputes with other subsidiaries slowed Vydec's ability to develop new products in the time frame required to be competitive. Ultimately, the acquired company began losing money, the founder-entrepreneur departed, and Vydec was sold to Lanier Business Products. In such situations, the acquiring organization may have to take specific, explicit actions to "protect" the acquired organization from encroachment by functional entities of the acquiring firm. Clear communication of the desired degree of integration is essential in these situations.

Summary. Since 1981, the number of mergers and acquisitions has risen steadily. However, many of these mergers simply do not work. Often the reason for failure is the lack of attention to human and organizational considerations. Merger-related stress and problems of integration can be minimized through better preplanning and communication and through the design and implementation of effective postmerger integration activities. A phased, evolutionary approach to integration employing techniques discussed in this section is likely to enhance employee identification and organizational acculturation.

Emerging Employment Trends

The problems that employment managers will face in the future derive from the pattern of demographic and technological shifts this country is now experiencing. The pattern of births in this country following the end of World War II is having a strong influence on the availability and expectations of today's work force. At the same time these changes are taking place, the nature of work is changing as well.

The "Baby Boom" Generation. The "baby boom" was a major demographic shift. The United States experienced unusually high population growth during the period 1946–1964 as the total fertility rate (live births per woman) soared. Baby boomers have had a tremendous influence on the economy as they matured. The impact was initially felt by companies selling baby products, then by elementary schools and firms selling toys, clothing, youth furniture and so on. As the baby boomers entered the work force, they also had an impact on employers—the number of persons in the work force increased by 31 million from 1972 to 1986, a 35 percent increase (Kutscher, 1987).

Businesses and government services grew rapidly to keep pace with the population growth. This provided young people with many opportunities for good jobs and for rapid advancement. As a group, they were the best educated workers America had ever seen. They came to expect regular promotions as a sign of their capabilities. However, because of changes in the pattern of growth, brought on in part by the end of the baby boom, the same opportunities for advancement no longer exist.

Instead of facing a future of continuously expanding opportunities, many in this generation have plateaued—reaching a level in the organization from which they will advance only slowly, if at all. One of the increasingly difficult problems faced by human resources managers is how to deal with these high expectations for career growth in the face of diminished opportunities.

The "Baby Bust" Generation. At the same time that the baby boom is causing human resources managers one set of problems, the "baby bust" or "birth dearth" (Wattenberg, 1987) is causing problems of another sort. These problems are brought about by the lack of young people now entering the work force. After reaching a peak of 3.77 in 1957, the total fertility rate steadily declined to 1.8 in 1975 and has remained near this point since. This rate is below the 2.1 rate required to replace population losses. These low fertility rates will translate into a shrinking population in the near future. From 1990 to 2000 the population in the age group twenty-five to thirty-four will decrease by 18 percent (Wattenberg, 1987). A number of other changes are outlined in Table 12.

The effects of this population change are being attenuated by the increase in work force participation rates (the percentage of a population category that actually joins the work force) by several demographic groups, particularly women. The participation rate for women has increased dramatically since 1972. The number of women in the work force increased from 39 percent in 1972 to 45 percent in 1986, and women are expected to constitute more than 47 percent of the work force in the year 2000 (Kutscher, 1987, p. 4).

Although the main impact of the birth dearth will be felt several years from now, some parts of the economy are already

Table 12. Projected Population Changes Among Various Demographic Groups, 1986 to 2000 (numbers in thousands).

Group	1986		2000		Change 1986–2000	
	Number	Percent	Number	Percent	Number	Percent
Total	117,837	100.00	138,775	100.00	20,938	100.00
Men						
16+	65,423	55.52	73,136	52.70	7,713	36.84
16–24	12,251	10.40	11,506	8.29	–745	–3.56
25–54	44,406	37.68	53,024	38.21	8,618	41.16
55+	8,766	7.44	8,606	6.20	–160	–0.76
Women						
16+	52,414	44.48	65,639	47.30	13,225	63.16
16–24	11,117	9.43	11,125	8.02	8	0.04
25–54	35,159	29.84	47,756	34.41	12,597	60.16
55+	6,138	5.21	6,758	4.87	620	2.96
White	101,801	86.39	116,701	84.09	14,900	71.16
Black	12,684	10.76	16,334	11.77	3,650	17.43
Other	3,352	2.84	5,740	4.14	2,388	11.41
Hispanic	8,076	6.85	14,086	10.15	6,010	28.70

Source: Adapted from Kutscher, 1987, p. 4.

feeling some effects. In some areas of the country, fast food restaurants are having great difficulty in finding enough young people to operate the fryers and cash registers, construction firms face a shortage of entry-level workers, amusement parks have a hard time getting enough summer workers, and enrollment in engineering and other technical programs producing highly sought after graduates has peaked. More severe shortages of entry-level workers and skilled professionals are just around the corner and will cause difficult problems for many organizations.

Some organizations that have already been affected by a reduced entry-level work force are dealing with the shortages creatively. McDonald's and Kentucky Fried Chicken are actively recruiting retired people to work in their restaurants. McDonald's has even used national advertising to point out the benefits of working for the company. The ads stress the feelings of self-worth that working can bring to a retired person. Kentucky Fried Chicken hopes to use its retired persons program to help young workers value work by having the older workers serve as positive role models for youngsters from homes or segments of society with limited work experience.

To take advantage of the increasing number of women in the work force, many companies have begun to make it easier for women to work. These companies provide free or reduced-cost child care, flexible working hours, career advancement opportunities, and an attractive work environment. Other companies such as Digital Equipment and Hewlett–Packard offer campuslike workplaces with such facilities as jogging trails and health clubs and flexible work schedules that permit employees to enjoy these facilities.

Changing Nature of Work and the Work Force. As the economy shifts from traditional manufacturing activities to high-technology manufacturing and services, different skills and abilities are required of the work force. Unfortunately, the U.S. educational system has not kept pace with the change. Various signs of the system's failure can be observed. For example, a twenty-year slide in college entry scores has only recently been turned around. The number of functional illiterates is on the rise. William Brock, former secretary of labor in the Reagan administration, says that we have a "vocational system that is still training people for jobs that existed 10, 15, 20 years ago" (Numec, 1987).

Not only is the total work force less well prepared than in the past, but its composition is changing as well. By the year 2000, 80 percent of entrants into the work force will be women, minorities, and immigrants. The changing composition raises questions about the suitability of a number of current human resources practices.

Child care, training, recruitment, organizational culture, and health care costs are among the many issues that will require closer attention by human resources managers in the future. As an example of the effect of these trends, consider the fact that women will account for 63 percent of the work force growth from 1986 to 2000. Employers must be prepared to adjust to the requirements of a predominantly female work force. This may include providing convenient, low-cost child care; more flexibility in work hours and entrance and exit from the work force; different career advancement paths; and additional training for nontraditional jobs.

An analysis (Kutscher, 1987) of educational requirements for various occupations indicates that between now and the year 2000 the greatest growth will occur in those occupations requiring a year or more of college. Occupations requiring a high school education will experience a slight decline and occupations requiring less than high school will experience a sharp decline. A comparison of jobs currently held by blacks, Hispanics, and, to a lesser extent, women shows these groups to be overrepresented in those occupations requiring the least education.

The comparison of occupational requirements and population projections in Table 12 indicates that for the fastest growing and most technically demanding job categories traditional workers (white males) will not be available in sufficient numbers to meet the needs of private business and government. Organizations must more actively anticipate their needs through strategic human resources planning and take more long-term approaches to securing the work force of the future. Such measures may include working with local, state, and federal attempts to attract blacks, Hispanics, and women to occupations that they have not previously sought in large numbers. This may mean working with local groups to get junior school high school or younger children interested in the courses that would prepare them for jobs requiring a college education and specifically a technical education.

Immigrants will account for more than 23 percent of the work force growth between 1986 and 2000. This will help to reduce the impact of the birth dearth but at the same time will challenge firms to effectively use these resources. Non-English-speaking immigrants will need to be integrated into mainstream employment opportunities. Given the shifts in skill requirements, immigrants are likely to be poorly prepared to take the jobs employers most want to fill. As with the groups mentioned earlier, firms must assist this group so that they can enter the labor force with the skills required to operate modern businesses.

In the near term, firms can do several things to lessen the current impact of these trends and at the same time deal with other problems as well. One method is the increased use of temporary workers. If a company employs certain workers only during those times when their services are actually needed, other companies can use these services at other times. An example is found in the computer services/data-processing field. Thousands in this field work on a relatively short-term basis (less than one year) for the using organization but work for an extended period for the firm that contracts them out. The growth of specialized temporary employment agencies provides other evidence of the effectiveness of this approach.

The use of retired employees is also becoming much more prevalent. As the quality of health care improves and the life span of the average American increases, more people are able and willing to continue some type of work after retirement. As mentioned earlier, some firms are readily taking advantage of this fact to solve labor shortage problems. One significant obstacle stands in the way of even greater utilization of retired workers. This obstacle is the earning limitation placed on recipients of Social Security. Under the law in effect at the beginning of 1988, recipients were able to earn only $8,160 before their Social Security payments were reduced. Although the secretary of health and human services has called for revision of the law, to date no action has been taken by Congress.

Another solution to the labor shortage is possible—the substitution of technology for manpower. This substitution is seen in a variety of industries, from automatic french-frying machines in fast food restaurants to automated bank tellers to robotic devices assembling IBM personal computers. However, in some of the fastest growing industry sectors such as the business services sector, there are severe limits on the amount of substitution that can be made now or in the foreseeable future.

Summary. The forecasted effects of known demographic factors are not just vague speculations. They are based on statistics that account for people already born and project their numbers into the future. These demographic factors require that human resources managers systematically analyze their environments and the forces acting on their firms. Only through a regular review of the firm's position with respect to key environmental elements can human resources managers anticipate changes and plan effective organizational responses.

Corporate Terrorism

Corporate terrorism is an issue of increasing significance to employers. In 1985, according to the U.S. Department of State, terrorists killed 17 Americans and wounded more than 150. There were sixty-seven separate attacks against U.S. businesses and business personnel in 1985 (Willis 1986a). These statistics mark a 33 percent increase over the number of like incidents reported for 1984. The extent of loss is even greater when property damage and ransom payments are considered. According to Risks International, 1.72 million dollars in property damage was caused by terrorist attacks against U.S. businesses in 1985. And, an additional 6.1 million dollars was paid in ransom for the release of three kidnap victims (Willis, 1986a).

Large multinational corporations are particularly vulnerable to the often indiscriminate acts of terrorism. Consequently, the multinationals now include antiterrorist countermeasures as part of their risk management portfolio and as part of their corporate security program. The succeeding paragraphs discuss targets of terrorism, sources of terrorism, and security measures that can be taken to reduce the risks of terrorism.

Targets of Terrorism and Terrorist Tactics. In using violence as a systematic means of persuasion, terrorists choose their targets among people, buildings and installations, and modes of travel. Their tactics range from extortion and kidnapping to bombings and assassinations. Terrorists operate widely and boldly overseas; however, their activities are less frequent and confined largely to buildings and installations in the United States. Terrorists also operate by a set of rules that seem barbaric and exceptionally cruel to most Americans. They frequently conduct unprovoked attacks against women and children, for example, to demonstrate the limitless vulnerability of their targets. Terrorists also make extensive use of unconventional tactics to enhance their image of ruthlessness and power in seeking recognition and concessions for their varied causes.

American executives and managers are most vulnerable to extortion and kidnapping for ransom. Terrorists regard American corporations as a primary means of financing their operations.

They correctly believe that corporations are likely to accede to demands for money in exchange for the release of a hostage or the promise to spare a building from physical damage. On occasion, terrorists will demand that some social good be performed in exchange for the release of a hostage. The Symbionese Liberation Army's demands in the case of Patty Hearst several years ago constitute an example of extortion and kidnap in return for some act of social benevolence. Americans are least likely to be assassinated. With the exception of prominent executives in certain foreign countries, threats of assassination are few and actual attempts even fewer.

When installations are the targets of terrorists, bombing is most frequently the mode of attack. Bombs accomplish two key objectives. First, they create a visible demonstration of serious damage. Second, they create a pervasive sense of fear among employees of the targeted organization. Terrorists attempt to concentrate the damage in areas of operation vital to the business too. Destroying a computer center, communication center, or central distribution point would extend the psychological effect of damage to a serious disruption of the organization's ability to function. In the case of public utilities, power generation and transmission stations are prime targets. In 1977, for example, the New World Liberation Front and the George Jackson Brigade conducted ten separate bombing attacks against Pacific Gas and Electric Company facilities in California, and they bombed a Puget Power and Light facility in Washington State once (Willis, 1986a). The most frequently targeted industrial corporations are IBM, Citibank, ITT, Xerox, Coca-Cola, and Exxon.

The greatest threat from terrorism occurs overseas. Americans are most likely to be the targets of terrorist attack, moreover, when they are traveling. The concern is so great that several prominent companies have issued bulletins and pamphlets on foreign travel to their employees. Johnson and Johnson has asked their employees to limit foreign travel to essential business only. AT&T provides an instructional booklet on ways to cope with terrorist attacks while in terminals and as a passenger aboard an airliner. To be as inconspicuous as possible while traveling overseas, many companies encourage their employees to use foreign airlines. Swiss Air and Lufthansa are frequently preferred because of their stringent security procedures, which supplement those of airport authorities (D'Amore and Anuza, 1986). Israel's El Al Airline is regarded as the most secure air carrier when traveling to the Middle East. Symbols or behavior that would identify a traveler as a business executive or representative of a prominent American company should be avoided. For instance, flying economy and coach class and staying at major hotels in standard accommodations are common practices to avoid attention.

Sources of Terrorism. Those who perpetrate acts of terrorism against American businesses and their employees are primarily international zealots who are opposed to capitalism and its consequences. Occasionally, mercenaries also pose a risk. Mercenaries can operate inconspicuously in completing a particularly difficult assignment in which security measures are known to be stringent. Zealots such as Germany's Baader-Meinholf Gang conduct continuous operations against both industrial and government targets overseas. Of little threat to American businesses are separatist and nationalist groups. Such groups as the Irish Republican Army and the Palestine Liberation Organization, for example, focus their terrorist activities against incumbent political powers and adversarial rivals for national power in a particular region. Unless these groups are provoked by an antagonistic act, therefore, they pose little risk to American businesses.

The risk of terrorist attack is greatest in certain areas of the world. In 1985, more than half the attacks on businesses occurred in Latin America. More than one-third occurred in Western Europe. Six countries—Colombia, Chile, Peru, Bolivia, Spain, and Belgium—accounted for two-thirds of all attacks (Willis, 1986a). The turbulence in Latin America can be attributed largely to strong leftist groups and wholesale trafficking in narcotics. Kidnappings and extortion plots represent the greatest danger to American businesses in Latin America. The largest ransom known to be paid is $14.2 million for the manager of Argentina's Exxon refinery (Willis, 1986a).

In Europe, Paris, London, and Rome are centers of terrorist activity. From information obtained in raids on terrorist hideouts, West German authorities know of 100 businessmen targeted for terrorist attack. Bombings represent the largest threat to American businesses in Western Europe. The Middle East poses a continuing and serious threat to American interests largely because of the instability of the region and the large number of extremist political parties. Asia and Africa are relatively calm by comparison.

In North America, occasional bombings and kidnappings by a small number of extremist groups and psychotics or criminals acting alone constitute the extent of terrorist activity. American businesses and their employees are clearly more vulnerable to terrorist activity in foreign countries.

To reduce the risk of terrorist activity and to contain the damage of a terrorist assault, employers need a mix of countermeasures and insurance. Insurance and active countermeasures combine as part of a company's risk management and security program to provide the most effective defense against damage and harm from what has become one of the major risks of doing business as a multinational.

Protection Against Terrorism. About $21 billion is spent annually by American businesses on security according to the Rand Corporation. Each year a larger percentage of the security budget is allocated to combat terrorism (Willis, 1986a). Comprehensive programs to combat terrorism often combine insurance, education and training, and active countermeasures that range from elaborate detection systems, to bodyguards, to the careful design and location of facilities. Insurance is most often purchased to indemnify losses incurred from ransom and extortion payments. Other lines of coverage include bomb damage, sabotage, and product tampering. Insurance can cover losses resulting from threats as well as physical damage and harm to employees. Many terrorists exploit business's vulnerability to product withdrawals with threats to contaminate a product in selected market areas. In these situations businesses suffer the loss of sales plus the costs of product disposal and, frequently, a ransom to the terrorist.

Insurance for kidnapping, ransom, and extortion (K,R&E) is expensive. Premiums of $1,000 to $500,000 per year buy coverage worth $100,000 to $50 million (Willis, 1986a). The coverage usually extends to loss in transit of a ransom payment, consulting expenses, reward bounties, and other reasonable expenses. When property or product extortion is at issue, the coverage includes business interruption losses, product recall expenses, and consequential losses suffered from the extortion (Morphew, 1986). The liabilities can be very large. In 1982, for example, a large U.S. pharmaceutical company's facility in Peru suffered $30 million in property damage from a terrorist attack. The Swedish office of a large U.S. airline was bombed. Of course, insurers, of which there are few, advise corporations on reducing the risks of terrorism. Advice typically includes risk assessment, loss prevention, and crisis management.

Insurance, though a prudent measure for large multinational companies, merely transfers the risk of terrorism in financial terms to the insurer. Reducing the risk requires an active program of countermeasures. Companies can combat the risks of terrorism by actively employing countermeasures that deter terrorist attacks and contain damage resulting from terrorist strikes. Such measures include passive detection and containment devices, facility design, construction, location, and training of employees to detect and respond to potentially risky situations. In some instances, bodyguards are also useful. Bodyguards are very expensive, however, and often are less obtrusive to a trained terrorist than corporations may believe. Reputable bodyguards cost $600 to $800 a day plus expenses (Willis, 1986a), and require time in advance of an assignment to become thoroughly familiar with the person being guarded and the mission to which the protected person is being assigned.

In developing an antiterrorist security plan, a company should employ a full-time director of security working with people trained in antiterrorist tactics. Those organizations needing outside expert help can obtain a list of reputable consulting firms from the American Management Association. Depending on its nature and scope, the plan may include actions and precautions to take while traveling, while residing in foreign countries, and while working. Note these points:

At Work

- In high-risk areas overseas, all access and entry points should be under constant surveillance.
- During hours of operation, guards should be posted at all entry

control points. Visitors should be escorted and wear identification badges at all times while on company property.

- When the risk warrants, metal detectors should be employed.
- Periodic security audits should be conducted to ensure that antiterrorist measures fit the circumstances defining the threat. These audits should also confirm the ability of the organization to implement successfully the plans in place to counter an antiterrorist attack.
- Outside buildings, proper lighting, and alert systems should be positioned and periodically tested.
- Training should be conducted to ensure that reaction forces can respond effectively to an actual attack by terrorists. Training should provide certification exercises for both individuals and integrated teams.
- Training should also be provided for employees who are on the premises during an attack. Employees should be able to execute properly both evasive actions, such as avoiding high-impact areas from bomb damage, and escape actions, to avoid physical contact with terrorists.

At Home

- Employees and their families should be able to report correctly to proper authorities phone calls threatening abduction or property damage.
- Employees and their families should vary their habits and avoid predictable patterns of behavior to reduce the risk of being abducted.
- Living quarters should be easily accessible from several different routes of entry to facilitate rescue attempts and escape plans.
- A watchdog should guard the premises from inside the house.
- Family members should avoid going to windows and doors to observe a commotion or disturbance in public areas adjacent to the premises. Sometimes these events are staged by terrorists to draw a victim into position for an attack.

While Traveling

- Aisle seats on aircraft should be avoided; they attract more attention from hijackers.

- An armored car should be used if ambush is a threat while en route.
- Public ground transportation and traveling alone in taxis or limousines should be avoided.
- Public displays of wealth or prominence should be avoided in all foreign countries; such displays attract attention that could ultimately lead to discovery by a terrorist or terrorist sympathizer and informant.
- Outside walls near windows or doors in restaurants or shops should be avoided.
- In public places, employees and their families should sit with their backs to the wall whenever possible, to have a full view of the surrounding area.

Terrorism against U.S. businesses and their employees will continue to be a significant threat to the safety, morale, and risk management operations of large corporations. Therefore, corporate executives must plan for these risks to maintain their control over operations and the prospects for continued economic success.

Summary. Multinational corporations are increasingly vulnerable to terrorism. Damages, currently confined to very large and well-known organizations, total in the millions of dollars annually. Even the threat of terrorism is disruptive and costly. It can discourage activities which, without the presence of a threat, would enhance the growth and profitability of a company.

Businesses combat the risk of terrorism with a variety of measures. The most common are insurance for ransom, kidnapping, and extortion; active countermeasures such as anti-intrusion devices and the design and location of facilities; and training employees and their families to reduce their vulnerability to terrorist acts.

For many large companies, contending with terrorism has become an active part of their risk management policy and portfolio. As political turmoil around the world intensifies, so will the risk of terrorism for a growing number of American companies doing business in foreign countries. As international competition for product and capital markets increases, the need for an antiterrorist policy will become evident to a growing number of companies.

11

Strategic
Human Resources Planning:
Linking HRM
to Business Strategy

Previous chapters in this book have identified and discussed several human resources issues presently of concern. Through their impact on employee availability, employee skill, employee productivity, and employee cost, these developments have significant potential to affect employee welfare and the competitive advantage an employer enjoys within an industry.

Although diverse in content, these issues share many features. First, their boundaries are not clearly defined. They tend to be complex. The total potential impact is not clear. Thus, easy solutions are difficult to find. Second, they tend to involve conflicting values and interests. Various stakeholders view and respond to the issues quite differently. Thus, logic alone provides insufficient basis for effective organizational response. Put another way, expert knowledge cannot automatically resolve these issues. This is the third shared feature. Fourth, the issues are usually stated in value-laden terms. Hence, they tend to be presented and examined in ways that evoke conflict and emotional response. Finally, however, trade-offs are possible and workable solutions can be developed. Often this involves assessing the benefits and costs of various response options and negotiating acceptable outcomes with affected stakeholders. Because of these features (that is, complexity, lack of expert knowledge, value bias), organizational response to issue development may be slow. Consequently, the longer the lead time an organization has to develop an informed response, the more likely it is to achieve external and internal benefits. For this reason, some companies have adopted a more active role in the process known as strategic human resources planning.

Definitions, Perspectives, and Practices

There is no generally accepted definition of strategic human resources planning. One review of the literature (Milkovich, Dyer, and Mahoney, 1983) identified more than twenty definitions of human resources planning and more than twenty-five human resources planning models. Some authors focus on forecasting as the core element (Burack and Mathys, 1980; Dyer, 1982; Walker, 1980). Others (for example, Mirvis, 1985; Ulrich, 1987) take a more comprehensive perspective, seeing human resources planning as the way management gains competitive advantage and comes to grips with ill-defined and tough-to-solve human resources problems.

Despite the variation in perspectives, today the element that most clearly distinguishes "strategic" human resources planning from previous forms of human resources planning is the attempt to link the human resources planning process directly to business strategy. Nearly all large business organizations now develop five-year business plans to steer the enterprise into the uncertain future. Historically, these plans have focused primarily on financial, marketing, and technical considerations. But, with increasing dynamism and complexity in the social and legal arenas, many organizations discovered their plans to be less effective than anticipated. As a result of their failure to assess the impact of financial, marketing, and technical decisions on the personnel function, employers frequently found that their plans were delayed or could not be implemented effectively.

Because of the negative consequences of exclusion of human resources considerations in business planning, companies began to seek more human resources input into the business planning process. Typically, this involvement consisted of post facto review of proposed business plans. Gradually, it became apparent that earlier human resources involvement could provide valuable insights into the business planning process itself. Not only could obstacles be eliminated, but opportunities could be better exploited through a more informed perspective of human resources attributes.

As the human resources function became more involved in the long-term business planning process, necessary changes became apparent in the management of human resources. Primarily, it was noted that human resources managers needed to view their function less parochially and to define their role in the organization relative to the strategic purpose of the business. Thus, human resources managers had to develop a more informed operating perspective, a need that is still discussed in many planning circles. In essence, human resources practitioners were urged to reconceptualize their role in terms of dollars and cents rather than recruiting, training, wage and salary administration, and other traditional personnel functions.

As a result, human resources departments became more involved in planning. The primary outcome of these planning processes was a human resources action plan that ensured the availability of properly qualified employees. The primary purpose of current strategic human resources planning is essentially to ensure that the organization has the right people, at the right place, at the right time, with the desired skills and abilities to carry out the tasks the organization has to perform.

Elements of Strategic Human Resources Planning

As noted previously, a variety of human resources planning models have been proposed. Despite variations in their specific form, they share in common three major elements: (1) environmental analysis of human resources opportunities and threats, (2) forecast of the demand for human resources, and (3) forecast of the internal supply of human resources. Each element is addressed in greater detail.

Environmental Analysis: The Process. Most organizations recognize that analysis of the firm's macroenvironment is required in business planning. However, few recognize the need to scan this same environment for its human resources implications. Although the specific environmental interests vary with the industry and the business strategy, companies typically tap social, educational, demographic, political/legal, and economic trends and events.

In the social arena, for example, organizations should be alert to changes in societal values and worker attitudes and their impact on workplace innovations (for example, the evolution of flex-time practices, day-care provision, quality circles). Chapters Two and Three shed light on the impact of two contemporary social trends (substance abuse and AIDS) on human resources policies and practices.

Educational trends suggest the potential degree of difficulty in recruiting a qualified work force and, perhaps, the degree of organizational involvement required in training. Chapter Nine indicated the general concern for workplace literacy and, specifically, for specialized training and retraining that permit the organization to gain a competitive advantage through the incorporation of advanced technology.

The availability of an adequate number of workers will become a major issue as demographic patterns continue to shift. For example, changes in age, birth rate, gender patterns, and geographic distribution influence the size and nature of the work force. As more women enter the work force, the issues of comparable worth and sexual harassment increase in significance. Even employee benefit strategies are affected. The aging of the work force and the growing number of retirees affect health care costs.

With respect to political and legal trends, new concerns in addition to OSHA and Title VII loom on the horizon. As indicated in Chapter Seven, the employment-at-will doctrine is being challenged through judicial interpretation. On a broader scale, political differences in the international arena have resulted in an upswing in terrorist activities, often resulting in attacks against American firms or their employees. Also, recent changes in ERISA and other governmental programs such as Medicare have resulted in additional demands on human resources.

Finally, analysis of economic conditions and trends can provide useful information for planning wages, health care costs, alternative employment opportunities (turnover), and the likelihood of employment growth or decline within an industry.

Employers also need to explore microenvironmental trends and conditions. At least five microconsiderations are important. (1) What is the specific competitive situation of the firm in its industry? (2) What are the long-range organizational plans of the firm? (3) What is the present and desired managerial philosophy of the organization? (4) What trends exist in employee attitudes and behaviors? (5) What technological trends are evident?

Without exploring these areas in depth, it is easy to see that the first two factors significantly affect the number and type of personnel needed. Chapter Six examined the situation faced by a firm whose competitive situation and plans call for downsizing. Trends in managerial and worker attitudes influence the type and magnitude of human resources responses to environmental needs. Technological trends dictate choices regarding the type of employee and the skill level required. Corollary choices affect the degree of worker displacement, recruiting, training, and retraining necessary in the organization.

Up to this point we have discussed only the focus of the environmental scanning process. Equally important is the frequency of this activity. Three options are available: irregular scanning, regular scanning, and continuous scanning. Naturally, there are advantages and disadvantages to each option. The more continuous the scan, the greater the cost of information and the larger the scanning staff required. Usually under continuous scanning conditions, specialized individuals or departments are assigned full-time responsibility for the activity.

The form of scanning appropriate for an organization depends on the degree of complexity and rate of change in the firm's environment and the particular environment being scanned (that is, economic, legal, social). Firms in more dynamic industries, impacted by a broader range of environments, require higher scanning frequencies than firms in less dynamic industries subject to fewer environmental issues. However, it is evident today that to successfully meet emerging human resources challenges, firms need to engage in regular (for example, annual) scanning practices at a minimum. It was noted earlier in this chapter that earlier trend detection increases the likelihood of developing positive response

Table 13. An Environmental Scanning Framework.

	Scanning Approach		
	Irregular	Regular	Continuous
Media for scanning	Ad hoc studies	Periodically updated studies	Structural data-collection and -processing systems
Scope of scanning	Specific events	Selected events	Broad range of environmental systems
Motivation for activity	Crisis initiated	Decision and issue oriented	Planning process oriented
Temporal nature of activity	Reactive	Proactive	Proactive
Time frame for data	Retrospective	Contemporary	Prospective
Time frame for decision impact	Current/near term	Near term	Near term/long term
Organizational responsibility	Various staff functions	Various staff function	Environmental scanning unit

Source: Unknown.

options and taking more informed action. Table 13 presents a descriptive framework for categorizing scanning activity.

As soon as the environmental analysis is completed, human resources planners are prepared to develop forecasts of human resources demand and supply.

Demand Forecasting. Demand forecasting attempts to predict, given alternative sets of business developments, the number and type of employees required. In other words, given the results of our external and internal environmental analyses, and our business plan and strategy, we must now translate our information into manning requirements.

Demand forecasting is a two-step process. First, the demand for an organization's products or services must be determined. This is usually obtained from the business plan. Second, the demand for people is determined. Thus, the demand for human resources is essentially a derived demand. A typical manpower forecasting procedure involves six basic steps (Burack and Mathys, 1980):

1. Forecasting the activity level (in dollars, units, and so on) for each period, usually one year, over the total planning period (1 to 5, 10, or even 20 years).
2. Converting activity levels into the corresponding numbers of direct labor (salesperson, nurse, and so on) hours required to meet the forecasted number of (direct) labor hours per unit of service or dollar of sales.
3. Adjustment for productivity improvement that reflects new methods, use of computers, new production technologies, and so on. Thus the initial calculation of required hours is reduced by this productivity correction.
4. Adjustments for nonproductive time, lost time, and so on. These adjustments reduce any gains made in productivity. At times, lost hours resulting from absenteeism, poor training, or even excessive turnover can cancel the entire savings from productivity improvements.
5. Calculation of supervisory staff or administrative requirements. These calculations are usually based on the adjustment figures from direct labor calculations using ratios of indirect to direct personnel.
6. Distribution of required employees. The detail and refinement of this calculation depend entirely on organizational need. Relevant classifications include exempt/nonexempt, departmental/divisional, line/staff, administrative/professional, technical/line, managerial/professional/technical, and so on.

    In addition to points 3 and 4, other adjustments should also be considered. For example, adjustments to traditional translation factors should be considered for changes in organizational structure, for example, change from a functional to a project form or elimination of a level of management, merger or acquisition activity that may involve the elimination of substantial duplication of personnel, or changes in internal company policies or practice (for example, increased use of subcontracting).

Supply Forecasting. After the need for manpower is determined, the organization must determine how it will ensure that the employees required are available at the proper time. This is the supply side of the forecasting process. Manpower can be supplied from both within and outside the organization. Neither source can be determined purely on the basis of quantitative analysis. Managerial assumptions and judgments are necessary.

The internal labor supply is determined by projecting various anticipated losses from current manning levels. Quits, discharges, retirements, deaths, and leaves (for example, military, educational) are all sources of aggregate loss. Although these losses can be numerically estimated through historical ratios, age profiles, actuarial tables, and the like, the calculations are not exact. For example, the quit rate can be influenced by changes in general economic conditions (unemployment rate, home mortgage interest rates), increases in the number of area employers, or changes in the wage practices of area firms. The quit rate can also be influenced by changes in company policies (provision for financial support for continuing education, benefit packages). Retirement rates can be influenced by the provision of early retirement incentives or by changes in retirement legislation or Medicare provisions. Even death rates have the potential to be altered by changes in company benefit programs, for example, early detection, fitness, and wellness programs and changes in the enforcement of safety and industrial hygiene rules. The more dynamic the nature of these external and internal changes, the greater the difficulty of making aggregate forecasts of internal supply.

Beside aggregate forecasting, firms must forecast the availability of various classifications of employees (for example, managerial, professional, sales, technical, clerical/administrative, and direct labor). Thus, the rate of internal movement between various job classifications must be considered and the net effect of these movements within each job category must be calculated.

Frequently, supplemental supply analyses are required for special groups. One such group may be hard-to-recruit occupations such as technical and computer specialists. Another might be females and blacks to ensure fulfillment of EEO/AA requirements.

A third might be executives holding "key" positions within the organization.

Once the internal manpower supply is determined and compared with the labor demand, the organization can turn its attention to the external labor supply. Demands that cannot be met internally must be supplied through external market actions (for example, recruitment, subcontracting, establishment of cooperative education programs, temporary services). Thus, it is incumbent on organizations to develop an environmental sensitivity to trends in the external labor market and to establish programs and relationships within the relevant labor markets to secure needed personnel. As noted in Chapter Ten, many firms have had to develop innovative labor market strategies because of changes in traditional sources of supply. McDonald's, for example, has begun recruiting "seniors" to fill gaps caused by a deficient labor supply within the traditional "teens" market.

Supply side calculations can be especially useful in determining the form of company response to decreases in the demand for products or services. An accurate supply side manpower model permits an organization to ask "what if" questions in testing alternative employment actions. For example, if downsizing is determined to be necessary, supply side calculations can determine the effect of normal attrition on the company's roll. This permits the firm to estimate whether layoff is necessary or to determine the potential effect of offering an early retirement package. A description of the internal distribution of manpower may also provide the employer with insight into the employment groups to target for layoff, transfer, or other personnel action. Figure 5 summarizes the manpower planning process in model form.

Using the Model. As evidenced in the processes just described, a primary requirement for strategic human resources planning is having a strong business planning process in place. Strategic human resources planning is an extension of that process.*

In practice, use of the model involves two steps: (1) moving

---

*Ideas in this section are heavily influenced by materials presented by Myron Roomkin in a seminar on Strategic Human Resources Planning, June 1982, Northwestern University.

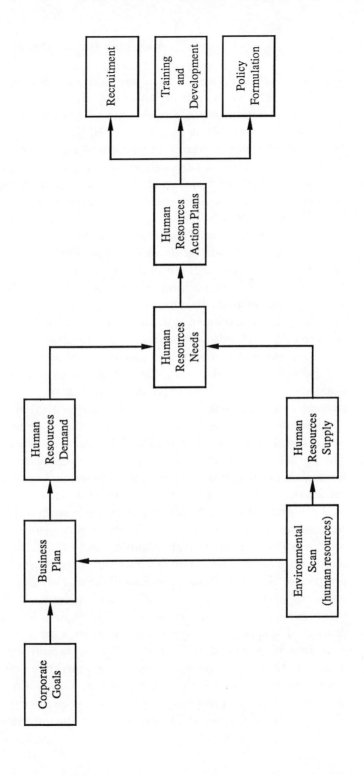

Figure 5. Strategic Human Resources Planning Model.

from the business plan to human resources and (2) moving from human resources to the strategic business plan.

Step 1 recognizes that every strategy has human resources implications. Whether it is a strategy of growth, stability, or retirement, human resources implications are apparent in the quality and quantity of labor, geographic location of employees, motivation, employee morale, organizational design, productivity, labor relations, and the like. Assessment of these implications is the process of translation.

Once the implications inherent to the business plan are identified, plans should be developed that reflect the most cost-effective combination of traditional human resources techniques: recruitment, selection, training and development, compensation, and employee relations. In other words, human resources strategies and plans can be developed to manipulate the internal and external labor market mechanisms to achieve a cost-effective response.

As noted previously, the rationale for strategic human resources planning is that sufficient lead time is necessary to use the fluctuations (growth or decline) in the internal labor market to meet strategic business objectives. Time is often critical in making effective use of external labor markets too. Market segments must be cultivated over years to produce an adequate yield when needed. The greater the lead time, the greater the options available to the human resources group to manipulate internal and external labor markets to achieve a cost-effective mixture of skills.

Turning to step 2—moving from human resources to the strategic business plan—we note that the environmental scanning process is common to strategic planning and to human resources planning. The business planner views the environment from the perspective of business opportunities and threats. Although human resources planners focus on similar environmental sectors (for example, economic, technical, political, social), their focus is quite different. For example, in an economic forecast, a business planner is likely to be interested in the projected cost of capital and rates of inflation, as they may affect the costs of acquired materials or the pricing opportunities for the firm's products. On the other hand, an economic forecast from a human resources perspective might note how changes in the inflation rate or the unemployment rate could affect the labor force participation of married women and the retirement decisions of persons fifty-five and older. Timely access to the strategic planning process with this kind of information would allow human resources planners to alert strategic planners to potential errors in their assumptions about the availability of human resources and project more accurately the impact of human resources functions on the bottom line.

To improve the effective implementation and use of these planning processes, business can take several steps:

1. Employ better qualified human resources specialists. These specialists will require knowledge of environmental, business, and statistical concepts and practices.
2. Educate human resources managers and planners as to the organization's business practices and functions (financial goals, marketing strategy, manufacturing processes, and so on).
3. Familiarize line managers and business planners with the human resources assumptions inherent to the business planning process.
4. Involve key line managers in the design of the human resources planning process.
5. Involve human resources planners early in the strategic planning process.
6. Establish realistic expectations for the implementation of the human resources planning system. The entire process does not have to be installed at once.
7. Be prepared to change and modify the system. Flexibility is necessary to accommodate shifting business environments.

Toward the Future: Building Competitive Advantage

A great deal of variety exists in the practice of human resources planning. Much of the variation results from the fact that human resources planning is in a state of evolution. Several frameworks have been advanced to capture the direction in which this process is moving.

Stages of Planning. Gluck, Kaufman, and Walleck (1982) have noted that most strategic business planning systems go through four stages as they evolve: (1) budgeting, (2) financial forecasting, (3) externally oriented planning, and (4) strategic management. Their conclusion is based on a study of planning systems of a number of large companies by McKinsey and Company. They also note that the compelling force behind the continuing evolution of planning—particularly the leap between stages 2 and 3—appears to be the increasing complexity of business problems and the pace of change in the environment.

The analogy between the evolution of strategic business planning and strategic human resources planning seems obvious. Many human resources systems currently function at stage 1: annual program budgeting. Stage 1 human resources planning consists of determining what human resources programs to implement next year and what budgets are needed to implement them. Most organizations are at this stage.

At stage 2, human resources planning is linked to the business plan, but only in a reactive sense. That is, the business plan is reviewed to determine what human resources programs and activities are required. The jump to stage 3—externally oriented planning—represents a major leap forward in planning capability. For the human resources function this would consist of scanning the external environment and using the observations as input to the business planning process and to a human resources supply-and-demand analysis. Only a few well-managed organizations consistently function at this level. English (1984) reports that less than 10 percent of major firms develop human resources plans prior to, or concurrently with, the business planning cycle.

As Gluck, Kaufman, and Walleck (1982) note, stage 3 planning signals top management that explicit choices are being made, and have historically been made, at lower levels of the organization, and that these choices have the potential to affect the company's strategic capability. The knowledge that strategic decisions are being made without their involvement often propels top management to greater participation in the planning process. This impetus can lead to full-fledged strategic human resources management (that is, stage 4).

Transitional Phases. Ulrich (1987) suggests that during the past twenty years transitions in strategic human resources planning have paralleled transitions in the underlying theory. Consequently, he identifies three evolutionary planning phases based on the guiding human resources concepts of regulation, control, and shaping.

Early human resources planning efforts had as their goals compliance with regulations and policies. Human resources plans were developed to ensure compliance with governmental regulations such as EEO, wage and salary, and labor laws. With this focus, planning emphasized operational rather than strategic practices. Many, if not most, organizations remain in this phase.

Current efforts to match human resources practices with business strategies characterize the second phase—control. Unfortunately, in most human resources circles, linking strategy to human resources management is perceived as a goal in itself. As Ulrich notes, if organizations hope to move beyond this phase they need to view this bridge between strategy and human resources management as only one step toward a higher goal, that is, competitive advantage.

This higher goal is achieved through the human resources concept of shaping. According to Ulrich, creation of competitive advantage requires that human resources plans shape, not merely regulate, behavior. In essence, shaping is the development of human resources programs that generate employee commitment. Through shaping, such human resources functions as staffing, training and development, and wage and salary administration are integrated and focused on creating a corporate culture leading to a market advantage. During this phase, human resources professionals become strategic partners in business planning and implementation. Sobol (1983) notes that this focus is reflected in IBM's creation of a core culture based on excellence, customer service, and respect for employees.

A Functional Perspective. As Roomkin (1982) and others have pointed out, the human resources function currently follows the same path trod by other staff functions in the past. For example, the finance function once had a subordinate status equivalent to that experienced by human resources today. The financial metamorphosis occurred when managers recognized the time value of money and the opportunity costs associated with its use. To date, few human resources managers and specialists have perceived their role in terms of opportunity costs and return on investment. However, as more organizations experience greater worldwide competition and a more dynamic external environment replete with threats and opportunities, they will embrace the concept of strategic human resources planning to secure a competitive advantage or to avoid significant opportunity costs. Readers interested in learning more about how human resources can be presented in financial terms should consult the pioneering work of Cascio (1982), Flamholtz (1985), and Spencer (1985).

When human resources professionals become thoroughly familiar with the full range of business activities associated with the design, manufacture, and sale of the firm's products or services, and are able to relate their contribution to the bottom line in dollars and cents, they will probably become significantly involved in the shaping of business strategy. It is also incumbent on line managers to develop a more informed perspective of the potential of human resources if strategic unity is to be achieved.

Issue Management

Although manpower forecasting is an essential aspect of current human resources practice, many strategically significant issues do not directly impact quantitative projections. Rather, the impact of many issues is far more subjective. In these instances, insight gained from the issue management process (Coates, Coates, Jarratt, and Heinz, 1986) can be helpful.

The purpose of issue identification and issue management is to anticipate and identify unfolding trends likely to have significant impact on the organization and to frame a positive response that serves the organization's needs in light of the new reality engendered by the trends. It is an outgrowth of futures research and is best and most usefully applied when directly linked to the analysis of policy implications.

Issue management, as an organizational process, incorporates four basic elements: (1) It identifies and defines developing issues that may affect an organization. (2) It analyzes the implications of these issues. (3) It produces a range of options available to the organization and specifies the benefits and costs of each option.

(4) It sets in motion short- and long-term operational and strategic actions to deal with these issues.

Two major assumptions underlie these processes. First, early identification of an issue permits the development of a wider range of options. Second, by anticipating or identifying issues early, an organization enhances its likelihood of developing a positive response, that is, a response that supports its strategic goals or produces a comparative advantage.

In some respects, issues management is similar to problem solving; however, they are different processes. Problems can often be solved by the application of structured diagnostic methods and expert knowledge. Issues (as we have defined them at the beginning of this chapter) can almost never be definitively and completely resolved to the satisfaction of all parties. Instead, successful issues management is most often characterized by negotiation, compromise, and trade-offs. Resolution requires some dynamic balance in interests or mutual accommodation.

In addition to the obvious conflict evident in the processes necessary to develop effective responses, several other conflicts are inherent to the acquisition of organizational foresight. Nine such tensions are identified by Coates, Coates, Jarratt, and Heinz (1986):

1. *Expanding Needs Conflict with the Constraints on Acquiring New Knowledge.* The need of policymakers for new knowledge is without limit. Each new body of knowledge seems to create a demand for further knowledge. Each new tool demands its extension to some new limit. Furthermore, the required data are not always available, easily collected, or cheap, and converting data into knowledge through analysis, understanding, and presentation is often slow and expensive.

2. *Pressure for Action Conflicts with the Uncertainty of Outcomes.* Although policy decisions can be deferred, sooner or later action is called for and must be made in the context of uncertainties about the success of the policy or plan and the outcome of the actions thereby triggered.

3. *Rapid Change and Increasing Complexity Conflict with Our Limited Human Ability to Think About Large Numbers of Factors Simultaneously.* The tendency, therefore, is to oversim-

plify complex situations or to use such aids as mathematical modeling to increase our insight into complexity. Although oversimplification often enters into the analysis of extremely complex situations, a further simplification is likely as the results of a foresight activity are briefed and transmitted from person to person in ever diminishing detail.

4. *The Pressure for Quick Response Conflicts with the Needs for More Data.* Every issue involves data and every analysis calls for data. Consequently, a general policy is to anticipate the need for and gather and stockpile data. When the data are not fully in hand one often makes more or less wise estimates. Data and time, however, also come in conflict in that it takes time to act and, in turn, time for responses to develop from actions. Consequently, foresight requires the continuing collection of data with regard to past and new actions, to determine their consequences and to put us in better shape for managing the future.

5. *Preference for Quantitative Data and Mathematical Analysis Is at Odds with the Need for Some Qualitative Data and Subjective Evaluation.* Numbers have a purported degree of reliability and public character that make them the preferred policy coinage. But the underlying significance of the number often is obscure and tells only part of a complex story. Often the most critical policy aspects of a potential development or venture hinge upon what can only be described in conjectural, "what if" or discursive fashion, such as the likelihood of the participation of the key actor, the uncertain interaction of complex social or political variables, or the poorly understood points of weakness in a potential venture.

6. *The Need for Efficiency and Effectiveness Conflicts with the Need for Flexibility.* The need to allow alternative forms of analysis to flourish is very important in policy research. Striking a balance between, on the one hand, centralization, which promises efficiency and effectiveness, and, on the other hand, flexibility is difficult. Useful analysis requires the simultaneous exploration of alternative approaches.

7. *Science as a Rational Process Often Conflicts with Ideological and Political Factors.* The attempts to make policy analyses

scientific, objective, and rational clash with the practical constraints of ideology and the practical realities of political judgment. The risk of centralized analyses in a politically charged environment is that ideology and politics too often swamp knowledge and objectivity.

8. *Short-Term Factors Are Almost Always in Conflict with Long-Term Factors.* Every decision maker, public or private, elected or appointed, is continually beleaguered by pressures for short-term action, even though he or she may know that longer-term outcomes and actions may be more important in shaping the future.

9. *The Pressure for Certainty Is in Conflict with the Contingent and Hypothetical.* Good policy analysis, whether it involves quantitative or qualitative techniques, must continually answer the question "What if?" and must continually traffic in "let us suppose" information and data. These needs are particularly at odds with rigid organization, bureaucracy, narrow specialization, and ideological preconception.

Although these tensions can inhibit the assimilation of issue management processes, a number of other factors simultaneously drive organizations toward more proactive environmental involvement. These pressures include environmental turbulence, heightened worldwide competition, and organizational pluralism.

Issue Management and Policy Implementation

Human resources responses to emerging issues require the development of action plans, and often new policies, to meet future work conditions. Thus, an understanding of the opportunities and pitfalls inherent to policy development and implementation is important for effective management of human resources.

Many organizations fail to effectively meet the challenges posed by new issues. As we stated earlier in this chapter, often the issues are complex and involve conflicting values. Thus, insular policy development within a human resources or personnel department is likely to be unsuccessful in evoking effective response. More frequently, today's issues require collaborative analysis and response.

For example, in responding to the issue of performance management, one large manufacturing organization developed and implemented an employee performance appraisal system. Although the system, including a new performance appraisal instrument, was approved by top management before implementation, few affected constituencies within the organization participated in its development. Consequently, implementation of the much needed program met with a great deal of resistance.

Subsequent to the implementation of the program, it was discovered that several departments and a few remote facilities had developed their own performance appraisal systems. They resented having to give up their own systems which, some felt, were superior to the corporate system, and being excluded from participating in the design of the corporate program.

In addition to evoking general resistance to the program, the personnel department had failed to plan for detailed implementational procedures or training for affected departments. Thus, operating departments did not have the guidance necessary for effective implementation of the policy change.

These problems could have been avoided if several steps had been taken before implementation:

1. Involve a representative sample of managers from affected business segments. Involvement overcomes resistance to change and builds commitment to an agreed course of action. It also offers the potential for development of a higher-quality response.
2. Solicit "informed" opinion. Many emerging issues (for example, substance abuse, AIDS, terrorism) are outside the experience range of human resources professionals. Even though these issues are just emerging, "experts" are available who can guide an organization in developing a more informed perspective and more effective response options. These experts should be sought during the early phases of response development.
3. Determine if a pilot program is feasible and desirable. As we

have stated previously, many human resources issues are complex and the impact of alternative courses of action is impossible to assess in advance with certainty. To the extent possible, responses should be "action tested" before implementation on a companywide basis. For example, in the case of the performance management program discussed earlier, a test of the new appraisal system in one division of the company would have reduced the risks inherent to its introduction and permitted response modification, that is, "fine tuning," prior to companywide introduction.

4. Plan and organize the implementation or revision to ensure smooth transition through advance communication and training, if necessary. Advance communication is necessary if implementation is to produce the desired results. Effective advance communication informs constituencies of the action being planned, solicits feedback from potentially affected constituencies, and allows adequate time for those impacted by the change to employ supportive measures.

5. Monitor the success of the transition and posttransition phases. This is especially necessary if a pilot program is not feasible. Problems are always encountered in the implementation of new policies and procedures, especially when they are complex and involve value-laden issues. To ensure a successful implementation, a formal system for providing feedback should be incorporated into the advance communication or policy. Managers, employees, or affected constituencies outside the company (for example, customers, vendors) should have a vehicle for informing those who will implement the action of any negative impact (anticipated or real).

Summary

In this chapter we have described the dynamic and complex environment in which the human resources function operates. And we have encouraged organizations to adopt strategic human resources planning practices to provide the lead time necessary to develop effective responses to emerging issues, to develop human resources management policies that create a competitive advantage, and to develop human resources practices that assure the availability of an adequate and qualified work force.

Obviously, the field of strategic human resources planning is still in its infancy. But, it is evolving. Today's emphasis on linking human resources planning to the long-range business plan is welcome and necessary. However, much more remains to be done. Planning tools and techniques can be improved, but the predominant need is for a shift in management attitude. Operating managers must perceive the human resources function as a strategic partner in achieving the firm's business plan. And human resources managers need to refocus their attention from the execution of traditional human resources activities to strategy, the bottom line, and competitive advantage.

The future is certain. The shifts in thinking called for will occur. Some organizations will wait until they are forced to act and will develop hasty and ill-conceived responses. Strategically focused organizations will see the need, make the necessary changes, and achieve the competitive advantage necessary to assure future survival and economic prosperity.

References

Adler, J. N. "Reductions in Force." In C. T. Norback (ed.), *The Human Resource Yearbook (1987 Edition)*. Englewood Cliffs, N.J.: Prentice-Hall, 1987.

Alcaire, A., and McGowan, D. T. "Alliances for Healthcare Cost Management." *Management Review*, Oct. 1986, pp. 30–35.

American Management Association. *Drug Abuse: The Workplace Issues*. New York: American Management Association, 1987.

Association for Fitness in Business. "Health and Fitness Personnel Update." In C. T. Norback (ed.), *The Human Resource Yearbook (1987 Edition)*. Englewood Cliffs, N.J.: Prentice-Hall, 1987.

Barrett, P. F. *The Human Implications of Mergers and Takeovers*. London: Institute of Personnel Management, 1973.

Bell, C. S. "Comparable Worth: How Do We Know It Will Work?" *Monthly Labor Review*, Dec. 1985, pp. 5–12.

Bellak, A. O. "Comparable Worth: A Practitioner's View." In U.S. Commission on Civil Rights, *Comparable Worth: Issue for the 80's*. Vol. 1, June 6–7, 1984, pp. 75–82. Washington, D.C.: U.S. Government Printing Office, 1984.

Bennigson, L. A. "Managing Corporate Cultures." *Management Review*, Feb. 1985, pp. 31–32.

Bensinger, P. B. "Drugs in the Workplace." *Harvard Business Review*, 1982, *60* (6), 48–53.

Bensinger, P. B. "Drugs in the Workplace: What Lies in the Future?" Chicago: Bensinger, Du Pont, and Associates, n.d.

Bernstein, A. "How IBM Cut 16,200 Employees—Without an Ax." *Business Week,* Feb. 15, 1988, p. 98.

Bittel, L. R., and Ramsey, J. E. "New Dimensions for Supervisory Training and Development." *Training and Development Journal,* 1983, *37* (3), 12–20.

Bompey, S. H. "How to Develop a Company AIDS Policy." *Boardroom Reports,* 1986, *15* (13), 1–2.

Bové, R. "Retraining the Older Worker." *Training and Development Journal,* 1987, *41* (3), 77–78.

Bracker, J. S., and Pearson, J. N. "Worker Obsolescence: The Human Resource Dilemma of the '80's." *Personnel Administrator,* 1986, *31* (12), 109–116.

Burack, E. H., and Mathys, N. J. *Human Resource Planning: A Pragmatic Approach to Staffing and Development.* Lake Forest, Ill.: Brace-Park Press, 1980.

Carroll, S. J. "Management by Objectives: Three Decades of Research and Experience." In S. L. Rynes and G. T. Milkovich (eds.), *Current Issues in Human Resource Management: Commentary and Readings.* Plano, Tex.: Business Publications, 1986.

Cascio, W. F. *Costing Human Resources: The Financial Impact of Behavior in Organizations.* Boston: Kent Publishing, 1982.

Castro, J. "Battling Drugs on the Job." *Time,* 1987, *128* (30), 43.

Chapman, F. S. "AIDS and Business: Problems of Costs and Compassion." *Fortune,* Sept. 15, 1986, pp. 122–127.

Chase, M. "Corporations Urge Peers to Adopt Humane Policies for AIDS Victims." *The Wall Street Journal,* Jan. 20, 1988, p. 31.

Coates, J. F., Coates, V. T., Jarratt, J., and Heinz, L. *Issues Management: How You Can Plan, Organize, and Manage for the Future.* Mt. Airy, Md.: Lomond Publications, 1986.

College Placement Council. *Preemployment Drug Screening: A Survey of Practices Among National Employers of College Graduates.* New York: College Placement Council, 1986.

Collingwood, H. "What AIDS Will Cost Insurers." *Business Week,* Jan. 11, 1988, p. 49.

Comarow, A. "AIDS: A Time of Testing." *U.S. News and World Report,* Apr. 20, 1987, pp. 56–59.

Committee on the Effective Implementation of Advanced Manufacturing Technology, Manufacturing Studies Board Commission on Engineering and Technical Systems. *Human Resource Practices for Implementing Advanced Manufacturing Technology.* Washington, D.C.: National Academy Press, 1986.

Condon, M. "The Ins and Outs of Displacement." *Training and Development Journal,* 1984, *38* (2), 60-65.

Cook, M. F. "Mergers and Acquisitions." In C. T. Norback (ed.), *The Human Resource Yearbook (1987 Edition).* Englewood Cliffs, N.J.: Prentice-Hall, 1987a.

Cook, M. F. "Layoffs, Terminations, and Outplacement." In C. T. Norback (ed.), *The Human Resource Yearbook (1987 Edition).* Englewood Cliffs, N.J.: Prentice-Hall, 1987b.

Coombe, J. D. "Employee Handbooks: Assets or Liability?" *Employee Relations Law Journal,* 1986, *12* (1), 4-17.

Coopers and Lybrand. *1983 Group Medical Plan Cost Survey.* Dallas, Tex.: Coopers and Lybrand, 1983.

Dalton, G. W., and Thompson, P. H. "Accelerating Obsolescence of Older Engineers." *Harvard Business Review,* 1971, *49* (5), 57-67.

D'Amore, L. J., and Anuza, T. E. "International Terrorism: Implications and Challenge for Global Terrorism." *Business Quarterly,* 1986, *51* (3), 20-29.

"Do Mergers Really Work." *Business Week,* June 3, 1985, pp. 88-94.

Dowdle, J. L., and Eide, S. R. "Avoiding Severance Pay Disputes." *Personnel,* 1987, *64* (11), 8-12.

Dube, L. E. "Planning for Defensible Discharges." *Management Review,* Mar. 1986, pp. 44-48.

Dyer, L. "Human Resource Planning." In K. M. Rowland and G. R. Ferris (eds.), *Personnel Management.* Boston: Allyn & Bacon, 1982.

Dyer, L. "Linking Human Resource and Business Strategies." *Human Resource Planning,* 1984, 7 (2), 79-84.

Employers' Health Costs Savings Letter. *The Employers' Health Costs Management Guide.* Wall Township, N.J.: American Business Publishing, 1986.

English, J. W. "Human Resource Planning: The Ideal Versus the Real." *Human Resource Planning,* 1984, 7 (2), 67–72.

Ewing, D. W. "Your Right to Fire." *Harvard Business Review,* Mar./Apr. 1983, pp. 32–42.

Extejt, M. M. "The Use of Pre-Employment Drug Testing: Pros and Cons." *SAM Advanced Management Journal,* 1987, 52 (4), 10–14.

Feuer, D. "A World Without Layoffs: Wouldn't It Be Wonderful?" *Training,* 1985, 22 (8), 23ff.

Feuer, D. "AIDS at Work: Fighting the Fear." *Training,* June 1987, pp. 61–71.

Finkel, M. L., Ruchlin, H. S., and Parsons, S. K. *Eight Years Experience with a Second Opinion Elective Surgery Program.* Washington, D.C.: U.S. Health Care Financing Administration, 1981.

Flamholtz, E. G. *Human Resource Accounting: Advances in Concepts, Methods, and Applications.* (2nd ed.) San Francisco: Jossey-Bass, 1985.

Fulmer, W. E. "How Do You Say, 'You're Fired'?" *Business Horizons,* Jan./Feb. 1986, pp. 31–38.

Galagan, P. "Here's the Situation." *Training and Development Journal,* 1987, 41 (7), 20–22.

Geidt, T. E. "Drug and Alcohol Abuse in the Workplace: Balancing Employer and Employee Rights." *Employee Relations Law Journal,* 1985, 11 (2), 181–205.

Geis, A. A. "Making Merit Pay Work." *Personnel,* Jan. 1987, pp. 52–60.

Gelb, B. D. "When and How to Use Outplacement." *Business Horizons,* Sept./Oct. 1986, pp. 55–59.

Gertner, M. "There's a New World Coming—Third Generation of Health and Welfare Plans." *Employee Benefits Journal,* Mar. 1983, pp. 22–26.

Gluck, F., Kaufman, S., and Walleck, A. S. "The Four Phases of Strategic Management." *Journal of Business Strategy,* Winter 1982, pp. 9–21.

Goldbeck, W. B. "Health Care Coalitions." In P. D. Fox, W. B. Goldbeck, and J. J. Spies (eds.), *Health Care Cost Management: Private Sector Initiatives.* Ann Arbor, Mich.: Health Administration Press, 1984.

Gomez-Mejia, L. R., and Balkin, D. B. "Dimensions and Characteristics of Personnel Manager Perceptions of Effective Drug Testing Programs." *Personnel Psychology,* 1987, *40* (4), 754–763.

Goozner, M. "Job Training at Crossroads: Activists Push Industrial Skills." *Chicago Tribune,* Mar. 8, 1987, Sec. 7, p. 6.

Gould, W. B., IV. "Stemming the Wrongful Discharge Tide." *Employee Relations Law Journal,* 1988, *13* (3), 404–425.

Greller, M. M. "Subordinate Participation and Reaction to the Appraisal Interview." *Journal of Applied Psychology,* 1975, *60,* 544–549.

Grider, D., and Shurden, M. "The Gathering Storm of Comparable Worth." *Business Horizons,* July/Aug. 1987, pp. 81–86.

Guinn, K. "Performance Management: Not Just an Annual Appraisal." *Personnel,* Aug. 1987, pp. 39–42.

Hall, D. T. *Careers in Organizations.* Pacific Palisades, Calif.: Goodyear Publishing, 1976.

Handel, B. *New Directions in Welfare Plan Benefits: Instituting Health Care Cost Containment Programs.* Brookfield, Wis.: International Foundation of Employee Benefit Plans, 1984.

Harris, P. R., and Moran, R. T. *Managing Cultural Differences.* Houston, Tex.: Gulf Publishing, 1979.

Hayes, R. H., and Abernathy, W. J. "Managing Our Way to Economic Decline." *Harvard Business Review,* 1980, *58* (4), 67–77.

Helfgott, R. B. "Can Training Catch Up with Technology?" *Personnel Journal,* 1988, *67* (2), 67–72.

Herzlinger, R. E., and Calkins, D. "How Companies Tackle Health Care Costs, Part III." *Harvard Business Review,* Jan./Feb. 1986, pp. 70–80.

Herzlinger, R. E., and Schwartz, J. "How Companies Tackle Health Care Costs, Part I." *Harvard Business Review,* July/Aug. 1985, pp. 69–81.

Holley, W. H., and Walters, R. S. "An Employment-at-Will Vulnerability Audit." *Personnel Journal,* Apr. 1987, pp. 130–138.

Horton, T. R. "If Right to Fire Is Abused, Uncle Sam May Step In." *The Wall Street Journal,* June 11, 1984, p. 26.

Horvath, F. W. "The Pulse of Economic Change: Displaced Workers of 1981–1985." *Monthly Labor Review,* 1987, *110* (6), 3–12.

Ivancevich, J. A., Schweiger, D. M., and Power, F. R. "Strategies for Managing Human Resources During Mergers and Acquisitions." *Human Resource Planning*, 1987, *10* (1), 19-35.

Jesperson, F. "The Fall of the Raise." *Business Monthly*, Nov. 1987, p. 18.

Kandel, W. L. "AIDS in the Workplace." *Employee Relations Law Journal*, 1986, *11* (4), 678-690.

Kane, J. S., and Freeman, K. A. "MBO and Performance Appraisal: A Mixture That Is Not a Solution (Part I)." *Personnel*, Dec. 1986, pp. 26-36.

Kane, J. S., and Freeman, K. A. "MBO and Performance Appraisal: A Mixture That Is Not a Solution (Part II)." *Personnel*, Feb. 1987, pp. 26-32.

Kanter, R. M. "From Status to Contribution: Some Organizational Implications of the Changing Basis for Pay." *Personnel*, Jan. 1987, pp. 12-37.

Kanter, R. M., and Seggerman, T. K. "Managing Mergers, Acquisitions, and Divestitures." *Management Review*, Oct. 1986, pp. 16-17.

Koeth, B. "Expressly American: Management's Task Is Internal Development." *Management Review*, Feb. 1985, pp. 24-29.

Kutscher, R. E. "Overview and Implications of the Projections to 2000." *Monthly Labor Review*, Sept. 1987, *110* (9), 3-9.

Landy, F. J., Barnes, J. L., and Murphy, K. R. "Correlates of Perceived Fairness and Accuracy in Performance Evaluation." *Journal of Applied Psychology*, 1978, *63*, 751-754.

Latham, G. P., and Wexley, K. N. *Increasing Productivity Through Performance Appraisal*. Reading, Mass.: Addison-Wesley, 1981.

Latham, G. P., and Yukl, G. A. "A Review of Research on the Application of Goal Setting in Organizations." *Academy of Management Journal*, 1975, *18*, 824-845.

Lawler, E. E. *Pay and Organizational Effectiveness*. New York: McGraw-Hill, 1971.

Lee, R. "Business-Health Coalitions." *Compensation and Benefits Review*, Jan./Feb. 1986, pp. 18-25.

Lefton, R. E. "Performance Appraisal: Why They Go Wrong and How to Do Them Right." *National Productivity Review*, 1986, *5* (1), 55-63.

Letchinger, R. S. "AIDS: An Employer's Dilemma." *Personnel,* Feb. 1986, pp. 58-63.

Lord, L. J., and others. "The Staggering Price of AIDS." *U.S. News and World Report,* June 15, 1987, pp. 16-18.

McAuliffe, K., and others. "AIDS: At the Dawn of Fear." *U.S. News and World Report,* Jan. 12, 1987, pp. 60-69.

McGregor, D. "An Uneasy Look at Performance Appraisal." *Harvard Business Review,* 1957, *35* (3), 89-94.

Mann, P. "The Hidden Scourge of Drugs in the Workplace." *The Reader's Digest,* 1984, *124* (742), pp. 55-61.

Mark, J. A. "Technological Change and Employment: Some Results from BLS Research." *Monthly Labor Review,* 1987, *110* (4), 26-29.

"Maryland to Publish First Statewide Doctor Fee Directory for Consumers." *Hospital Week,* Jan. 10, 1986, p. 3.

Masi, D. A. "AIDS in the Workplace: What Can Be Done?" *Personnel,* 1987, *64* (7), 57-60.

Maxwell, R. B. "The 'Graying' of America—Implications for Business." *Vital Speeches of the Day,* 1987, *53* (23), pp. 711-713.

Merritt, N.L. "Bank of America's Blueprint for a Policy on AIDS." *Business Week,* Mar. 23, 1987, p. 127.

Meyer, H. H. "The Pay-for-Performance Dilemma." *Organizational Dynamics,* Winter 1975, pp. 39-50.

Meyer, H. H., Kay, E., and French, J.R.P., Jr. "Split Roles in Performance Appraisal." *Harvard Business Review,* 1965, *43,* 123-129.

Milkovich, G. M., Dyer, L., and Mahoney, T. "HRM Planning." In S. J. Carroll and R. S. Schuler (eds.), *Human Resource Management in the 1980's.* Washington, D.C.: Bureau of National Affairs, 1983.

Milkovich, G. T. "The Emerging Debate." In E. R. Levernosh (ed.), *Comparable Worth: Issues and Alternatives.* Washington, D.C.: Equal Employment Advisory Council, 1980.

Mirvis, P. H. "Formulating and Implementing Human Resource Strategy: A Model of How to Do It, Two Examples of How It's Done." *Human Resource Management,* Winter 1985, pp. 385-412.

Mitchell, C. "A Growing Shortage of Skilled Craftsmen Troubles Some Firms." *The Wall Street Journal,* Sept. 14, 1987, p. 1.

Mobley, W. H. "The Link Between MBO and Merit Compensation." *Personnel Journal,* 1974, *53,* 423–427.

Morano, R. A., and Deets, N. "Professional Retraining: Meeting the Technological Challenge." *Training and Development Journal,* 1985, *39* (5), 99–101.

Morphew, A. J. "Terrorism and Corporate Insurance." *Management Review,* 1986, *75* (11), 29–30.

Naugle, D. G., and Davies, G. A. "Strategic-Skills Pool and Competitive Advantage." *Business Horizons,* 1987, *30* (6), 35–42.

Nemeroff, W. F., and Wexley, K. N. "Relationships Between Performance Appraisal Interview Outcomes by Supervisors and Subordinates." Paper presented at the annual meeting of the Academy of Management, Orlando, Fla., 1977.

"New Blueprints in the Drive for Job Security." *Business Week,* Jan. 9, 1984, pp. 91–92.

Nielsen, J. "Sick Retirees Could Kill Your Company." *Fortune,* Mar. 2, 1987, pp. 98–99.

Numec, M. M. "Workforce 2000: Dramatic Changes and a Shortage of Skilled Workers." *Industrial Engineer,* Jan. 1987, pp. 26–31.

Oaxaca, R. "Male–Female Wage Differences in Urban Labor Markets." *International Economic Review,* Oct. 1973, pp. 693–709.

O'Connell, J. M., and Hoerr, J. "There Really Are Jobs After Retraining." *Business Week,* Jan. 28, 1985, pp. 76–77.

O'Connor, M. "Steel Braces for Blast of Bad Tidings." *Chicago Tribune,* Dec. 28, 1986, Sec. 7, p. 1.

Opalka, D. P., and Williams, J. B. "Employee Obsolescence and Retraining: An Approach to Human Resource Restructuring." *The Journal of Business Strategy,* 1987, *8* (2), 90–96.

Penzkover, R. C. "Building a Better Benefit Plan at Quaker Oats." *Business and Health,* Oct. 1984, pp. 33–36.

Philips, J. "Enough Talk: What Can Employers Do About Drug Abuse?" *The Wall Street Journal,* Nov. 17, 1986, p. 34.

Polachek, S. W. "Occupational Segregation Among Women: Theory, Evidence, and a Prognosis." In C. B. Lloyd and others (eds.), *Women in the Labor Market.* New York: Columbia University Press, 1979.

Polachek, S. W. "Women in the Economy: Perspectives on Gender Inequality." In U.S. Commission on Civil Rights, *Comparable Worth: Issue for the 80's.* Vol. 1, June 6–7, 1984, pp. 34–53. Washington, D.C.: U.S. Government Printing Office, 1984.

Pollack, M.-A., and Bernstein, A. "The Disposable Employee Is Becoming a Fact of Life." *Business Week,* Dec. 15, 1986, p. 15.

"Protection for AIDS Victims." *Business Week,* Mar. 16, 1987, p. 46.

Raitt, J. "Retrain to Retain: A Prescription for the 1980's." *Training and Development Journal,* 1982, *36* (2), 48–52.

Reisler, M. "Business in Richmond Attacks Health Care Costs." *Harvard Business Review,* Jan./Feb. 1985, pp. 145–155.

Robbins, M. A., and Norwood, N. "State Wrongful Discharge Law: Are Unionized Employees Covered?" *Employee Relations Law Journal,* 1986, *12* (1), 19–32.

Romberg, R. V. "Performance Appraisal, 1: Risks and Rewards." *Personnel,* Aug. 1987, pp. 20–26.

Roomkin, M. Course notes and materials, Strategic Human Resources Planning Program, Northwestern University, 1982.

Russell, G. "Rebuilding to Survive." *Time,* Feb. 16, 1987, p. 44.

Rynes, S., Rosen, B., and Mahoney, T. A. "Evaluating Comparable Worth: Three Perspectives." *Business Horizons,* July/Aug. 1985, pp. 82–86.

Sales, A., and Mirvis, P. H. "When Cultures Collide: Issues in Acquisitions." In J. R. Kimberly and R. E. Quinn (eds.), *New Futures: The Challenge of Managing Corporate Transitions.* Homewood, Ill.: Dow Jones–Irwin, 1985.

Sanderson, S. R., and Schein, L. "Sizing Up the Down-Sizing Era." *Across the Board,* Nov. 1986, pp. 15–23.

Saporito, B. "Cutting Costs Without Cutting People." *Fortune,* May 25, 1987, pp. 26–32.

Sawhill, I. V. "The Economics of Discrimination Against Women: Some New Findings." *Journal of Human Resources,* 1973, *8,* 383–395.

Schein, E. *Career Dynamics.* Reading, Mass.: Addison–Wesley, 1978.

Schlesinger, J. M. "GM's New Compensation Plan Reflects General

Trend Tying Pay to Performance." *The Wall Street Journal,* Jan. 26, 1988, p. 39.

Seib, G. F. "Debate Rages over AIDS-Test Policy: Advocates See Need to Track Diseases Spread." *The Wall Street Journal,* June 18, 1987, p. 33.

Seligman, D. " 'Pay Equity' Is a Bad Idea." *Fortune,* May 14, 1984, pp. 133–140.

Semarad, R. D. "2000: Labor Shortage Looms." *Industry Week,* 1987, *232* (3), 38–40.

Shrivastava, P. "Postmerger Integration." *Journal of Business Strategy,* Summer 1986, pp. 65–76.

Simpson, J. C. "A Shallow Labor Pool Spurs Businesses to Act to Bolster Education." *The Wall Street Journal,* Sept. 28, 1987, p. 1.

Siwolop, S., and others. "AIDS Research: Where the Battle Stands." *Business Week,* Mar. 23, 1987, pp. 128–132.

Sobol, R. *IBM: Colossus in Transition.* New York: Bantam Books, 1983.

Somers, R. L., Locke, E. A., and Tuttle, T. C. "Adding Competition to the Management Basics: An Application in the Defense Department." *National Productivity Review,* 1986, *5* (1), 7–21.

Spencer, L. M., Jr. "Calculating Costs and Benefits." In W. R. Tracey (ed.), *Human Resources Management and Development Handbook.* New York: AMACOM, 1985.

Taldone, N. J. "Federal Preemption of Wrongful Discharge Claims of Union Employees." *Employee Relations Law Journal,* 1986, *12* (1), 33–45.

Tomasko, R. M. *Downsizing: Restructuring the Corporation for the Future.* New York: AMACOM, 1987.

Ulrich, D. "Strategic Human Resource Planning: Why and How?" *Human Resource Planning,* 1987, *10* (1), 37–56.

U.S. Public Health Service. *Surgeon General's Report on Acquired Immune Deficiency Syndrome.* Washington, D.C.: U.S. Department of Health and Human Services, 1987.

U.S. Senate. *Hearings on the Equal Rights Amendment.* Washington, D.C.: Committee on the Judiciary, 1984.

Verespej, M. A. "Retraining for What?" *Industry Week,* 1986, *231* (5), 68–70.

Wagel, W. H. "A Positive Approach to Alcohol and Drug Abuse." *Personnel,* 1986, *63* (12), 4-11.

Wagel, W. H. "Performance Appraisal with a Difference." *Personnel,* Feb. 1987a, pp. 4-6.

Wagel, W. H. "Keeping the Organization Lean at Federal Express." *Personnel,* Mar. 1987b, pp. 4-12.

Waldholz, M. "Drug Testing in the Workplace: Whose Rights Take Precedence?" *The Wall Street Journal,* Nov. 11, 1986, p. 39.

Walker, J. W. *Human Resource Planning.* New York: McGraw-Hill, 1980.

Wanous, J. P. *Organizational Entry: Recruitment, Selection, and Socialization of Newcomers.* Reading, Mass.: Addison-Wesley, 1980.

Wattenberg, B. J. "The Birth Dearth: Dangers Ahead?" *U.S. News and World Report,* June 22, 1987, pp. 56-63.

Williams, R. E. "Comparable Worth: Legal Perspectives and Precedents." In U.S. Commission on Civil Rights, *Comparable Worth: Issue for the 80's.* Vol. 1, June 6-7, 1984, pp. 148-161. Washington, D.C.: U.S. Government Printing Office, 1984.

Williams, R. E., and McDowell, D. S. "The Legal Framework." In E. R. Levernosh (ed.), *Comparable Worth: Issues and Alternatives.* Washington, D.C.: Equal Employment Advisory Council, 1980.

Willis, R. "Corporations vs. Terrorists." *Management Review,* 1986a, *75* (11), 16-28.

Willis, R. "What's New with Comparable Worth?" *Management Review,* Mar. 1986b, pp. 40-43.

Wohl, S. *The Medical Industrial Complex.* New York: Harmony Books, 1984.

Zucker, S., and others. *The Reindustrialization of America.* New York: McGraw-Hill, 1982.

Index